Islam in Modern Turkey

Religion, Politics and Literature in a Secular State

Edited by
RICHARD TAPPER

I.B. Tauris & Co Ltd
Publishers
London • New York

Published in association with
THE MODERN TURKISH STUDIES PROGRAMME
of the
CENTRE OF NEAR AND MIDDLE EASTERN STUDIES,
SCHOOL OF ORIENTAL AND AFRICAN STUDIES
(UNIVERSITY OF LONDON)

First published in 1991;
paperback edition
published in 1994 by
I.B.Tauris & Co Ltd
110 Gloucester Avenue
London NW1 8JA

175 Fifth Avenue
New York
NY 10010

In the United States of America
and Canada distributed by
St. Martin's Press
175 Fifth Avenue
New York
NY 10010

First published in the UK in 1982;
reprinted 1984, 1990, 1993.

A CIP record of this book is available from the British Library.

Library of Congress Catalog card number 90–60627
A full CIP record is available from the Library of Congress

ISBN 1–85043–833–1

Printed and bound in Great Britain by
WBC Print Ltd, Bridgend, Mid Glamorgan

CONTENTS

Editor's Foreword   v

1. *Introduction* – Richard Tapper   1

Part I: Islam and Nationalism as Political Ideologies

2. *Religion and Political Culture in Turkey*
   İlter Turan   31
3. *Religion, Education and Continuity in a Provincial Town*
   Richard Tapper and Nancy Tapper   56
4. *Mosque or Health Centre?: A Dispute in a Gecekondu*
   Akile Gürsoy-Tezcan   84
5. *Ethnic Islam and Nationalism among the Kurds in Turkey*
   Lâle Yalçın-Heckmann   102
6. *The Nakşibendi Order in Turkish History*
   Şerif Mardin   121

Part II: Turkish Muslim Intellectuals and the Production of Islamic Knowledge

7. *Islamic Education in Turkey: Medrese Reform in Late Ottoman Times and Imam–Hatip Schools in the Republic*
   Bahattin Akşit   145

8. *Muslim Identity in Children's Picture-Books*
   Ayşe Saktanber   171
9. *The New Muslim Intellectuals in the Republic of
   Turkey*
   Michael E. Meeker   189

**Part III: Islamic Literature and Literacy in Contemporary
   Turkey**

10. *Traditional Sufi Orders on the Periphery: Kadiri
    and Nakşibendi Islam in Konya and Trabzon*
    Sencer Ayata   223
11. *Pluralism Versus Authoritarianism: Political Ideas
    in Two Islamic Publications*
    Ayşe Güneş-Ayata   254
12. *Women in the Ideology of Islamic Revivalism in
    Turkey: Three Islamic Women's Journals*
    Feride Acar   280

Notes on Contributors   304

Index   308

EDITOR'S FOREWORD

This book derives from a workshop held at the School of Oriental and African Studies (SOAS), University of London, in May 1988 as part of the Modern Turkish Studies Programme of the Centre of Near and Middle Eastern Studies. Apart from the Introduction, all the chapters are revised versions of papers delivered at the workshop; Ahmet Evin and Gencay Şaylan also delivered papers, neither of which, unfortunately, were available for publication here.

I would like to thank the Research Committee of SOAS, the Nuffield Foundation and the British Academy, for generous grants which helped bring participants together for the workshop. Thanks are also due to the following for assistance in organizing the workshop: Clement Dodd, Chairman of the Programme, and co-convenor of the workshop; Tony Allan, then Chairman of the Centre Near and Middle Eastern Studies; Martin Daly, Secretary of SOAS Research Committee; and Rita Duah-Sakyi, Bridget Harney and Anne Mackintosh for valuable administrative assistance.

I am most grateful to all the contributors to the book, who have been patient with my suggestions for revision and with the delays in bringing the book to publication; they are not responsible for the way in which I have characterized their chapters and linked them together in the Introduction.

1

Introduction

Richard Tapper

Among the many recent studies of Islam as a social and political phenomenon, few have specifically discussed the Turkish case. Those which have, seeking to explain the apparent revival of Islam in modern – supposedly secular – Turkey, mostly focus on the role of Islam in the political process, especially on the most visible manifestations of 'Islamic revival' such as political party activity and events which have attracted foreign media attention. The question most often asked has been whether Islamic revival poses a political 'threat' to the survival of the modern Turkish state; the hidden agenda is the age-old Western fear of Islam, now shared by many Turks, and the rarely articulated role of this fear in determining Turkey's relation to Europe.

Much of this discussion is abstract and speculative; what is usually missing is any detailed knowledge of how religion has been practised by the broad mass of the Turkish people during the decades of the Republic, or of its meaning and importance in their lives today. There are few detailed studies of the way Turkey has shaped and been shaped by such 'Islamic institutions' as schools, Sufi orders, intellectual activities, and pious literature.

This book attempts this kind of broad coverage, filling the gap by looking at constructions of Islam in some less accessible areas of daily life and as they appear in popular and religious literature. Turkey has long stood out as a unique case in the Islamic world, and the authors hope that, by exploring the nature of some of the important manifestations of Islam in Turkey today, and their place in the context of other aspects of Turkish society, they can shed light on matters of importance to the general social scientific study of Islam: the conflict between, and possible intersection of, secular and re-traditionalizing appeals; socialization and mobilization through agents of education and popular culture; and the competition of Islamic idioms. The book raises the question of whether Turkey may still be said to be so different from other Muslim societies, the exception that proves the rule.[1] How far is the self-designation 'secular state' still appropriate, either as a description or as a political principle, to modern Turkey?

In the pages that follow, I make no pretence at a comprehensive survey of the complexities of politics, religion and literature in recent Turkish history; rather, the rest of this Introduction is intended both as a background to the other chapters, and as a means of highlighting their arguments and the way in which they contribute to an improved understanding of Turkish Islam.

Since the republican revolution of 1923, Islam in Turkey has been redefined. Secularism ('laicism') emerged as one of the key principles of Atatürk's new state, and religious expression came under strict government supervision and control. With the abolition of the Caliphate, the outlawing of the powerful Sufi tarikats (orders/brotherhoods) and the discouragement of mystical forms of Islam, Turkish Islam in effect became more standardized, circumscribed and compartmentalized, while republican ideology and associated institutions came to dominate much of everyday life.

The new centre-right Democrat Party government elected in 1950, widely supported by the Anatolian peasantry and small townspeople, whose religious lives had been less affected than those of city-dwellers, brought an easing of the repressive attitude to religion. Over the following decades there was a growth in manifestations of popular religious sentiment, evidenced both in the building of mosques and religious schools and in the semi-clandestine activities of mystical groups, whether the older Sufi tarikats such as the Nakşibendis and Kadiris, or the more recent Nurcu and Süleymancı movements. This resurgence in religious consciousness and activity became particularly evident in the

1980s, with an apparent shift in government attitudes and a remarkable proliferation of religious newspapers, periodicals and other literature.

Many aspects of the role of Islam in republican Turkey have been debated, among Turkish commentators as well as among foreign observers. Contrasting and changing interpretations of the apparent revival in Islamic consciousness have been suggested. One constant theme of discussion has concerned the sources, nature and depth of Turkish 'laicism', a principle which has indeed been subject to competing definitions ever since the foundation of the Republic. How does 'laicism' differ from 'secularism' as understood elsewhere? Does it mean separation of religion from the political arena, or should it rather mean control of religious affairs by the state? How free from state interference should an individual's religious beliefs and practices be?[2]

Official understandings and propagations of state secularism for long blinded the educated republican élite and middle classes to the continuing vigour of Islamic belief, practice and identity among the mass of the population. The strength of the Islamist movements of the 1980s ran counter to the expectations of many republican academics and intellectuals, for whom the revival of religious activity since the 1950s had merely confirmed prejudices about the continuing cultural backwardness of the peasants, which would in due course be remedied by education and modernization. Educated opinion in Turkey has been divided as to the depth of ordinary people's commitment to secularism, and whether or not Turkey could ever experience an 'Islamic Revolution'. There is considerable debate over the meaning of manifestations of 'Islamic revival' in Turkey, and how far they are the product of external material or ideological influences: financial support from Muslim oil-states, or direct or indirect inspiration from fundamentalist movements in Iran, Egypt or elsewhere. Other debates have focused on whether there are specifically Turkish constructions of Islam, rooted in Turkish culture, political history and geography, which might explain or provide a model for current revivalist movements.

Some conclusions are generally agreed; for example, that Islam in Turkey always was, and continues to be, multi-dimensional. Secondly, that neither modern manifestations of Islam, nor republican secularism, nor the relation of religious institutions to the Turkish state, can be understood without some reference to their Ottoman roots.

A number of writers have examined the origins of republican secularism and nationalism in Ottoman Islamic culture, society and politics. Islam in the Ottoman Empire was not a unified, monolithic set of beliefs and practices; it was complex, hetero-geneous and changing, and its different manifestations were related to different aspects of Ottoman society. The Ottomans ruled a polyglot, multi-faith Empire. After seizing the Caliphate in the early sixteenth century, they established a Sharia-based official orthodoxy. In Anatolia, dervishes, Sufism and the Shi'ite minorities – heirs of the old shamanistic tribal religion of the Turks – were marginalized into an oppositional or protest role. Three main clusters of Sunni Islam emerged: the official orthodoxy of the more influential Ulema, the mystical orders (the tarikats) and heterodox elements, and the traditional Islam of the bazaars and guilds. Meanwhile, the roots of secularism were early evident in the Sultans' *kanun* legislation, and in the eighteenth century a secular bureaucracy rose to power.[3]

Faced with the threat of European economic and political expansion and a shrinking empire, nineteenth-century Ottoman reformers determined to 'modernize' the state, abandoning Islamic political principles for a Western model of enlightened despotism. During the Tanzimat period of reforms (from 1839), the military, education, administration and the judiciary were transformed through further radical secularization.

Several scholars have pointed out how the Ottoman centraliza-tion of power and economics impeded the horizontal integration of society. Ottoman Islamic culture, as Mardin has strikingly analysed, was based on a model of society as person-based, and on personalized social relations.[4] As in other Mediterranean and Middle Eastern societies, both politics and personal relations were characterized by informal patronage networks. With the break-down in the nineteenth century of traditional Ottoman social institutions like the craft guilds, the tarikats and local religious and landlord hierarchies, there were no political institutions, no central ideology or value system, to bridge the gulf between the various élites (military, bureaucratic and legal–educational) and the ordinary people. Religion and Islamic ideology could fill this gap, but in complex ways: both the conservative official religion and the more liberal religion of the dervishes could, like the modern state, link the ruler to the ruled; but they could also offer the ruled an alternative, a focus of protest.[5]

In effect, the Tanzimat reforms, by depersonalizing the Ottoman system and reducing the place of Islam, widened the gulf between governors and governed, and the need began to be felt for a central value system, a 'cultural anchor', a source of identity, with which to mobilize the masses and maintain the legitimacy of Ottoman rule. The Young Ottomans (in the 1870s) sought to base an Ottoman constitutional state on Islamic premises. Sultan Abdülhamid II (r. 1876–1909) also sought to use Islamic culture and ideology, through building mosques and promoting the tarikats, but he also extensively secularized the administration, justice and education. While accepting the advantages of Western technology as the door to progress, he rejected the necessity to adopt Western ideas. These too, however, were promoted by the Young Turks (1908–18), who with their positivist Durkheimian sociology established a constitutional government and continued the secularizing process, accompanied by lively debates over the role of Islam in Ottoman society and over the confrontation between materialism and idealism.[6]

The secularization introduced under the Ottomans largely involved the separation of religion from politics by the creation of parallel state institutions. Paradoxically, however, as the recognition of its role as 'social cement' grew, Islam became politicized and ideologized; at the same time, with the secularization of the functions of the state, religion became both more specialized and more important at the personal and family level.[7]

The process of secularization continued under the Republic. Mustafa Kemal, however, was not content with separating Islam from politics: he wanted to remove its power base and subordinate it to the state, thereby (he hoped) depriving the old élite of the ability to fight back.[8] He was aware of the dual functions of religion: the private one of giving intellectual and emotional meaning to life, an ethics, an eschatology and the promise of salvation; and the public function of providing a political ideology, a cultural and communal identity and social solidarity. He was not openly against Islam in the former role, but (like many of his predecessors) strongly disapproved of the latter – even though he and others had made use of Islam as a rallying cry against the invaders in the War of Independence.[9] His solution to the Ottoman reformers' quest for a unifying value system was the extreme one of replacing religion with a modern secular ideology and the values of republican nationalism. His reforms even further restricted Islam to the private, personal sphere: individuals should worship alone, even without the leadership of imams; the social and political side of Islam, including the tarikat orders and local and unofficial Islamic practices, were outlawed and driven underground.

Significant events and legal changes affecting Islam under the Republic began with the abolition of the Sultanate in 1922 and of the Caliphate in 1924. Islam was deleted from the Constitution in 1928, and the state was officially declared secular in 1937. In 1924, the Sharia was abandoned (to be replaced by the Swiss civil code in 1926), the Vakf (religious endowment foundation) was abolished, courts and education were unified and the medreses (religious schools) were closed. The next year saw the closure of the tarikats, and the adoption of Western forms of hats, clothing and calendar. In 1928 a romanized alphabet and in 1931 the metric system were adopted. Westernization was further enforced by the introduction in 1934 of family names and of Western music in schools, and the next year Sunday was adopted as the weekly holiday.[10]

Mardin argues that the republican revolution was primarily a change of values.[11] Until recently, however, it was presented, like its counterparts elsewhere, as a radical break from the institutions and structures of the past. The Ottoman roots of major republican reforms, and the continuities between Ottoman–Islamic and contemporary Turkish culture, were disguised, and a focus was placed instead on specifically Turkish language, history and culture. Starting in 1925, revolts against the reforms broke out but were suppressed. The regime came to associate them with Sufism and with ethnic (linguistic–cultural) separatism, especially the Nakşibendi order and the Kurds of the East.[12] Religion in general, as it increasingly articulated popular discontent, came to be seen as subversive and reactionary. A simple conceptual opposition was encouraged between 'republican' (= modern, secular, European) and 'Islamic' (= backward, decadent, Ottoman). As Yalman notes, 'an entire generation was educated thinking religion to be some evil and irrational force of mere orthodoxy and blind tradition'. This construction of Islam seems to have coincided with the secular ambitions of the state: 'the intellectuals from Istanbul and Ankara had for political reasons completely misunderstood what Islam or religion was all about'.[13]

If Kemalist republican nationalism was a public ideology, it was supported by a variety of public rituals and came to constitute a 'civic religion', to an extent that Islam probably never did under the Ottomans, and more on the model of 'civic religions' that were introduced in other countries in the first half of this century.[14] But it is not surprising if, in the Turkish context, the new civic religion perpetuated some functions, forms and fundamental values of Islam: it was the overt structure, ideology, orientation, and the personnel that changed.

The new civic religion was poor in ritual forms and conspicuously failed to attract the rural population. Recently several scholars have argued that Kemalist republican nationalism, as a dominant ideology, could not replace the multi-level appeal of Islam. It was no alternative to Islam in providing identity and organizing principles of life. At the public level, it was no substitute for the divine laws of Islam; at the individual level, it could not meet intellectual needs for an ethics and an eschatology, and its ideology and values were inadequate, shallow and thin.[15] In sum, as Mardin writes, Islam has persisted since 1945, following twenty-five years of secularism, because there was something missing from the materialist values of Kemalism which religion continued to supply.[16]

Intellectual and political life in Turkey have however never been characterized by stark, simple oppositions between materialist and religious values, or between Islamic and republican nationalist ideologies. On the one hand, after the 1920s, there was a considerable diversity of constructions of both Islam and secularism, and indeed nationalism, in Turkish intellectual circles: different emphases, varied discourses, and contested definitions and meanings. Indeed, under the Turkish Republic, as under the

Ottomans, Islam took different forms. On the other hand, some argue that all these forms or structures may be seen as expressions of a single underlying ideology or value system. As Toprak writes: 'the cultural distance between the secularist and the traditionalist forces may not be as wide as it is assumed to the extent that both sides, in a latent or manifest fashion, approach politics with a value system that may be at its roots consensus-oriented'.[17] The history of Islamic societies, as of other civilizations and movements, shows a constant interplay between such alternative structures. As many have argued, the apparent conflict between the alternatives is an essential enabling mechanism of change.[18]

Turkey has seen rapid developments since the death of Atatürk in 1938: economic growth and diversification, population increase, urbanization, the spread of universal education and mass communications. The framework for all these was laid by Atatürk, but the effects were not felt until the 1950s when the process of rural–urban migration began on a large scale. One major effect is usually identified as the general change in social experience from 'community' to 'society', begun under the Tanzimat but now rapidly accelerated.[19]

From the introduction of multi-party politics in 1946, and the first genuinely free elections in 1950, until the military intervention of 1980, the political centre ground was disputed between Atatürk's own Republican People's Party (CHP) and the Democrat Party (DP) and its successor the Justice Party (AP). The CHP had a more left-of-centre, socialist programme, supported mainly by urban workers and intellectuals, but in the republican political context it was associated with the more 'conservative' secular position.[20] The right-of-centre DP/AP, being economically oriented to Western capitalism, became identified as more 'progressive', while being more supportive of religious freedom. On the political and religious extremes, the far left was supported by Shi'ites (perhaps a quarter of the population), while Sunni fundamentalists formed a part of the extreme right, notably (from 1969) the National Order Party (MNP) and its successor (from 1972) the National Salvation Party (MSP), which attracted largely rural support for its explicitly religious, anti-Western, antisocialist – though highly 'progressive' – programme.[21]

The 1950 elections brought in the DP in place of Atatürk's CHP. Sometimes thought to be identified with religious conservatism, early DP success has been shown to have had little to do with Islam, and more with the revolt of the periphery against the centre. The DP did not take on a clearly religious character until the late 1950s, following the emergence of economic problems.[22] An 'Islamic revival' did, however, coincide with the introduction of multi-party politics. Already before 1950, religious courses were brought back into education, government support for the Hajj was restored, shrines were reopened and training for religious officials was restarted.[23]

Several writers have discussed the debates inside and outside parliament concerning the interpretation of secularism, and how far rival parties appealed directly or implicitly to religious elements in the population.[24] Heper quotes studies from the 1950s to the 1970s, all showing how deep-rooted are secular attitudes to religion, ranging from educated atheism to protestant, 'modern', personal Islam.[25] A consensus emerged around 1980 that Turkey, unlike most Islamic countries, had become used to secularism (in the sense of the separation of Islam from politics), participatory democracy, and political and religious fragmentation and pluralism.

In the late 1960s and the 1970s, the problem of Islam was commonly seen as a matter of party politics (the threat of MNP/MSP) and the revival of tarikat activity. However, analysis of election results shows that few voters supported parties with an explicitly religious programme; the notoriously conservative provincial petty bourgeoisie do adhere to the tarikats, but continue to vote for broad centre-right parties.[26] Toprak shows that religious parties appeal most 'to either very traditional or to rapidly changing communities'. This is explained, she says, by Ahmed Yücekök, who in his study of small-town voluntary mosque associations and the roots of conservatism argues that

religion plays a dual role in Turkish society. In the less developed areas, it functions to defend the interests of dominant social or economic groups. In the more developed regions, on the other hand, it functions as a protest movement for individuals or groups who have been ill-affected by rapid development. In either case, the religious manifestation of support or protest against the status quo, in his view, is conservative in nature.[27]

However, Heper and others writing around 1980, by focusing on party politics, failed to recognize how far religious revival was already moving from these geographically and socially peripheral locations into the centre. Since the 1950s, but particularly during the 1970s and 1980s, this movement has taken a variety of forms. There has been a massive increase in Islamic publishing activity, including both intellectual treatises and popular prayer-manuals, tarikat journals, and other literature.[28] Media attention – both in Turkey and in the West – has been particularly drawn to visible symptoms of Islamic activity and identity, such as women's headscarves and men's facial hair, mosque-building and the formation of Islamic communes, and the growth of religious education (including unofficial Koran courses).[29] Some of these phenomena, notably the last, have received government support.

Indeed, after the military intervention of 1980, government attitudes changed. Without abandoning the basic principle of secularism, the generals, as well as the powerful intellectual élite of judges, professors and administrators who controlled the media, adopted a new approach to protecting it. A tacit admission of the failure of the ideology and forms of Kemalist republicanism led to a reassessment of its elements and a perception of the need for reinforcing an unchanging national culture and eliminating foreign influences. A departure from strict traditional secularism was supported by the newly active tarikats and substantial Islamic funding from abroad, channelled into educational facilities and huge budget increases for the Directorate of Religious Affairs.[30]

The tarikats had never died, but had gone underground; the Nakşibendis and Kadiris remained active especially in the East, where they catered for religious education through the underground medrese network, supporting the family and economic enterprises and providing jobs and social mobility. The recent tarikat revival, especially of the Nakşibendis, has been prominent in western Turkey, where newer orders like the Nurcu and the Süleymancı have also flourished. Some of the new Muslim intellectuals support one or other tarikat – though others are against them. Several orders have received foreign Islamic funding, channelled into religious education facilities. On the whole, the tarikats in Turkey inculcate a conservative morality, focusing on belief, not practice, and encouraging self-improvement rather than political activism. They project Islam as a protest ideology, a counter-culture, and the newer orders may call for the restoration of the Sharia, but they appear for the most part to be non-revolutionary, despite some popular images, and have recommended followers to vote for the centre-right Motherland Party (ANAP) and True Path Party (DYP), though Nakşibendi and Kadiri support has also gone to the MNP/MSP and increasingly to their successor the Welfare Party (RP).[31]

After 1980, the tarikats and other religious elements became influential in the military, the bureaucracy, education and government, dominating one wing of Turgut Özal's ruling (from 1983) ANAP. Particularly prominent were the Intellectuals' Hearth (Aydınlar Ocağı), and the movement known as the Turkish–Islam Synthesis (TIS), which wished to bring supposedly traditional shared values to the surface, to peel away the false Western veneer, which was so shallow, so seductive, so corrupting, and to recognize (under the label of Turk and Islam) a national synthesis of fundamental values.[32] Proponents of the TIS wanted an authoritarian but not an Islamic state: religion, the essence of culture and social control, must be fostered in schools, but it must not be politicized. They wished to re-personalize social relations, and to use religion much as Sultan Abdülhamid did. In effect they were seeking to activate the common ideological structure mentioned above as underlying both Ottoman Islam and republican nationalism.[33] In the late 1980s, however, the TIS was intellectually discredited, and there was evidence of a backlash from strict secularists, while the Islamic 'threat' was defused by the integration of religious ideals into the programmes of most political parties. At the same time, religiously motivated violence appeared to be increasing, with the assassination of some key secularists.

Once again, secularism, the relation between the state and religious education, and the role of religion in politics, is being redefined.

The five chapters in Part I consider how both Islam and nationalism have been treated as political ideologies in recent

Turkish history. Three local case-studies, from a provincial town, a city squatter-settlement and the tribal hinterland,[34] are framed by a general state-level discussion and a survey of the political history of the main Sufi order.

İlter Turan examines the framework of Turkish political culture and the religious basis of the state ideology of control, finding a common Ottoman source. He applies the tools of political science to the analysis of how religion has influenced political culture in modern Turkey. Islam is in theory a 'total religion', but in practice its effects on political life have never been total, and were certainly substantially reduced during the last century of Ottoman rule, reaching a nadir in the early years of the Republic, though they have increased since. Surveying the processes of secularization under the Ottomans and their culmination in the Kemalist reforms, Turan notes the debate between Islamists and Westernists as to whether culture could be separated from technology. He examines different aspects of political culture: the changing role of Islam, and of Islamic notions of 'community', in defining the political community. Formally, Islam is not relevant under the Republic, though many citizens continue to think of themselves as Muslims first, and Turks afterwards: for most people, Turk is equated with Muslim. As for political legitimacy, Turan notes that the Ottoman state legitimated religion, as much as the reverse. Religion acts as a constraint on government, though it may be a tool of the state and a source of symbols. Generally, the state has treated religion as a resource.

Ideologies of secularization and modernization sought to reduce the impact of Islam on politics, but allowed Islam to become an ideology of opposition and conservatism, and Islamic groups to provide a refuge for marginal people suffering deprivation and alienation from state and society at large. With multi-party politics, and particularly from the 1960s, religion again emerged into the political arena, though in no homogeneous fashion. Recently, all parties have incorporated religious ideas and shown tolerance, with the result that religion has a reduced impact on political ideology. Turan shows the difficulties of testing the impact of supposed Islamic values – such as authoritarianism or egalitarianism – on political values and styles. There is much to be said for the notion that the Ottoman Ulema, their conceptions of Islamic knowledge and their modes of reasoning (the use of sacred texts for guidance; analogy; the importance of consensus) provided a model for the westernizing élite, and continued to do so even after they had been abolished by the Republic, though this has declined in recent decades.

The continuity Turan identifies between Islamic and republican values at the level of the intelligentsia and state leadership is also found by Richard and Nancy Tapper in a provincial town. They find two discrete sets of values, but with close underlying links that suggest they are aspects of a single ideology of social control. Provincial towns play a mediating role between cities and the countryside, in various ways, not least in providing a meeting-place for city-sourced republican values and province-based religious conservatism. Nationalism is associated with Islam in a kind of 'fundamentalist' ideology; the associations are manifest in a variety of accommodations, some explicit and some hidden. Hidden accommodations are found, for example, in attitudes to hard work; in ritual parallels; in the 'cults' of Atatürk and Muhammad; and in the discourses of knowledge and of education. In this provincial town, republican principles such as secularism have taken root and are closely defended, but their local construction and character, like the soil in which they are embedded, remain firmly Islamic.

Other local-level cases of Islamic–secular confrontation present a different picture. Akile Gürsoy-Tezcan's chapter discusses religion as idiom of opposition to the state, where there are perceived conflicts between local/family and national interests. She outlines a project in progress to examine the cultural causes of infant mortality in Turkey, and describes a case encountered during the research which exemplifies many of the local-level conflicts that exist in Turkish life today. Infant mortality rate (IMR) is a commonly agreed indicator of level of development: yet Turkey, like several other Middle Eastern countries, has a far higher IMR than expected in relation to another commonly agreed indicator, GNP per capita. Studies of IMR in the literature pay little attention to possible socio-economic, political or cultural determinants, and the project in question set out to do just this, in an Istanbul *gecekondu* (squatter settlement). First, environmental and demographic factors were considered – for example the apparent association of high IMR with extended patriarchal families. The possibility that cultural practices, as well as local political pressures, might play a major role in determining infant survival and child health, came sharply into focus during the course of a dispute which arose when the temporarily vacated site of a mother–child Health Centre was taken over by male members of a religious group who started to build a mosque; this in a district with no schools and no other Health Centre. Repeated deputations by the mayor, his daughter, and groups of women failed to stop the mosque-building and reinstate the Health Centre.

Numerous similar cases, reported and cartooned in the national press during the 1980s, caught the popular imagination as epitomizing the conflict of religious traditionalism versus the modernizing ambitions of the state. Elsewhere in the Islamic world mosques were traditionally associated with institutions of both health and education. The building of mosques (or religious schools) is not necessarily an indication of religiosity, but when, as in Turkey, it is contrasted with the building of schools and the provision of health facilities, the concern of the state, it clearly indicates a set of political oppositions in society as a whole. According to Gürsoy, the reactions of the local and national press, local politicians and state agencies revealed the deep contradictions 'between traditional and modern, culture and politics, local and national, and male and female interests, both in Turkey and also in other parts of the world'.

Lâle Yalçın-Heckmann raises the same question of the religious idiom of local resistance to the state, but in remotest Hakkari, at the other end of Turkey from both the Istanbul *gecekondu* and the town studied by the Tappers. Here the question is, how 'Islamic' (as opposed to ethnic, tribal, or nationalist) are Kurdish uprisings against the state? Van Bruinessen saw local support for the Shaikh Seit uprising of 1925 as a matter of rivalries between Sunni tribal chiefs; the Alevis held back, since they saw a future for their religious identity in the Republic. In effect the rising was both religious, tribal and nationalist.

Yalçın considers Islam and ethnic nationalism as ideologies in Kurdistan. Are supposedly conflicting loyalties actually perceived as conflicting at the local level? The motivations of leaders, as of followers, are complex. Is religion incompatible with nationalism/tribalism/ethnicity? 'When do people start expressing their economic, social and political differences as being due to ethnic, national or religious differences? And why do they express their differences in an ethnic, national or religious discourse?' Islam is the dominant force in Hakkari daily life and discourse. Numerous types of religious leadership validate the significance of Islamic values, and explain the social structure of gender, class and age differences, and the incidence of misfortune; but 'the teachings of Islam can be used to argue both for and against the existence of differences in social status and prosperity'. Essentially these elements constitute an ethnic/national religion: Kurdish Islam. Meanwhile, the state is now more relaxed about religious than ethnic identity and dissociates the former from the latter; it refuses to concede that rebels might be religiously motivated – they are not Muslims, but Marxists and separatists. At the same time, Kurdish nationalist activists are increasingly acknowledging the power of religious and tribal ideology.

Şerif Mardin approaches a similar theme – the politics of religious opposition to the state – through a brief history of the Nakşibendi. Popularly, and in the view of the state, the Nakşibendi are considered inherently subversive, though recent apologists have shown them to be highly orthodox in orientation and sought to portray them as non-political, and indeed their characteristic sobriety and inward discipline do not fit with popular images of Sufi mystics. Mardin says neither view is adequate, but that attention should focus on their internal dynamic and their changing involvement in politics. He looks at the lives and ideas of a number of Nakşibendi leaders of the Mujeddidi and Halidi branches, showing that while concerned with spiritual renewal and purification they have been very much involved politically in the affairs of this world. Recent examples include the founder of the Nurcu sect, Said Nursi, who was much influenced by both Mujeddidi and Halidi, and the Halidi shaikh Mehmed Zahid Kotku, who became the Nakşibendi leader in Istanbul and whose circle included intellectuals as well as politicians such as the founder of the MNP/MSP Necmettin Erbakan and President Özal's brother Korkut.

Nakşibendi were indeed interested in power, for higher Muslim interests, and they have had remarkable political success both in popular mobilization and in influencing intellectuals. Mardin argues that they drew organizational strength from their heritage in Central Asia and their esoteric discourse; they appealed to the just versus the unjust, and were open to modern influences. At the same time: 'The Nakşibendi contention that one should not establish too close a relation with politicians is a sincere Islamic cry of the heart based on the correct conviction that Islamic faith will by itself put one on the political warpath without any abrupt transition from faith to ideology.'

In Part II, three chapters examine different aspects of the production of Islamic knowledge in Turkey, through education, religious books for children and the writings of Muslim intellectuals.

Bahattin Akşit focuses on education, a key state institution and focus of reform, arguing that the increase of religious schools at all levels, and of publications and of religious endowments, are further 'clear indications of the official as well as non-official institutional proliferation of Islam'. Since multi-party rule, governments have tolerated and even sponsored religious schools, which have shown a much higher growth rate than secular education and are not just producing religious functionaries as originally intended. There are continuing debates about the implications: Islamist groups argue over whether these schools are to be welcomed as useful for recruitment or rejected as instruments of state control; secular groups differ over whether they exemplify a dangerous radicalism or the rationalization of religion; meanwhile opportunists use religious education as a channel for social mobility. Akşit considers the available evidence on the origins and motivations of students in religious schools. There are few from the tribal groups in the East, the urban proletariat, the wealthy élite and farm labourers; rather, many come from areas of rapid and recent industrialization and urbanization, with centre-right political inclinations. A high proportion are from families of farmers and self-employed small traders and craftsmen, who seem to be seeking an alternative to the extremes of Western materialism and Eastern spiritualism; people of a practical orientation, but conservative over gender issues.

The debates are not new. Akşit sketches the history of medrese reform under the late Ottomans, and the lively debates of the time, particularly on how Western modernist education and traditional Islamic sciences could be integrated. He then reviews a number of recent books and periodicals which discuss the same themes, concluding that 'little advance in resolving the problem of reconciling Islam, modernism and the nation-state has been made since the time of Ziya Gökalp'.

If, as is commonly held, Islamic resurgence in Turkey is a response to the failure of modernization, then, Ayşe Saktanber argues, we need to ask, why Islam? 'One way of doing this is to seek to explain how Islamic ideologies transform individuals and construct them as Muslim subjects. This construction not only defines the Muslim subject as an "ideal type" but also delineates Muslim identity within the specific social context.' This can be achieved by looking at religious education in the home, through children's picture-books – a form of popular literature. Saktanber surveys a range of children's books, classifying them as traditional, modern or religious, and focusing on the latter and how they inculcate norms and values relating to gender and authority roles: men are portrayed as active in a range of occupations in the outside world; women are passive, dependent mothers of sons – girls figure only as recipients of religious learning, taught by fathers and never by mothers. The antithesis is the selfish, ignorant, hypocritical modern woman. Modernity is painted as the antithesis of Islam. Morality (good and bad, rewards and punishments) and the father's authority are based on God; patriotism is approved, but not the Republic as such. There is little realism about environment or society. Social roles derive from essential qualities of age and sex. Children live in a world of sin, whose consequences come in this world; the emphasis is on the development of self, personal loyalty to God, and the rejection of modern Western values.

With the new Islamic literacy, these children's books are one important modern medium for the transmission of the 'popular knowledge of Islam', whose earlier vehicles are discussed elsewhere by Mardin.[35] At a more reflective level, Islamic knowledge is being freshly produced by the new Muslim intellectuals, considered by Michael Meeker. Though rooted in nineteenth-century Islamist resistance, they are modern products distinguished by the secularist environment in which they operate, but of varied backgrounds. The typical Muslim intellectual is provincial in origin, urban, educated, in young middle-age,

familiar with the West. He is treated as a spokesman for Islam on
the media, and as essentially parallel to his secular counterparts.
He rejects assimilation with the West, or evaluation by Western
values, calling for a distinctive Islamic outlook; modern humanist,
scientist, secularist thought is dangerous unless guided by religion.
'While he must engage secularist intellectuals on their own ground
to develop a strong case for the Muslim point of view, he risks
losing contact with the ordinary Muslim as he traffics in the
concepts and problems of his secular counterparts.' He is tainted
with the same 'leftist' brush as the latter.

Meeker discusses the work of three Muslim intellectuals in some
detail. Ali Bulaç, who had a religious education and currently
works as a journalist, proposes Islamic alternatives to failed
Western ideologies. He is concerned with the role of Muslim
intellectuals in reformulating Islam, to revive the community in
modern life. Rasim Özdenören is a civil servant, with a degree
from the United States and familiarity with Western ideas, known
as a writer of fiction as well as volumes of essays on Western
culture and contemporary Islam. He focuses on the issues of
cultural identity and the need to clarify the Turkish Muslim
tradition and to understand the failures of the West. İsmet Özel, a
leftist poet and essayist who turned to Islam, seeks the
reconstruction of an Islamic way of life after the failures not just
of the West but of the Turkish responses to it; but action should
come from the individual, not from the state.

In Meeker's analysis, 'Muslim intellectuals are responding to the
"constructedness" of social relations and personal identity in
contemporary Turkish experience.' Like other countries in the
process of modernization, Turkey is experiencing the passage from
Gemeinschaft to *Gesellschaft* and the consequent identity void.
Ideological maps are needed, especially by youth moving to the
cities and exposed to secular Western culture. Muslim intellectuals
interpret this differently: in Islamic civilization 'they see the
contractual and fictional side of society (*Gesellschaft*) to be more
perfectly rooted in moral conventions and moral solidarities
(*Gemeinschaft*)' – this does not just apply to old Turkish
traditions, however. 'Islam is a social discourse which represents
an *alternative* to the Western and secular *Gesellschaft* in
contemporary Turkey, one which would be free of the emptiness
and injustice they attribute to modern society.'

The three chapters in Part III analyse the contents of a variety of Islamic journals published during the 1980s, representing the views of different Sufi orders and Islamist groups. While agreeing generally on the rejection of Western culture and values, the journals differ significantly on issues such as whether technology can be separated from culture, whether revival should be locally or internationally based, whether the individual is responsible or needs guidance by a leader, and how far to accommodate to the secular state.

Sencer Ayata examines in detail two journals published in provincial cities, the one (*Ribat*) by an extremist and activist branch of the Nakşibendi, the other (*İcmal*) by the Kadiri order. He analyses the conceptions of human nature and the world and its evils (especially individual desires, Western 'materialism', and 'Satanic' forces) and the role of Islam projected by the writers of each journal, and compares their conceptions of withdrawal from the world and personal and political struggle against evil. *Ribat* takes a radical rejectionist attitude to the material joys of the world, yet enjoins commitment to political action to change it, if necessary by martyrdom. *İcmal*, though also rejecting the world, does so for esoteric reasons – in order to attain greater spiritual purity – and also rejects the use of force. Kadiris accept that they live in a world of matter, but try to change themselves by rising above it morally; *İcmal* sees its primary aim as moral education, under the supreme guidance of the Perfect Man.

Ayşe Güneş-Ayata discusses the political ideas represented in two further journals. *Girişim* (described elsewhere by Mardin as 'a radical and intellectually extremely interesting Islamic periodical')[36] is new, modernist in outlook and approach, encouraging theory and discussion and modern means of communication. Though fundamentalist in its use of scripture, it is politically leftish, adopting a conflict model of society, and realistic concerning previous and present conditions in Turkey. It advocates tolerance, appealing to educated youth. It proposes the theory of 'calling': the West can be defeated by arguing on its own terms – see how it has failed in practice; Islam, if developed, can provide the answers. It is pluralist, and against authority. Leaders are needed, but must be of the people. By contrast, the journal *İslam*, coming from the central Nakşibendi, is much more traditional. Addressed mainly to youth and women, it gives instructions, advocating preaching and action, not discussion. It is optimistic in outlook, authoritarian, with a consensus model of society. The original Islam is still valid; the concepts of Hijra ('withdrawal') and Jihad ('struggle') are central, the mujahidin in Afghanistan are the model to follow. Although modern technology can be used, Western culture is imperialistic and to be avoided. Muslim schools and media must be developed to counter Western dominance. The journal favours internationalism, with Turkish leadership. The individual is responsible, but needs guidance by a leader.

Finally, Feride Acar examines three Islamic women's journals for their conceptions of women's position in the ideal alternative society and their role in revivalism. Women in this alternative ideology are symbolically important, and a key: partly because 'emancipation' was a central focus of Kemalist secularism, partly because Islam too revolves around the position of women, and partly because, with the contradictions resulting from Kemalist reforms, women themselves are active in revivalism, so that revivalists turn the woman issue on its head. *Kadın ve Aile* is another Nakşibendi journal, aimed at middle-class urban women experiencing role conflict. Didactic, not reasoned, it projects women as home-makers, bastions of Islamic values; it favours (segregated) education for women, but not employment out of the home. Anti-Western, it resembles conservative women's journals of the west. Quite different is *Bizim Aile*, a new journal from the Nurcus, which enters intellectual debate with the secularists. Pluralist in outlook, it adopts democratic discourse and values; concerned with meaning and the priority of belief, it is preoccupied with veiling but gives reasons for it. It appears modern and liberal, though not in its prescriptions, where it is ambiguous. Different again, and extremist in its focus on women, is *Mektup*, an independent (though near-Nakşibendi) journal from Konya, uncompromising in its hostility to secularism and the West. Appealing to educated but oppressed women, *Mektup* underlines the martyrdom, pain and suffering caused by the 'pharaohs', including husbands, though the latter must be protected. Despite advocating heavy veiling, in some ways *Mektup* is 'progressive': men and women are equal in the home and women's role in the Jihad is very important.

The success and influence of the new Islamic movements should not be exaggerated. Turkey is politically and intellectually much more heterogeneous than most (perhaps all) of the countries in which Islamic movements have recently played a dominant role. Although several writers have maintained that Kemalist secularization had merely a superficial effect on the religiosity of the mass of the population, there is increasing ethnographic evidence to support Heper's conclusion in 1980 (see above, p. 9) that political pluralism, and the separation of religion from politics, have indeed become deeply rooted in much of Turkish society.[37] A wide range of non-religious ideologies and political programmes are popularly supported. Despite the prominence of new Islamic literature, education, mosque-building and other phenomena, Islamic groups receive the active support of a small minority of the population, and they are besides, as the chapters in this book make clear, far from united among themselves. Further, field-studies have shown how apparently 'Islamic' behaviour often reflects local-level political and economic rivalries; a new adherence to Islamic values and practices is evidence less of religious fanaticism than of a renewed ability of Islamic discourses to articulate structural conflicts, attitudes to the state and the process of change.[38]

None the less, the substantial growth in the public recognition and expression of Islam requires further assessment and explanation. What is new about Islam in Turkey today? How revolutionary are the new movements – do they seek an 'Islamic state'? Has there been there a 'resurgence' of something dormant, or a 'revival' of something dead? If there is revival, what is its source and character? Is it an expression of a wider phenomenon, whether Iranian, Middle Eastern, or a world movement? What is specifically Turkish about it? If there is continuity, are the same questions being asked, or are there new values and vocabulary, debates and discourses?

'Islamic revival' can involve 'real' change, or merely changed perceptions through the greater availability of information about Islam or more sensitization to religious and political issues.[39] Most writers on the subject, including contributors to this book, regard the Islamic movements in modern Turkey specifically as expressions of a search for identity among people who feel their rulers have compromised it in aligning themselves too closely with a West whose values, while seductive, are at the same time both alien and unattainable. More generally the movements are seen as expressions of Third World reaction to the materialism and secularism associated with Western and Soviet civilizations. Just as the Turkish revolution of 1908–23 was 'one of the many echoes of a global upheaval . . . a Turkish answer to the great turmoil that marked the end of the nineteenth century',[40] so the revival of Islam in Turkey of the 1970s and 1980s is part of wider late-twentieth-century movements such as anti-materialism and perhaps post-modernism.[41]

Yet the 'Islamic revival' in Turkey is also distinctively Turkish, and its different phases and expressions can be attributed to more specific factors. For example, increasing Islamic consciousness after 1950 owed much to the expansion of education and politicization,[42] which brought greater popular awareness, both of the country and its relative position in the world, and of Islamic movements elsewhere, such as in Egypt, Iran and Afghanistan. Equally, Islam as an ideology of opposition flourished in the official circumstances of state secularism in the decades up to 1980, while the more pragmatic government attitude to Islam adopted after the military intervention, including promotion of the Islamic element in Turkish national identity, has certainly allowed far greater freedom of expression.[43] As Mardin has insisted, 'Islam' in Turkey is and always has been heterogeneous and multi-dimensional, including both orthodoxies and the tarikats and neo-orders, with different forms and functions, varying with region and class, and both personal–moral and ideological–political dimensions.[44] Indeed, in the new circumstances of the 1980s in Turkey, Islamic revival has taken on quite new forms, which are socially and ideologically not necessarily the same as any previous version; they are even more varied than before, both in their manifestations, and in their differences from revivalism elsewhere.[45]

Other explanations of the Islamic revival in Turkey have pointed to radically new economic conditions; to the reluctance of post-1980 youth to follow the secular line of their parents' generation; to external Islamic sources of funding; and to modern media – the new Islamic literature and openly available audio and video-cassettes can supplant or supplement the knowledge purveyed through state-dominated radio and television, allowing unprecedented popular familiarization with and then criticism of the West.[46]

If a major element in Islamic revival in Turkey is the quest for identity, or for a non-capitalist, non-socialist ideology, the dominant factor in this is Turkey's relation with the West. Turkey today is not a Muslim state, but it is a country with an overwhelmingly Muslim population. Of Muslim countries other than those with oil-based economies, Turkey is the most industrially and technologically advanced, and the closest economically and culturally to Europe and the European Community. Discussions of the place of Turkey in the modern world rarely fail to indicate the importance of its geographical location in both Europe and Asia, and its historical, economic, political and cultural ties with both the Christian West and the Muslim Middle East.

Opposition to Turkey's entry into the European Community focuses explicitly on the economic gap, the political questions of Cyprus and the Aegean dispute with Greece, and the issues of human rights and democracy (including the legacy of the Armenian massacres and more recent Kurdish problems). Implicitly, it seems more often to be based on culture, religion and pseudo-history. Advocates of entry note that the Islamic identity of Turks (if not of Turkey) does not significantly differentiate them from other countries of Europe which have non-religious constitutions and multi-faith populations. Turkey's relationship with Muslim Middle Eastern nations as fellow-Muslims is no more grounds for ideological solidarity than is the Christian identity for the nations of Western Europe. History shows centuries of Ottoman alliance with Europe, before Atatürk made his direction clear. Turkey's opponents have a powerful lobby in the West, while Turks have been notoriously bad at lobbying for themselves, and myths of 'the terrible Turk', whether or not realistically based, continue to be perpetuated through Byron, *Lawrence of Arabia* and *Midnight Express*.[47]

The momentous events of the winter of 1989–90 in Central and Eastern Europe and the Soviet Union, and of the summer and autumn of 1990 in the Gulf, have radically altered political alignments and assumptions, in the Middle East as elsewhere.

Turkey has committed herself to the common front against Iraq, and the question of Islamic revival is for the moment in abeyance. At the time of writing it is too early to tell whether Turkey will emerge with its strategic role as a front-line member of NATO, and its prospects for eventual full-membership of the European Community, diminished or (as seems more likely) enhanced.

NOTES

1. See e.g. James Piscatori, *Islam in a World of Nation-States*, Cambridge University Press, 1986.
2. On different types of 'secularization', see Turan (Chapter 2 below).
3. On Islam in Ottoman society, see Bernard Lewis, *The Emergence of Modern Turkey*, 2nd edn, London, Oxford University Press, 1968; Niyazi Berkes, *The Development of Secularism in Turkey*, Montreal, McGill University Press, 1964; Metin Heper, 'Islam, polity and society in Turkey: a Middle Eastern perspective', *Middle East Journal*, 1981, pp. 345–63; Binnaz Toprak, *Islam and Political Development in Turkey*, Leiden, Brill, 1981, pp. 24–31; Ahmet Evin, 'Communitarian structures and social change', in Ahmet Evin, ed., *Modern Turkey: Continuity and Change*, Opladen, Leske, 1984, pp. 11–24; Şerif Mardin various, esp. *The Genesis of Young Ottoman Thought*, Princeton University Press, 1962; 'Ideology and religion in the Turkish revolution', *International Journal of Middle East Studies*, 2, 1971, pp. 197–211; 'Religion in modern Turkey', *International Social Science Journal*, 29, 1977, pp. 282–3, and Chapter 6 below.
4. Most recently, Şerif Mardin, *Religion and Social Change in Modern Turkey*, Albany, SUNY Press, 1989, pp. 11, 158f, and passim; see also Meeker (Chapter 9 below).
5. See Mardin, 'Ideology and Religion'; Evin, 'Communitarian structures'; Toprak, *Islam and Political Development*, p. 28.
6. See E. I. J. Rosenthal, *Islam in the Modern National State*, Cambridge, Cambridge University Press, 1965, Chapter 3; Nur Yalman, 'The center and the periphery: the reform of religious institutions in Turkey', *Current Turkish Thought*, 38, 1979; Toprak, *Islam and Political Development*, pp. 59f., 115; Evin, 'Communitarian structures'; Ergun Özbudun, 'Antecedents of Kemalist secularism: some thoughts on the Young Turk period', in Ahmet Evin, ed., *Modern Turkey*, pp. 25–44; Mardin, *Religion and Social Change*, pp. 91, 108, 112–3, 142; and see Akşit (Chapter 7 below).
7. See Mardin, 'Religion in modern Turkey', p. 284; *Religion and Social*

Change, pp. 103, 124f; Yalman, 'Center and periphery'; Toprak, *Islam and Political Development*, p. 33; Turan below.

8. Toprak, *Islam and Political Development*, p. 47.

9. Toprak, *Islam and Political Development*, p. 63f.; Mardin, 'Ideology and religion', p. 208.

10. See Mardin, 'Ideology and religion', pp. 286–8; *Religion and Social Change*; Toprak, *Islam and Political Development*, pp. 40f.

11. Mardin, 'Ideology and religion'; Toprak, *Islam and Political Development*, pp. 38f.

12. See Yalçın-Heckmann (Chapter 5) and Mardin (Chapter 6) below.

13. Nur Yalman, 'Islamic reform and the mystic tradition in eastern Turkey', *Archives Européennes de Sociologie*, 10, 1969, p. 47.

14. Cf. Şerif Mardin, 'Religion and politics in modern Turkey', in James P. Piscatori, ed., *Islam in the Political Process*, London, Cambridge University Press, 1983, p. 142. See also Richard and Nancy Tapper (Chapter 3 below), and Christel Lane, *The Rites of Rulers*, Cambridge, Cambridge University Press, 1981.

15. Toprak, *Islam and Political Development*, p. 70; Heper, 'Islam, polity and society'; Mardin, *Religion and Social Change*, pp. 25, 169, 229.

16. Mardin, 'Religion in modern Turkey', p. 279; *Religion and Social Change*, p. 179.

17. Toprak, *Islam and Political Development*, p. 57; see Ali Yaşar Sarıbay, 'Türkiye'de siyasal modernleşme, toplumsal yapı ve laiklik', MS, c. 1987; Turan (Chapter 2) and Tappers (Chapter 3) below.

18. E.g., Mardin, *Religion and Social Change*, p. 15, referring to Leach and Gellner. Cf. Richard Tapper, 'Introduction', in *The Conflict of Tribe and State in Iran and Afghanistan*, London, Croom Helm, 1983, on 'tribe' and 'state', and references there to other systems of alternatives within one single ideological structure.

19. See Evin, 'Communitarian structures,' and Meeker (Chapter 9) below.

20. Mardin calls them 'Kemalist jacobins', *Religion and Social Change*, pp. 1, 76.

21. On the MNP/MSP see Turan (Chapter 2) below; Binnaz Toprak, 'Politicization of Islam in a secular state: the National Salvation Party in Turkey', in Said Amir Arjomand, ed., *From Nationalism to Revolutionary Islam*, London, Macmillan, pp. 119–33; Ali Yaşar Sarıbay, *Türkiye'de Modernleşme, Din ve Parti Politikası: MSP Örnek Olayı*, Istanbul, Alan Yayıncılık, 1985. For analyses and overviews of Turkish multi-party politics, see C. H. Dodd, *Democracy and Development in Turkey*, Beverley, Eothen, 1979, and *The Crisis of Turkish Democracy*, Beverley, Eothen, 1983; and Andrew Finkel and Nükhet Sirman, eds, *Turkish State, Turkish Society*, London, Routledge/SOAS CNMES, 1990.

22. Toprak, *Islam and Political Development*, pp. 72ff., 85–8.

23. Ibid., pp. 77–8.

24. Notably ibid.
25. Heper, 'Islam, polity and society'.
26. Ibid., pp. 356–7; see Mardin, 'Religion and politics'; Toprak, *Islam and Political Development*, pp. 75f. and 'Religion as state ideology in a secular setting: the Turkish-Islamic synthesis', in Malcolm Wagstaff, ed., *Aspects of Religion in Secular Turkey*, University of Durham, Centre for Middle Eastern and Islamic Studies, Occasional Paper No. 40, 1990, pp. 10–15; see also Tappers (Chapter 3) below.
27. Toprak, *Islam and Political Development*, pp. 118–19, referring to Ahmet N. Yücekök, *Türkiye'de Örgütlenmiş Dinin Sosyo-Ekonomik Tabanı, 1946-1968*, Ankara, Sevinç Matbaası, 1971.
28. See Akşit (Chapter 7), Meeker (Chapter 9), Saktanber (Chapter 8), Ayata (Chapter 10), Güneş-Ayata (Chapter 11) and Acar (Chapter 12) below; also Binnaz Toprak, 'Islamist intellectuals of the 1980s in Turkey', *Current Turkish Thought*, 62, 1987; Şerif Mardin, 'Myth, literature and the modernization of Nakşibendi discourse', paper at international round-table, *Horizons de pensée et pratiques sociales chez les intellectuels du monde musulman*, Paris, 1987, and 'Culture and religion towards the year 2000', in *Turkey in the Year 2000*, Turkish Political Science Association, Ankara, Sevinç Matbaası, 1989, pp. 163–86.
29. See Gürsoy-Tezcan (Chapter 4) and Akşit (Chapter 10) below.
30. See Erkan Akın and Ömer Karasapan, 'The Rabita affair', 'Turkey's tarikats', 'The "Turkish–Islamic synthesis"', *Middle East Report*, 18 (3), 153, July–August 1988, pp. 15–18; Turan (Chapter 2) below. See also Andrew Mango, 'The consolations of religion in Turkey', in Wagstaff, ed., *Aspects of Religion*, pp. 16–21.
31. Mardin (Chapter 6), Ayata (Chapter 10), Güneş-Ayata (Chapter 11), Acar (Chapter 12) below; Akın and Karasapan, 'Turkey's tarikats', p. 16; cf. Yalman, 'Islamic reform', and 'Center and periphery'; also Toprak, 'Religion as state ideology'; John Norton, 'Turkish Sufis, saints and subversives', in Wagstaff, ed., *Aspects of Religion*, pp. 4–9.
32. On the TIS see esp. Toprak, 'Religion as state ideology' and references there; see also Akın and Karasapan, 'The "Turkish–Islamic synthesis"', drawing on Gencay Şaylan, *Islamiyet ve Siyaset*, Ankara, Yayınlar 1988; Mardin, 'Culture and religion'; Ali Yaşar Sarıbay, 'Religion in contemporary Turkish society and polity', *Current Turkish Thought*, 58, 1986.
33. See note 17 above.
34. These cases are clearly not representative of the vast variety of Turkish social contexts, and indeed much work remains to be done on religious life in villages, the smaller cities, the metropolitan middle class, not to mention the Muslim and other minority groups.
35. Mardin, *Religion and Social Change*, pp. 5f, referring to Nazif Shahrani's MS, 'Local knowledge of Islam and social discourse in Afghanistan and Turkistan'.
36. Mardin, *Religion and Social Change*, p. 4.

37. See Tappers (Chapter 3), Gürsoy-Tezcan (Chapter 11) and Yalçın-Heckmann (Chapter 5) below; and studies of provincial towns by Fatma Mansur, *Bodrum: a Town on the Aegean*, Leiden, Brill, 1972; Peter Benedict, *Ula: an Anatolian Town*, Leiden, Brill, 1974; and Paul Magnarella, *Tradition and Change in a Turkish Town*, New York, John Wiley, 1974.
38. See for example Gürsoy-Tezcan (Chapter 11) and Yalçın-Heckmann (Chapter 5) below, and Arnold Leder, *Catalysts of Change: Marxist versus Muslim in a Turkish Community*, Austin, University of Texas Middle East Monographs, 1976.
39. İlter Turan in discussion.
40. Mardin, 'Ideology and religion', p. 211.
41. Toprak, 'Religion as state ideology'; Mardin, *Religion and Social Change*, p. 24.
42. See Saktanber (Chapter 8).
43. See Acar (Chapter 12).
44. Mardin, 'Religion in modern Turkey', p. 280.
45. See Güneş-Ayata (Chapter 11).
46. Cf. Malcolm Wagstaff, 'Introduction', in Wagstaff, ed., *Aspects of Religion*, pp. 1–3.
47. See Sir Bernard Burrows, 'Turkey and Europe: the cultural background', in Gordon Johnson, ed., *Turkey and Europe in a Cultural Context*, Cambridge, Centre of Middle Eastern Studies, 1988, pp. 1–8.

Part I

ISLAM AND NATIONALISM AS POLITICAL IDEOLOGIES

2

RELIGION AND POLITICAL CULTURE IN TURKEY

İlter Turan

INTRODUCTION

Political culture – that is, political attitudes, values, ideas, feelings, information and skills[1] – constitutes a framework within which people engage in political behaviours. A study of political culture, therefore, enhances our ability to explain current and predict future behaviour.

To the extent that politics is one of the several areas of societal life, the elements of culture which pertain to it are distinct from those which belong to other domains. Yet because societal life is not rigidly compartmentalized, but comprises a connected, if not totally integrated, whole, the elements of culture in one area of societal life are connected with, and influence, those in others.

The particular topic this chapter intends to examine is the relationship between religion and political culture, more specifically how religion has influenced political culture[2] in a specific context: Turkey. Toprak has rightly complained that 'the degree to which Turkish political culture is shaped by religious values has remained unstudied. ... The Islamic emphasis on communal solidarity and its consequences for politics', she adds, 'is an important topic that ought to be investigated.'[3]

In recent years, there have been frequent references to an 'Islamic resurgence'. These can be traced to the emergence of the so-called 'militant Islam'.[4] Although the phrase evokes a powerful

31

image – which is used indiscriminately to describe and analyse the changing political role of religion in all societies in which the prevalent religion among the population is Islam – it is an imprecise term.[5]

It may be useful to study each country individually to understand how religion and politics are related, and how religion influences political culture and why. Turkey is an interesting case in this context, because, since the founding of the Turkish Republic, a conscious effort has been made to separate the religious and political domains of societal life.

HISTORICAL BACKGROUND

Islam is frequently viewed as a total religion; that is, not only as a religion in terms of theological belief and worship but also as a way of life which guides political, economic and social behaviour.[6] Such an observation often derives from a reading of theology. Any empirical examination of societies with predominantly Muslim populations would belie its validity. A more accurate way of looking at the relationship between religion and social life in general, and politics in particular, would be to suggest that religion affects social life (politics) very significantly in some societies, significantly in others, moderately still in others, and very little in the remainder. In the case of Muslim societies[7] we are likely to find more societies in the first two categories. We may also note that societies change, and they may move either way in the classification at a given moment in time.

If we turn to Turkey within this framework, we find that religion affected political life in the Ottoman Empire significantly until the nineteenth century, but a process of change rendered that effect moderate during the nineteenth and early twentieth centuries. Shortly after the founding of the Republic, the influence of religion was reduced to insignificance in terms of politics. Currently, it is thought that religion has a moderate but, some say, an increasing role in Turkish political life.

The Ottoman Empire was never a fully Islamic state. Confronted with the challenge of holding together a multi-ethnic and multi-religious empire which spread across three continents, the Ottoman rulers needed flexibility, which was achieved by developing a body of traditional law (*örfi hukuk*) which did not derive from religious law (the Sharia). Care was taken, however, that religious laws would not be openly violated.

Persistent defeat necessitated the introduction of comprehensive and sustained change. Expressed differently, the Empire needed to modernize; that is, to place a high value upon advanced material technology, use advanced techniques of organization and adopt a favourable attitude towards change.[8] As the Empire continued to fail despite efforts to change, the solution was found not in moving away from modernization but in rendering it even more comprehensive. During the nineteenth century, in most areas of public and political life, ideologies other than Islam were being pursued: societal life, including the political, was being secularized.[9]

Donald Smith has identified five types of secularization process that a society can experience.[10] Four of these had been taking place during the latter stages of the Ottoman Empire, namely: (1) polity separation secularization, meaning the institutional separation of religion and polity and the denial of the religious identity of the polity; (2) polity expansion secularization, meaning the expansion of the political system into areas of society formerly regulated by religion; (3) political culture secularization, meaning the transformation of values associated with the polity, and the replacing of religious by secular notions of politics, political community and political legitimacy; (4) political process secularization, meaning the decline in the political saliency of religious leaders, interest groups and issues. The fifth, polity dominance secularization, that is, the initiation of an open governmental attack on the religious basis of general culture, and the forcible imposition of secular ideology on the political culture, constitutes the essence of Kemalist reforms.

The modernizers themselves were divided from within as regards how to reconcile the conflicts that arose between the innovations being introduced to society and the basic tenets of traditional religion. The need for change was too evident to be debated, and there was consensus that without catching up with Western technology it would be impossible to turn the tide which had been running against the Empire. But commonalities ended here, and two rival modes of thinking emerged: the Westernist and the Islamist. Those subscribing to the Westernist mode argued that civilization was a unified whole and could not be broken into the two components of technology and culture; therefore, change could not be limited to the adoption of modern technology but must also include cultural transformation if the Empire were to be saved from disintegration and destruction. The Islamists rejected this line of reasoning: not only did they think that the adoption of technology without cultural transformation was possible, but they added that such transformation was tantamount to giving up what you had set out to preserve.[11] The cultural and political history of the Empire during the latter part of the nineteenth and the first two decades of the twentieth century is one of struggle between these two groups, with the Westernists gradually gaining the upper hand.

The ascent to political power of the Westernists led them to become keenly aware that religion was a big stumbling block in their efforts to effect a transformation of society on modern lines. As Mardin has astutely observed:

> The young revolutionaries of the 1900s were faced with religion under all of these headings: as a strongly anchored basis of community, as a philosophy and world view which seemed to perform more substantive function than ideas usually did, as one of the social and economic bases of power in the provinces, and as a state institution and ideology.[12]

It was the First World War, the defeat and break-up of the Empire, and the discrediting of the ruling house on account of its opposition to the National War of Independence, which gave the Westernists their definitive opportunity to deal with the religiously based opposition to cultural transformation. Shortly after the founding of the Republic, a major campaign was launched against the institutional and cultural basis of religion in society. The traditional institutions of religious education were closed down, all education was brought under the supervision of the Ministry of National Education, mystical orders were banned, a new civil code based on a Swiss cantonal code was adopted and many other similar changes were effected with surprisingly little resistance.[13]

The secularizing reforms of Atatürk, mainly in the cultural

domain, were instrumental in reducing the societal role of religion, but not so much that religion could not serve as a means of mobilization and protest against the single Republican People's Party when the transition to competitive politics took place.[14]

If we were to make a general observation, then, it might be said that religion provided a changing and declining input into Turkish political life and culture during the latter stages of the Ottoman Empire and the one-party period under the Republic. With the transition to competitive politics, the role of religion in politics has become more visible, but whether this in fact reflects an intensification in its political role needs to be analysed further.

CONTEMPORARY POLITICAL CULTURE: THE ROLE OF RELIGION

Almond and Powell have identified three broad aspects of political culture, which they have called system, process and policy aspects.[15] System aspects include people's notions about the nature of the political community, and the appropriate bases of political legitimacy. Process aspects deal, among other things, with the way people should relate to politics, and the way they should conduct politics. Finally, policy aspects pertain to people's ideology, their image of the good society and their ideas about the issues politicians should address.

In the following pages, the role of religion in certain elements of political culture will be examined. Specifically, the role of religion in the definition of political community, in the achievement of political legitimacy, in the formation of political ideologies and in the shaping of values and styles which pertain to politics will be taken up. While religion may provide inputs, as it inevitably does, into other aspects of culture, those that have been cited appear to me to be the most important.

RELIGION AND POLITICAL COMMUNITY

By 'political community' I mean a collectivity whose members feel they should be under the same government. The criteria on which feelings of membership in a political community are built have varied over time and across political systems.

In Islamic theology, all Muslims are supposed to constitute an *umma*, a community of believers who accept the divine basis of society. Because the Sharia regulates social relationships, there is no need for autonomous politics. Political community is synonymous with religious community, the state is its political organization.[16] In an Islamic state there may be non-Muslims: if so, they are extended protected status (*dhimmi*) but they do not have equal rights and duties with members of the *umma*. They are subjects of the state but not members of the political community.[17]

While such a theological model hardly corresponded to the realities of Ottoman society and politics during any stage of its existence, some basic elements of the model were characteristic of the Ottoman system. To begin with, Muslims and non-Muslims in the Empire were distinct political entities. Until the middle of the nineteenth century, if one were to participate in the 'political affairs' of the Empire, such as holding an administrative office or serving in the military, one had to be a Muslim. Members of the *millets*, that is, formally recognized non-Muslim communities with defined privileges and obligations, were free to practise their religion and their trade, but they were not members of the Empire's political community and they could not rule. They were to obey political authority.

To say that there were distinctions of a political nature between Muslims and non-Muslims should not be taken as sufficient evidence that the former were a unified political community. First, there were the Shi'a, whose political loyalty and commitment to the *umma* were always suspect. But there were, in addition, sects, cults, brotherhoods, orders, many of which were viewed as being subversive. They were not integrated into the political community, rather they were suppressed.[18]

With the advent of nationalism as put forth by the ideologues of the French Revolution and propagated by Napoleon in order to undermine the unity and power of the multi-ethnic empires, the stability of the Ottoman Empire was severely shaken.[19] Separatist nationalist movements quickly burgeoned in the western parts, first culminating in Greek independence, then spread to other areas. It became apparent that a new formula was needed to hold the Empire together.

The history of the Empire during the second half of the

nineteenth century was one of looking for ways and ideologies to prevent disintegration and dismemberment. The Tanzimat effort tried to render subjects into citizens, and worked to inculcate in them a sense of Ottoman nationality. The Muslims, on the other hand, found it difficult to accept an ideology that challenged their monopoly of politics and their superior social status.

As it became clear that non-Muslim *millets* could not be prevented from aspiring to form their own independent polities, Islam was turned to as a means of holding the Empire together; but to no avail. 'The political message of Islam was not sufficiently focused to keep many Muslims who made up [the] Empire united around a common purpose.'[20] The spread of the ideas of nationalism among the non-Muslims, then among the non-Turkish Muslims, prompted further revisions in the ideologies of integration; and ethnic Turkish nationalism came to dominate the Empire towards the end of its historical life.[21]

The National War of Independence was waged in the name of a political community, a nation, whose characteristics were not explicitly spelled out. Attention was focused on the defeat of the external adversary. With the successful completion of the war, and then the establishment of the Republic, efforts were launched to shape the population which remained within the boundaries of the state into a new political community.

Membership in the new political community was acquired by being a citizen of the nation-state. Citizens were expected to develop a Turkish national identity, in this way enhancing their feelings of attachment to the political community. This required changing the basis of community membership, which had been, up to that point, religious. The secularizing reforms of Atatürk were intended, as indicated earlier, to achieve that very purpose.

Has a political community emerged in Turkey, with members whose religious characteristics in no way affect their membership? At the formal–legal level, the answer is clearly, yes. All citizens are, by definition, members of the Turkish nation, they have equal rights. Religious affiliation is not mentioned in the laws as a criterion for membership in the political community. What, however, is the answer at the behavioural level?

Let us begin by noting that some segments of the Turkish population continue to view their society as a collectivity characterized by Islam. Although there has not yet been any comprehensive research on this, Mardin's study of workers in Izmir provides an indication of a basic cleavage in how the political community is perceived in Turkish society. In response to a question on how they viewed themselves, 50 per cent said that they viewed themselves as Turks, and 37.5 per cent as Muslims. Mardin observed that a person's self-perception also influenced how he viewed other people in the environment. Those who viewed themselves as Turks were much more likely to think of people around them as citizens than were those who saw themselves as Muslims. Conversely, the 'Muslims' were inclined to see others as 'brothers in religion'.[22]

Frey's study of peasant attitudes found that peasants were less likely to be oriented towards the nation than were urban Turks, but that this appeared to be mainly a function of educational differences. 'The school in rural Turkey seems to play a pronounced role in increasing national identification', he concluded.[23]

The rise of the 'nation' as the prevalent form of collectivity with which people identify tells us that Kemalist reforms may have been successful in helping redefine the nature of the political community. Contrary to Islamic ideology, which views all believers as belonging to a collective unit which is social and political at the same time, and which rejects the division of the *umma* into political communities without a religious base, such as nations, the republican ideology, taking the 'nation' as the appropriate unit on which to build the political community, appears to have permeated Turkish society. Put differently, most Turks, while being aware that they share a common religion with a number of other peoples in the Middle East, do not seem to think that this commonality warrants their incorporation under the same rule or political system.

But let us turn to the original question. Does the contemporary political community have some religiously-based attributes? Apart from a strictly legal sense which has been mentioned above, the answer is in the affirmative direction. More explicitly, a person who is not a Muslim is usually referred to as a minority person or as a Turkish citizen, but not a Turk.[24] 'Turk' designates an ethno-religious characteristic of the political community, an attribute which is not found among some of the citizens, albeit very few.

It is necessary to clarify what 'Muslim' means in this context.

My own observation is that the term implies no religiosity, and possibly not even belief, but the possession of what we may call 'Islamic credentials'. That is, if a person bears a name that sounds Turkish or Islamic, if his parents are thought to be Muslims, and if he does not profess belief in another religion, particularly a monotheistic one, then he is treated as a Muslim. Ironically, an agnostic or an atheist may qualify as a 'Muslim' if he is of an 'Islamic' background. Clearly, then, we are dealing with a cultural tradition not a belief system, a phenomenon found in other countries such as Israel and Greece.

There are several indicators showing the existence of an Islamic tradition dimension to the definition of the political community. We shall take up two of them. First, political leaders, including the president of the Republic, do not hesitate on occasion to talk about 'our religion' when in fact the political system is not supposed to possess such a characteristic. This is but a tacit way of identifying an attribute of the political community which is not accorded formal legal recognition. It should be added that 'our religion' is employed loosely to refer to all citizens with 'Islamic credentials' and does not carry with it sectarian connotations.

The second indicator relates to the way missionary activity and conversion to another religion are viewed in Turkey. Both are regarded with extreme suspicion. Such suspicion, particularly of missionary activity, may be understood in terms of the historical role that missionaries have played in fanning ethnic separatisms among the Christian populations of the Ottoman Empire, leading to its dismemberment. But more than 99 per cent of the population of the Republic are Muslims, and any fears based on historical experience are not well founded. In addition, historical experience does not explain why individual cases of conversion are also viewed as almost subversive acts.

We may have a clue to what is happening in Mardin's observation:

> The Republic ... secured the continuation of the umma structure. Patriotism, being united and resisting [external] others, were ways of fostering a feeling of umma. The emphasis on unity, togetherness, and communitarian integrity (*bütünlük*) in schools did not remove people too far from the umma idea.[25]

Unconsciously viewing the world in *umma* terms, and working to change the cultural orientations of a population that saw itself as an *umma*, the early republican leadership, in their effort to build a nation, may have produced a national *umma*. What was built, in other words, was a political community of Turks who were also Muslims. Islam did not legitimize the regime, nor was it necessarily the appropriate ideology on which to base political action, yet one's claim to membership in the political community, in behavioural terms, was validated by the possession of Islamic credentials.

It may be that Islam is an indispensable element in the definition of a Turk. The population of contemporary Turkey is composed of peoples of various origins who settled in the country under the Ottoman Empire. Many came as refugees after their lands fell under foreign (that is, Christian) domination. They came not because they were ethnic Turks, but because they were Muslims. In the building of a nation out of the conglomeration of people who inhabited the borders of the Republic, the integrative function of religion could not be ignored.

RELIGION AND POLITICAL LEGITIMACY

Until the emergence of modern nation-states, obedience to political authority was secured in great part by attributing divine qualities to it. The social system would be maintained because it was divinely ordained. In short, a religio-political system controlled both political and social behaviour, directing them to its support and harmonious operation.

The American and French Revolutions paved the way to the transformation of political systems such that the basis of political legitimacy shifted to secular bases. Although other secular legitimations of rule have been used, such as ideologically true government or effective government, by far the most popular legitimation of political power has been popular sovereignty. Governments are to be obeyed because they represent the will of the nation, or because they have been elected by a majority of the citizens, or because they represent the workers and the peasants.[26]

As a traditional bureaucratic political system, the Ottoman Empire initially creates the impression that it also was a political system which based its legitimacy on religion. A closer examination reveals, however, that such a hasty analysis may need to be refined. Heper has noted that 'the so-called Muslim institution in that polity was a prop for and subservient to the state'.[27] This implies a two-way relationship between religion and politics that is rendered more explicit by Mardin:

> The Ottoman bureaucrat saw as his duty the preservation of the integrity of the state and the promotion of Islam. This was expressed in the formula *din-ü devlet* . . . or 'religion and state'. But it was also understood that the viability of the state was essential for the preservation of religion. In the sense that the state was necessary to keep religion flourishing, it had priority over religion.[28]

In the light of these observations, it appears that the polity gave as much legitimacy to religion as religion did to the polity. Furthermore, the religion of the state was Sunni Islam, which accepted temporal power as being legitimate[29] and tended to accord legitimacy to whoever was in power. Therefore, political authority seems not to have been heavily reliant on religion as a source of legitimacy.[30] The prevalence of Sunni Islam over the heterodox cults, sects, mystical orders and the Shi'a, which characterized the countryside, was, however, dependent on its position as the state religion.

The conduct of the Turkish National War of Independence against the Allies, despite the open opposition of the Sultan–Caliph, illustrates that the primacy accorded to the state surpasses any claim of superior political legitimacy the Caliph might have pretended to have. This also explains why the shift in the basis of political legitimacy from religion to popular sovereignty, as depicted in the expression 'sovereignty belongs to the nation', was reasonably smooth.

As mentioned earlier, policies of cultural secularization characterized the earlier history of the Republic. Bans on attempts to base the political system on principles of religion were codified into law, and became part of subsequent republican constitutions. Can we then conclude that religion has no role in the political system's achievement of legitimacy?

We may say that the fundamental basis of legitimacy is not

embedded in religion but in the existence of a state. Religion is linked with the extension of legitimacy to the polity in several ways. First, religion provides a framework within which political power may be exercised. In other words, it is a constraint on what governments can do and still maintain their legitimacy. This function is not unique to Islam or Turkey, and is found in many countries and many other types of political system.

Second, religion is an element of social control which includes values such as being respectful of governmental authority and of public servants, and compliance with the government's commands.[31] In this way, religion is one of several ways through which obedience to political authority is secured.

Finally, religion is a source of symbols, ideas and meanings that are used to elicit positive political behaviours from society. A few examples may help to explain what is meant here. A person who dies in battle for the cause of religion is a *şehit* and goes directly to heaven. Now this symbol has been borrowed from religious vocabulary, and is used to describe any public servant who dies in the course of public duty; in this way, government service is elevated to the level of God's cause. Similarly, the Friday sermons are used to invite citizens to engage in acts supportive of government. The Directorate of Religious Affairs sends out model sermons to imams (preachers) which may encourage the citizens, for example, to pay their taxes, or to contribute to foundations established to assist the armed forces; thus, secular acts are identified as being religiously desirable, and they gain an aura of religious legitimacy.

In conclusion, it seems to me that the Turkish state, while not viewing religion as giving direction to its policies and actions, continues to treat it as a resource which may be mobilized for 'purposes of state' whenever it is found useful or necessary.

RELIGION AS POLITICAL IDEOLOGY

In many societies, religion is one of the bases of political ideology. Turkey is no exception.

Looking at the role of religion as a political ideology from a historical perspective, it may be recalled that the decline of the Ottoman state *vis-à-vis* the West was explained by two rival frameworks. Members of the bureaucracy and the military often tended to attribute the decline to the deterioration of the state apparatus, while men of religion explained it by a loss of faith and a move away from the basic requirements of religion.[32] The military bureaucratic élite who defined the causes of the decline as too much tradition (including religion) and not enough modernity, emerged as the victors. It is this group, as noted earlier, which established the Republic and engaged in energetic secularization as part of their overall modernization effort.

The centrally directed policies of cultural change, aiming to render religion a matter of private concern, unintentionally provided opportunities for religion to assume political functions, for several reasons. To begin with, the strategy of cultural change emphasized its consolidation first among the urban educated. The new values would then be disseminated by this élite to the countryside and the lower echelons of urban society. To the extent that the benefits of rapid cultural transformation were not immediately clear to the people of this periphery who constituted its target, a search for an ideology for resisting change was never lacking. Islam, in this context, was the most readily available ideological framework to which people could turn for guidance. During the early part of the history of the Republic, some rebellions in the name of Islam were indications of the presence of a counter-ideology to the compulsory modernization of the centre.[33]

Toprak has captured another dimension of Islam's tendency to become politicized in the face of policies of secularization. Noting that Islamic teaching does not differentiate between state and society, she argues that 'Kemalism not only made that differentiation, but also reversed the order of importance between the sacred and the political realms. Secularization as state policy, therefore, has a built-in tendency to envisage oppositional politicization of Islam.'[34]

It may be surmised that this is a two-way process. Whereas Islam was perceived as a source of political opposition, those who responded negatively to cultural change probably tended to perceive themselves as political actors guided by religion.

A third process through which Islam has ascended in political importance relates to the consequences of social and economic change. Sayarı has argued that the individual in mass society searches for communities in which he can gain identity and find security.[35] Religious communities such as orders or cults constitute one type of social organization in which such solace can be found. These communities offer their members alternative visions of society, and critiques of contemporary society, which inevitably bring them into the arena of politics.

Socio-economic change also creates winners and losers. For example, small merchants, craftsmen and small shopkeepers tend to be driven to economic and social marginality as change proceeds. Such people turn to religious groups as an avenue through which political dissent can be registered.[36] Feelings of economic and social deprivation need not always produce a religious response. Heper suggests that a religio-political response is more likely to occur if the nature of the deprivation is not accurately perceived.[37] What he is probably referring to is the fact that if people cannot explain what is happening around them or to them on rational grounds, they are likely to turn to traditional analyses and remedies. A poor, ignorant man may well attribute the rise in the price of groceries to the greed and unscrupulous behaviour of grocers, whereas the real cause might be an increase in transport costs because highways are too crowded. This man might then argue that if you hung a few grocers, or if the government inculcated a fear of God in them, price hikes might be brought under control. Of course, the broader point from the perspective of our problem is that socio-economic change produces outcomes that facilitate the politicization of religion in society.

The emergence of religio-political ideologies in Turkey has been a slow process. This is understandable. Initially, the religio-political responses to change occurred in the countryside and in small towns which had historically been on the fringes of the polity and did not have the resources and the skills to influence centrally determined and implemented policies. The occasional manifestations of violent protest against government authority could easily be put down.

The secular leadership had also rendered the bringing of religion into politics a heavily punishable crime. Committing a violation of the rule under the single-party system dedicated to rapid modernization would have been too hazardous to attempt.

A major change came with the transition to multi-party politics in the 1940s.[38] As each political party would now have to put together a winning coalition among the electorate to achieve power, the tendency to heed the religious preferences of the voters was considerably enhanced. Yet the initial attempts to politicize religion were not particularly successful. The Nation Party, for example, which represented the more religious wing of the opposition to the Republican People's Party, did not do well in the 1950 elections. Voters overwhelmingly supported the Democrat Party, which was secular in orientation but responsive to the pragmatic needs of the population, including those of the religious domain. It was not the religious basis of its political ideology, but its tolerant attitude towards religion, which made the Democrat Party popular among the voters.

Religiously-based political ideologies in Turkey began to proliferate towards the end of the 1960s. This evolution may constitute some evidence that rapid socio-economic change rather than cultural change is behind the conversion of religion into political ideology. Although it may in fact be true that Kemalism neither provided a 'social ethos that appealed to the heart as well as to the mind', nor addressed itself to man's 'basic ontological security',[39] it has been a background against which the hard consequences of socio-economic change have had to emerge before religion became ideology.

There is no single, religion-based political ideology in Turkey. The pluralistic nature of Turkish society is reflected also in its political ideologies of religious origin. I shall deal briefly with one example, the National Salvation Party, because it was represented in parliament between 1973 and 1980.

The National Salvation Party (MSP) had its origins in the National Order Party (MNP) established in 1969 and closed down after 1971 by the Constitutional Court for having used religion for political purposes. It re-emerged before the 1973 election under the MSP banner, and gained a position such that no parliamentary majority could form on either right or left without its support, giving it considerable leverage. The party was dissolved once again after the 1980 military intervention. Currently it is operating under a new name, the Welfare Party (RP). It did not achieve parliamentary representation in the 1987 elections because of the presence of severe cut-off provisions in the electoral laws.

This series of political parties – MNP, MSP, RP – have all represented the Islamization of life in Turkey. They have complained about the degeneration of morals in society, the rise in the use of alcohol, gambling and prostitution. These 'unfortunate' developments, they have argued, may be traced to the imitation of Western cultural patterns. While technology, the origins of which can be traced back to the scientific achievements of Islam during its first seven centuries, can be borrowed from the West, culture cannot be; if it is, society degenerates. Therefore, life should be lived according to the principles of Islam, and it is incumbent on the political authority to promote this.

In the field of economics, these parties have taken a strong line against interest, and also against foreign capital, except that which may come from other Islamic countries. They have opposed Turkish membership of the European Economic Community on the grounds that it is a Christian–Zionist plot.

A newspaper, *Milli Gazete*, often thought to represent the views of these parties, has complained that the current political system is not Islamic, and that society should not be ruled according to votes.[40] But the parties themselves have been more cautious in expressing their views for fear of being brought to trial for using religion for political ends. For example, they have called their viewpoint *Milli Görüş*, 'National Viewpoint', although what is clearly implied is a religious viewpoint.

Although the message of the MNP/MSP/RP has contained many religious elements, religion is only one of the components of an ideology which, while presumably rejecting materialism, has had to come to terms with the electorate's approval of industrialization. In campaign politics, therefore, heavy industrialization evenly distributed throughout the country has received more attention than questions of exclusively moral concern.

If we want to evaluate the role of religion as a political ideology, we may make the following observations. First, religion has been one of the elements of a political counter-culture. The content of this culture has varied along with social and economic changes in society. Those who have been attracted to this counter-culture appear to have been individuals who have been unable to cope with change and have been pushed into marginal status in society.[41]

Secondly, the political ideologies permeated by religious values are not homogeneous. While there may be consensus among them that traditional values including the religious should be given a greater place in political life, questions on which values, and to what extent, and in what ways, are answered differently among different groups.

Thirdly, the presence of competitive politics in society has served to reduce the militant secularist stand of the central government. Not only have all major political parties adopted a more tolerant attitude towards a public role for religion, but they have also sought to incorporate specific religious groups in the coalitions which they have tried to put together among the electorate. As a consequence, the role of religion as a determinant of political ideology has declined considerably. To the extent that religious–traditionalist orientations have been incorporated by larger political movements, their militancy and their sense of isolation have declined.

Religion, to be sure, will continue to serve as a source of political values in Turkey. It appears less and less likely, however, that it will provide a totally different alternative *Weltanschauung* to contemporary political ideologies.[42]

RELIGION, POLITICAL VALUES AND POLITICAL STYLES

Religion, sometimes unintentionally, may promote values, norms and styles which have a bearing on politics. It has been suggested that Islam may be instrumental in inculcating authoritarianism among individuals in societies where it is the predominant religion. A number of reasons have been offered as explanations. Mardin points to the fact that Islam requires total submission of oneself to God, which also means that one submits oneself to the Sharia.[43] Because rules are divinely ordained, one cannot challenge them; one has no choice but to obey them.

Bertrand Badie observes that the cultural code of Islam is monistic, placing extreme emphasis on the idea of unity and giving no room to pluralism, while Christianity, with its Holy Trinity, its hierarchy of saints and the blessed, represents cosmic pluralism. In addition, he notes that there is no delegation of power from Allah to anyone, nor intermediary powers between him and the believers, nor a division of labour.[44] Power emanates from Allah, but on earth the Islamic ruler holds it and practises it on his behalf. Since this is a divinely ordained rule, people are expected to obey. In theory, there is no need for communication to flow from society to the ruler. Therefore, the emergence of secondary structures which perform the function of political communication has neither been encouraged nor well received. What we have here, then, is an authoritarian framework in which obedience is expected and participation is not favoured.

Finally, we may find that grounds for authoritarianism derive from the identification of state with society. If this identification is made, it implies that religious differences are at the same time political differences; moreover, loyalty to a different version of the religion is tantamount to disloyalty to both polity and body politic.[45] Traitorous movements in any society are accorded little sympathy or understanding: they are crushed, usually in a heavy-handed fashion.[46]

While Islamic theology and organization may create tendencies towards authoritarian values, as the preceding discussion suggests, it should be recognized that we are dealing at best with a hypothesis. It would need to be demonstrated empirically that both individual religiosity and subscription to a religious ideology are positively correlated with socially learned authoritarianism, even when other possible sources of authoritarianism are controlled for. Otherwise, we run into the danger of attributing qualities to Islam which it may not possess, or mistaking patterns to be found in any traditional environment as being peculiar to Islam.

Another political value which some Islamic thinkers derive from religion is equality. Indeed much talk in sermons is devoted to the articulation of egalitarian values which, as Smith has suggested, 'should be favorable to the development of participant political systems'.[47] Yet this equality is only before God, and appears not to extend to worldly matters. As we know, Islam did not reject slavery, nor did it extend equal status to women, although it is possible that it helped improve the social status of women in the particular environment in which it was born.

An examination of other aspects of religion may well lead us to conclude that élite rule rather than political egalitarianism is what is transmitted through religion. We have already noted that equality obtains in submitting oneself to God, for Islam does not teach its followers to change society so as to provide believers either equality of condition or equality of opportunity. Social stratification is taken for granted and accepted. A static, stratified society is not, however, evidence of the presence of élitism as a value, if we mean by that term a belief that persons possessing specific characteristics ought to have a much greater say in the running of the affairs of a society.

More important has been the evolution through time of a group of Islamic scholars, the Ulema, who have assumed the responsibility for interpreting Islamic law. Technically, these men are not involved in law-making, rather they follow a well-established pattern of deductive logic to ensure the application of religious law in specific circumstances. In answering questions, they started by looking into the Koran; if they found no immediate and direct answer, they moved to the Hadith, the traditions of the Prophet. If there was no answer there, they engaged in the drawing of analogies (*qiyas*). If no analogies could be drawn, then the consensus (*ijma'*) of the community would be sought for an acceptable answer.

Although the Ulema were not any closer than other Muslims to Allah, they could tell others what to do simply because of their greater familiarity with matters of religion and knowledge of Islamic law. In the Ottoman Empire, the Ulema developed into an elaborate political stratum, whose functions included legitimization of political authority and the administration of justice. During the nineteenth century, as the Ottoman decline persisted, and as the Sultan failed to reverse this negative tide, some elements among the Ulema became critical of the way society was run. Their complaint was that the Sultan's government had moved away from adequate observance of the tenets of religion. This was occurring simultaneously with assertions by a small group of men who had received Western education that more comprehensive Westernization was the key to arresting decline. The Ulema and the Western-educated resembled each other in several ways. The Ulema presumably possessed the knowledge to define an ideal society, and had prescriptions on how to construct it. The Westernists had similar claims. In both instances, however, the logic was one of political élitism: the possession of education and knowledge would entitle a person or a group to have a greater say in how the affairs of their society would be run. It is likely that the role the Ulema played, or were expected to play, provided a model for the Westernists, guiding their evolution towards becoming essentially a Westernist Ulema.

The similarities between the two types of élites did not stop there. Both viewed themselves as transmitters of a truth which existed outside of them, which was absolute, and which could be discovered by humans. It is interesting that the Westernists saw themselves and were called by others *münevver* or *aydın*, that is 'enlightened'. The connotation here was that they had been exposed to a truth which others had not been exposed to.

As related earlier, the Westernists succeeded, after the founding of the Republic, in eliminating the Ulema. But in terms of how the modernizers related to the body politic, there did not exist major differences between themselves and the social category which they had worked so hard to eliminate. They were the 'enlightened'; they knew what was true and good, and the citizen's duty was to obey and do his part in the creation of an ideal society. Only this time, the ideal society was not Islamic but modern.

Mustafa Kemal was a charismatic leader who had not only a reasonably clear vision of what type of society he wished to create, but also the skills to mobilize the masses to support the changes he wanted to realize. His successors were more concerned with consolidation than with change. In this effort, they resorted to a deductive logic for political action which is reminiscent of the way in which the Ulema rendered opinions on necessary courses of action in the political arena. Kemalism was increasingly formalized into a set of books, writings from which guidance for contemporary needs would be drawn.

If only in a very general way, one cannot but find some similarities between the old deductive logic and the way Kemalist ideology has often been employed in recent years to offer guidance and legitimation for political action. The Great Speech of Atatürk has been raised, not infrequently, to the level of a holy book. If no direct or even indirect reference is found therein to the specific political problem in hand, then other speeches and sayings by Atatürk, or even accounts of what he said or did (allegedly sometimes the products of imagination), have been turned to for guidance. If a satisfactory basis for action has still not been found, analogies have been sought, or questions asked as to what Atatürk would have said or done under the given circumstances.

Ultimately, a consensus among the politically relevant publics has been needed, within which the ideas of Kemalism could be interpreted and applied under specific circumstances. Until 1960, such a consensus appeared to exist among the various parts of the Turkish intelligentsia, comprising the armed forces, the bureaucratic élite, and the university community. This consensus was eroded gradually during the 1960s, and more rapidly during the 1970s. The military has come to see itself as the real guardian of the Kemalist tradition. In other words, there is no longer a coherent body of republican 'Ulema' among whom a consensus obtains.

The military leadership from 1980 to 1983 made an attempt to compensate for the disappearing consensus on Kemalism by establishing an Atatürk Supreme Council for Culture, Language and History, which offers judgments on what Atatürk 'really' said or meant. As the influence of the military in daily politics has waned, the Council as an institution has become increasingly disregarded. In this way, the similarities between the deductive logic of religious ideology and the way guidance has been drawn from the modernist ideology of contemporary Turkey have been declining.

We may then conclude our discussion of how Islam may have influenced political values by summarizing our observations: Islam may be instrumental in promoting political authoritarianism, but this idea requires further investigation. It appears that the roots of political élitism, which continues to exist in contemporary Turkish political culture,[48] may be traced in part to Islamic understandings of knowledge, and the role of the Ulema in Islamic polity. Finally, there are remarkable similarities between the Ottoman Ulema and republicanism in how opinions are rendered about what is to be done and how what is done is legitimized; in both, a parallel deductive logic is employed.

CONCLUSION

Social systems are not closed systems. Religion in any society, including Turkey, influences politics, including political culture. In this chapter I have looked into four areas in which I have felt religion to have constituted an input into political culture.

Religion in Turkey appears to be an underlying dimension of membership in the political community, it has a moderate role in the achievement of political legitimacy, it is one of the bases of political ideology, and finally, it is a source of values which affect political goal-setting and behaviour in society.

The role religion has played in the shaping of political culture in Turkey has changed over time. Comparative studies need to be conducted to determine whether religion performs a unique role in the formation of political culture in Turkey, or whether there is a more general pattern which is specific to Muslim countries, or whether it is variables common to all religions or particular types of religions, rather than the unique characteristics of Islam, which account for the influence of religion in the formation of political culture.

NOTES

1. This definition comes from Gabriel Almond and G. Bingham Powell, *Comparative Politics Today*, 3rd ed., Boston, Little, Brown, 1984, p. 37.
2. I have purposely employed 'religion' rather than 'Islam' at this point, for it is certainly the broader concept 'religion' which is of theoretical relevance, and lends itself to comparison. Islam is one religion among many others, all of which influence political cultures in the specific environments in which they exist. To begin the discussion by referring to Islam may help reinforce an impression that Islam is a unique force in influencing political cultures of countries in which it is the prevalent religion. Such an impression, while clearly incorrect, approximates a mode of thinking commonly found among journalists, policy-makers and even academics in Western Europe and the United States.
3. Binnaz Toprak, *Islam and Political Development in Turkey*, Leiden, Brill, 1981, p. 57.
4. 'The wrath of militant Islam' is the subtitle of Robin Wright's book *Sacred Rage*, New York, Simon and Schuster, 1986, so the term has gained book-title status also.
5. Metin Heper, for example, offers four definitions that are currently used: the establishment of an Islamic republic by means of a mass movement; a more pronounced observance of the Islamic tenets among the masses; a focus of identity, a third-world state of mind; and a domestic Muslim revival which influences national politics. See

'Islam, polity, and society in Turkey: a Middle Eastern perspective', *Middle East Journal*, 35, 1981, p. 345.

6. See William E. Shepard, 'Islam and ideology: towards a typology', *International Journal of Middle East Studies*, 19, 1987, p. 308. Cf. also Bassam Tibi, 'The renewal of the role of Islam in the political and social development of the Middle East', *Middle East Journal* 37, 1983, p. 5. Ali Yaşar Sarıbay, 'Religion in contemporary Turkish society and polity', *Current Turkish Thought*, 58, 1986, p. 5.

7. I use 'Muslim societies' here and hereafter to denote simply those in which a majority of the population is identified as being Muslim. The usage implies no predetermined relationship between Islam and politics.

8. I have borrowed this definition of modernity from Shepard, 'Islam and ideology'.

9. For the definition of secularism, see ibid.

10. Donald E. Smith, ed., *Religion and Political Modernization*, New Haven, Yale University Press, 1974, p. 8. He first offered this classification in his *Religion and Political Development*, Boston, Little, Brown, 1970; but some terms were changed and clarified in his later work which I cite here. But cf. also the earlier work, pp. 8, 10, 85, 91, 96, 113–14, 119 and *passim*.

11. See Binnaz Toprak, 'Islamist intellectuals of the 1980's in Turkey', *Current Turkish Thought*, 62, 1987, p. 3.

12. Şerif Mardin, 'Ideology and religion in the Turkish revolution', *International Journal of Middle East Studies*, 2, 1971, p. 206.

13. See Heper, 'Islam, polity and society', p. 351. For explanation and analysis of these changes, see my 'Atatürk's reforms as a nation and state building process', forthcoming in *Southeastern Europe*. See also Ali Yaşar Sarıbay, *Türkiye'de Modernleşme, Din, ve Parti Politikası: MSP Örnek Olayı*, Istanbul, Alan Yayıncılık, 1985, *passim*, esp. p. 75. Smith, *Religion and Political Development*, p. 268. Toprak, *Islam and Political Development*, p. 40 and *passim*.

14. Toprak, *Islam and Political Development*, pp. 123–4; and Metin Heper, 'Islam, politics and change in the Middle East', in Metin Heper and Raphael Israeli, eds, *Islam and Politics in the Modern Middle East*, London, Croom Helm, 1984, p. 6.

15. Almond and Powell, *Comparative Politics*, pp. 32–40.

16. Toprak, *Islam and Political Development*, p. 24.

17. For a good discussion, see Daniel Crecelius, 'The course of secularization in modern Egypt', in Smith, *Religion and Political Modernization*, p. 82.

18. For an excellent analysis, see Şerif Mardin, 'Religion and secularism in Turkey', in Ali Kazancigil and Ergun Özbudun, eds, *Atatürk: Founder of a Modern State*, London, C. Hurst, 1981, p. 193.

19. For a discussion of the spread of nationalism and the channels through which it came, see my *Cumhuriyet Tarihimiz*, Istanbul, Çağlayan, 1969, pp. 19–25.

20. Mardin, 'Religion and secularism', p. 202.
21. The summary of the three ideologies has relied on my *Cumhuriyet Tarihimiz*, pp. 25–39.
22. Şerif Mardin, *Din ve Ideoloji*, Ankara, Siyasal Bilgiler, 1969, pp. 132, 134. 50.6 per cent of 'Turks' saw others as citizens, and 36.1 per cent as brothers; 89.2 per cent of 'Muslims', on the other hand, thought that others were brothers by religion.
23. Frederick W. Frey, 'Socialization to national identification among Turkish peasants', *Journal of Politics*, 30, 1968, pp. 941–45, 952. A similar observation is made by Robert F. Spencer, 'Aspects of Turkish kinship and social structure', *Anthropological Quarterly*, 33, 1960, pp. 1–11. See also Heper, 'Islam, polity and society', pp. 355–6.
24. See, for example, Shepard, 'Islam and ideology', p. 310. Bernard Lewis makes a similar observation in his *The Emergence of Modern Turkey*, London, Oxford University Press, 1961, p. 424. See also John Voll, *Islam: Continuity and Change in the Modern World*, Boulder, Westview Press, 1982, p. 281.
25. Mardin, *Din ve Ideoloji*, p. 139.
26. Smith, *Religion and Political Development*, pp. 115–16.
27. Heper, 'Islam, polity and society', p. 348. Similar ideas are advanced by Şerif Mardin, 'Religion and politics in modern Turkey', in James P. Piscatori, ed., *Islam in the Political Process*, Cambridge, Cambridge University Press, 1983, p. 139.
28. Mardin, 'Religion and politics in modern Turkey'.
29. Heper, 'Islam, polity and society'. Sarıbay, *Türkiye'de Modernleşme*, p. 62.
30. In a recent interview in the Istanbul weekly *Nokta*, 41 (19.10.1986), p. 37, Mardin makes the following interesting observation:

> In many Islamic countries, the head of the state has been seen as some sort of a Pharaoh. In the case of the Ottomans, however, owing to the existence of certain traditions which have their origins in Central Asia, the Umma is loyal to the state; it does not resist the authority of the state. This is not simply a function of the fact that the Padişah (the Sultan) is at the same time the Caliph. Societal culture is different.

31. See also Mardin, 'Ideology and religion', p. 205.
32. See idem, 'Religion and secularism', p. 195.
33. Turan, *Cumhuriyet Tarihimiz*, *passim*. İlkay Sunar and Binnaz Toprak, 'Islam and politics: the case of Turkey', *Government and Opposition* 18 (autumn), 1983, p. 426. Binnaz Toprak, 'Politicization of Islam in a secular state: the National Salvation Party in Turkey', in Said Amir Arjomand, ed., *From Nationalism to Revolutionary Islam*, London, Macmillan, 1984, p. 121.
34. Toprak, 'Politicization', p. 121.
35. Sabri Sayarı, 'Politicization of Islamic retraditionalism', in Heper and Israeli, eds, *Islam and Politics*, pp. 122–3.

36. Ahmet N. Yücekök offers some excellent examples in his study, *Türkiye'de Örgütlenmiş Dinin Sosyo-Ekonomik Tabanı*, Ankara, Siyasal Bilgiler Fakültesi, 1971, pp. 161, 175–92.
37. Heper, 'Islam, polity and society', p. 362.
38. For an analysis of the transition to competitive politics, see my *Cumhuriyet Tarihimiz*, pp. 105–7.
39. Mardin, 'Religion and politics', p. 156. Idem, 'Religion and secularism', p. 218.
40. See Türker Alkan, 'The National Salvation Party in Turkey', in Heper and Israeli, eds, *Islam and Politics*, pp. 91–3. See also Binnaz Toprak, 'The state, politics and religion in Turkey', in Metin Heper and Ahmet Evin, eds, *State, Democracy and the Military: Turkey in the 1980's*, Berlin and New York, de Gruyter, 1988, pp. 123–34.
41. For a comparative study on this point, see Michael M.J. Fischer, 'Islam and the revolt of the petite bourgeoisie', *Daedalus*, 111, 1982, pp. 101–25.
42. A survey by the weekly *Nokta*, 41 (19.10.1986), p. 32, showed that only 7 per cent of a national sample approved a statement that the country should be ruled by the laws of the Sharia.
43. Mardin, *Din ve Ideoloji*, p. 55.
44. Bertrand Badie, *Culture et Politique*, Paris, Economica, 1983, p. 83.
45. Mardin, *Din ve Ideoloji*, p. 72, remarks that 'the only way to free oneself from Islamic society is to esablish an alternative Islamic society'.
46. W. Montgomery Watt points out that small deviant groups are treated harshly precisely because they carry with them the potential danger of setting up a new state: *Islam and the Integration of Society*, London, Routledge and Kegan Paul, 1961, p. 172, cited by Mardin, *Din ve Ideoloji*, p. 54.
47. Smith, *Religion and Political Development*, pp. 269–70, and p. 187.
48. On political élitism in Turkish political culture, see my 'The evolution of political culture in Turkey', in Ahmet Evin, ed., *Modern Turkey: Continuity and Change*, Leske, Opladen, 1984, pp. 105–8.

3

RELIGION, EDUCATION AND CONTINUITY IN A PROVINCIAL TOWN

Richard Tapper and Nancy Tapper

INTRODUCTORY

In the 1970s, it was established republican dogma that 'laicist' values and institutions had replaced 'religious' ones in the structure of Turkish society. This dogma was reproduced among officials and educationists at all levels of society, even as late as 1979 when we first visited Turkey to initiate a research project on religion and society in a provincial town. In the 1980s the situation seemed to have changed. The 'religious revival' of the 1970s and earlier, so long dismissed officially as an extreme and fringe phenomenon and often attributed, like other extreme movements of the left and right, to external influences, was now taken more seriously both by government and in academic circles. However, apart from the major elements of the population for whom the official dogma reflected neither ideals nor reality, there had long been a dissenting minority of intellectuals who recognized the continuing importance, in the countryside if not in the cities, of religious values.

Our research in Turkey between 1980 and 1984, carried out mainly in the town of Eğirdir in Isparta province, had as a major focus an investigation of Islamic beliefs and practice, in the context of the dominant republican ideology, and in the light of the official dogma concerning the role of Islam in Turkey. Here we try to show that, although the townspeople treat republicanism and Islam as two discrete sets of values and associated activities, there are in effect close underlying links between them, and that it is useful to think of them as aspects of a single ideology.[1] The argument is developed in the context of philosophies and practices of education. It is suggested that the legitimacy of the republican ideology was bolstered through the modern secular educational system, but by means of the appropriation of key concepts from the Ottoman–Islamic philosophy of knowledge.

In a country like Turkey, towns (or rather certain people in them) play an intermediary role, in administrative, economic and cultural matters, between the metropolitan (and cosmopolitan) centres and the hinterland. Lloyd Fallers, for example, writing of Edremit, a 'provincial city' of 30,000 people on the Aegean coast of Turkey, suggested that it

> plays an important role as a meeting point and mediator between the outward-reaching national culture, institutions and processes on the one hand, and on the other, the increasingly self-assertive agricultural village majority. . . . In the metropolitan centers, where there is greater sociocultural differentiation, the tension [between modernist, nationalist intellectuals and village-backed men of religion] is more explicit. In the provincial towns, where persons of different social types exist in numbers too small to form subculturally insulated groups, the tension is held in check by cross-cutting personal ties.[2]

In Edremit in the 1960s, Fallers found the major *Kulturkampf* to be between religious and secular ideology, represented on the one hand by the religious preachers and on the other by the school-teachers and other modernist 'intellectuals', including army officers and government officials. The teachers have their public celebrations, such as the parades and fiercely patriotic speeches commemorating Atatürk's death. Religious officials are present, but only as guests, and the occasion is 'entirely "uncontaminated", as many teachers – and doubtless the Gazi himself – would say by "religious superstition"'. The men of religion and their supporters also have their celebrations: Friday prayers, Islamic feast days, and the fast of Ramazan. But Fallers was clear about the 'compromise, or synthesis, which emerges from the experience and experiment of everyday life in the microcosms of the provincial city', which he linked with the 'liberal democracy' which he felt to have taken root in Edremit.[3]

In villages of religious minorities in the rural hinterland of eastern Anatolia, however, Yalman found the main opposition to be between state-controlled orthodoxy and the semi-legal local religious leadership. 'The "official" religious organization of the hierarchy of *Imam* and *Müftü*, etc., connected to the General Directorate of Religious Affairs, is almost completely disregarded' and people preferred dealing with their local shaikhs. Communication between local people and the secularized intellectuals of the cities was only just beginning, and the interplay between their two positions, Yalman felt, was vital to understanding the basic problems in Turkey.[4]

EĞIRDIR – A PROVINCIAL TOWN

In Eğirdir things appeared rather more complex than either of these two cases.[5] On the whole, changes in provincial towns like Eğirdir have reflected the wider changes of the last sixty years, and indeed such towns may have played a crucial mediating role in reinterpreting the relation between the secular state and Islamic beliefs and practices. Eğirdir is a market and administrative centre for a sub-province of some 40 villages.[6] The town itself has a population (1981) of about 9,000, brought to a total of over 12,000 by two substantial national institutions, the Commando School (since 1926) and the Orthopaedic Hospital (since the early 1950s). The town lies on the shores of Lake Eğirdir, and fishing still brings in a proportion of the income, but by 1980 the economy of the town was based largely on the international export of locally grown apples.

Until the 1920s, Eğirdir was a poor local centre. Most of the population of the town, including a Greek minority, were involved in small-scale crafts and trade and were dominated by a few families of powerful landowners, wealthy merchants and religious leaders associated with the mosques and medreses in the town, which was also a centre for active branches of the Mevlevi and Nakşibendi (and earlier, Bektaşi) orders.

The development of Eğirdir was largely due to the spread of secular education, improved communications in the country as a whole, and the entrepreneurial efforts of local residents themselves. The apple economy started in the 1950s, and took off in the 1970s. All Eğirdir families traditionally owned vineyards outside the town, which were converted to apple orchards, and all have benefited to some degree from the apple boom, though large differences in wealth soon emerged. In terms of socio-economic status and life-style, there are distinct strata that one is inclined to call 'classes', though the townspeople themselves (like the Turkish state) maintain a self-image of classlessness. All but the poorest consider themselves 'middle class', and to the outsider they deny anything in the way of 'class conflict' in the town.

Eğirdir experienced almost no civil strife during the troubles of the late 1970s, and indeed contained few extremists of either right or left. People attributed this to a variety of factors. Some pointed to the fact, as they saw it, that there were few very rich or very poor among the local people. Others related the peace and prosperity of the town to the continuing respect for hard work and education: students from the main Eğirdir lycée, for example, have had unusual success in gaining entrance to universities.

Eğirdir has indeed a long tradition of educational achievement, dating well back into Ottoman times, when there were numerous medreses. Although not unique in this respect among provincial towns in Turkey, and not even in Isparta province (the tradition is even stronger in the town of Uluborlu), it is none the less striking for a town of its size, and many people of all persuasions in the town are conscious and proud of this tradition.[7]

Others attribute the self-conscious homogeneity of the population to the continuing strength of the values of family, hospitality and community support, which in turn are traced back to pre-republican religious institutions such as the *imaret-hane* associated with the local Sufi lodges. There is a dense and pervasive network of kinship and marriage linking the 7,000 to 8,000 locals (*yerli*): individuals count as relatives people from all walks of life. This undoubtedly operates as a powerful mechanism for social control. It has also, however, served to exclude strangers (*yabancı*) of all kinds – bureaucrats and other outsiders such as the soldiers in the Commando School and patients at the Hospital – who often find the locals unfriendly and grasping. In particular, the small proletariat is socially invisible: most manual labour is done by supposedly transient Kurdish immigrants from the west.

REPUBLICAN AND RELIGIOUS IDEOLOGIES

The people of Eğirdir are committed republicans. They have frequently chosen local officials (including their most successful recent mayor) from the Republican People's Party (CHP), though they have voted in national elections predominantly for Democrat Party (DP), Justice Party (AP) and True Path Party (DYP) candidates. They are also committed Muslims and are by and large religious: one dentist, who closes his office during Ramazan because dental treatment is held to break the fast, estimated in 1983 that 50 per cent of all men in town, and probably many more women, scrupulously keep the fast, but that another 30 to 35 per cent of men make only a show of doing so. The least religious people are said to be the high-status bureaucrats, while the most pious are reckoned to be found among the *esnaf*, the small traders and craftsmen of the bazaar.

The townspeople see republican values as underwriting most of their activities in this world, whereas they see Islam as mostly about the life hereafter. They often talk about a division between material (*maddi*) and spiritual (*manevi*) domains, and they treat republicanism and Islam as two separate ideologies, of which the former is of wider temporal scope.

This perspective leaves the townspeople unaware of, or actually inhibited by various taboos from seeing, many areas which suggest that republicanism and Islam in Eğirdir today are aspects of a single ideology. One of the most salient features of the relation between republicanism and Islam is its location at the centre of town values and activities. The ideology is thoroughly establishment in character. It creates and reproduces an orthodoxy and homogeneity, in which ideas about Turkey as nation-state and ideas about Islam are mutually reinforcing.[8]

Dissent from such a strong, unitary, centralizing value system is muted, or is likely to resemble treason, heresy, or both. About two dozen people, many of them of recent village origins, were considered by townspeople as 'extremists' (*aşırı*); they included adherents or sympathizers of the former main political parties of the extreme right and left as well as religious fanatics (*yobaz*). What is interesting is how, locally at least, these extremists adopted various strategies to avoid accusations of heresy or treason. Those of the right carried political orthodoxy to an extreme; those of the left adopted a diffuse, boundariless, heterodox ideology, a quasi-mystical socialism. The religious fanatics, who included some members of the two clandestine sects, the Nurcus and the Süleymancıs, do both: in their behaviour (for example, their clothing and insistence on sexual segregation) they resembled Western stereotypes of Islamic 'fundamentalists', but their beliefs were theistic and ecumenical in character.[9] In other words, in Eğirdir and probably widely in Turkey, the structure of the value system held by those considered by most people as 'fanatics' ('fundamentalists') can only be understood in terms of the value system of the local establishment, which itself has certain 'fundamentalist' characteristics.

We argue then that in Eğirdir, and probably elsewhere in Turkey, nationalism is associated with Islam in the form of a 'fundamentalist' ideology. In Eğirdir this ideology takes a relatively mild, open-ended form, but it is potentially hard-line, like that which surfaced in many Turkish communities before the 1980 military intervention. At present, its most obvious manifestation is the way in which conversations between townspeople on a wide variety of topics veer either into diatribes against Kurds, Armenians or Greeks, as threats to the integrity of the Turkish state, or into a paean for the unassailable virtues of Islam.

A wide variety of circumstances may cause embarrassment and intellectual confusion, and provoke such defensive reactions. These reactions seem directly related to those elements of the 'fundamentalist' ideology that concern the social construction of the self and personal identity. Certainly, patterns of socialization (in the home, in schools and in both religious and military training) are often arbitrary and authoritarian, and emphasize an individual's personal duties to the state or to God rather than a commitment to a broader social ethic. Failure and threats are often explained in terms of outsiders or external forces; where specific insiders are held responsible for anti-social actions, their behaviour is often concealed and ignored or the individual concerned may literally be ostracized from the town.

EXPLICIT ACCOMMODATIONS:
COMPARTMENTALIZATION AND BALANCE

The townspeople tend to treat both republicanism and Islam as separate monolithic wholes; there are, however, a number of important types of accommodation between them, which often give clues to the nature of the underlying ideology. First, there is a range of concepts which townspeople readily volunteered as key values by which they live, and which seem to contain or deflect any specific republican *or* Islamic interpretation that might be placed on them. Such concepts include *samimiyet* (sincerity, friendship), *insaniyet* (humanity), *komşuluk* (neighbourliness), *medeniyet* (civilization), *kültür* (sophistication), *misafirperverlik* (hospitality) and *hizmet* (community service). Frequently used but less often referred to is a further range of even more general and fundamental values, including *vazife* (duty), *saygı* (respect), *hürmet* (honour), *temizlik* (purity), and *irade* (self-discipline). It is perhaps significant that almost all these terms are of Arabic or Persian, not Turkish, origin, in spite of the efforts of fifty years to purge modern Turkish of such 'loan' words. This linguistic continuity suggests important social continuity with Ottoman values and forms of social control.

All these values allow for a wide area of agreement that can hide the complicated relation between customs and activities which people specifically do label as either national (*milli*) or religious (*dinî*). However, if one asks a question of republicanism and Islam which implies a comparison between them, one is liable to get an answer cast wholly in republican terms, in which Islam is associated with all that was formally outlawed by Atatürk: superstition, local custom, Sufi mysticism, and so on. There is also a tendency for people to apologize for Islam and religious allegiance by emphasizing that it is possible to be both a good Turk and a good Muslim. At first sight, loyalty to the state has priority and is the standard and foil against which religious allegiance is judged; as one notable republican leader, Celal Bayar, was able to say, 'our way of [religious] worship is to respect Atatürk' (*Atatürk'ün saygısı bizim ibadet-tir*).

In explicit statements, republican values appear to dominate social life, while the values that people would label explicitly religious are stated less often, less publicly, and in a more qualified manner. So, for instance, on national holidays and in public places throughout the town, banners, posters and inscriptions are displayed that express republican sentiments, often using Atatürk's own words. Perhaps the most well-known of these is inscribed on the back of the main Atatürk statue in town, and reads: 'How happy he who can say "I'm a Turk"' (*ne mutlu Türküm diyene*); and this sentiment is shouted out by school-children twice a day in their pledge of allegiance. By contrast, wherever religious ornaments are displayed, in shops or restaurants, a picture of Atatürk is even more prominently shown. Indeed, an exception that in effect proves this rule of the qualification of things religious by things republican is found in some of the religious activities which are associated exclusively with women and take place in the privacy of their homes, such as those associated with the tenth day of the Arab–Islamic month of Muharram (*Aşure günü*).

The townspeople are well aware that there have been considerable changes in the character of Islam in Turkey since the coming of the Republic; and of course an important republican concern has been secular 'consciousness-raising'. For most people, however, these efforts seem to relate to only a few specific areas of life, such as education, where they consider that traditional (religious) learning occurred only because children feared the physical punishment meted out by teachers; or the family, where men and women agree that in the past, with the sanction of Islam, relations between them and between adults and children were oppressive and tyrannical. No one regrets such changes.

In effect, the notion of republicanism has expanded, and is often treated as more or less synonymous with anything and everything that is thought new and different. It is as if the changes people have experienced have no antecedents in Ottoman history, and the Republic arrived all of a piece. So, for instance, there is an absence of detail or social realism in school textbook accounts or televised depictions of nineteenth-century Ottoman history, or even of the early Republic, which many people have experienced for themselves.

Moreover, because republican efforts at re-education focus on day-to-day social relations where those key values like humanism and friendship can apply, the townspeople fail to see other areas in which religious experience has also changed. For instance, few people seem aware that many of the town's shrines have gone, and that the complex sacred geography of the town has now altered and become very mosque-centred; or that some of the religious activities of individuals have become, paradoxically, more ostentatious during the same period. For example, inscribed tombstones are becoming fashionable among ordinary people, and nowadays charitable gifts which would previously have remained anonymous are often treated as news in local papers.

Since the coming of the Republic, the townspeople's religious experience has become much less shrine-centred, less ritualistic and more individualistic. Moreover, people's ideas about what constitutes 'religion' have narrowed. Now, normal accepted religious values and activities are seen as those which neither support nor impinge on republicanism.

Mevlûd recitals provide a good example of a compartmentalized religious activity that none the less allows for complex, varied statements about social identity. The *mevlûd* poem is a narrative account of the birth and life of the Prophet, and *mevlûd* recitals are arguably the most prominent religious services held in Turkey today. When they are performed in private homes as part of marriage and circumcision ceremonies, they have a confirmatory character and are particularly associated with men, as are those recitals sponsored on Islamic festivals by the local religious establishment and performed in local mosques to coincide with a nationally broadcast *mevlûd* on Turkish television. Most *mevlûd* recitals, however, are part of funeral and mourning rituals, and have a piacular character.[10] Women are particularly associated with these mourning *mevlûds*, but this very fact emphasizes the compartmentalization of religion in town life. Men tend to adopt the 'official' line in which the *mevlûd* poem and the associated hymns are said to be 'beautiful but unimportant' because they are not in the Koran. Indeed, for most men the only value of the *mevlûds* lies in the extent to which they serve as occasions for Koranic readings. Women insist that their services, and the rituals and hymn-singing associated with them, demonstrate that they are more caring and consciously religious than men. But the women's piety, and even the threat it might pose to state secularism, are dismissed by men as spurious, and the traditional stereotypes of women's social and religious inferiority are confirmed.[11]

Townspeople are aware of accommodation between republicanism and Islam in only certain limited areas. Three types of accommodation seem particularly common. The first involves the suggestion that some specific Islamic injunction was associated with a particular historical period or social problem, and that other Islamic values are more appropriate today: for instance, we were told that the Prophet forbade alcohol because he found all Arabs to be drunkards and could discover no other remedy for their excesses, but in fact Islam favours moderation in all things and if one can imbibe sparingly then one has no need to fear for one's soul.

A second type of accommodation is managed by arguing that republican institutions function in exactly the same ways as Islamic ones did and therefore are acceptable substitutes for them: for instance, people note that income and other taxes paid to the state go to support hospitals, education, the salaries of religious teachers and so on, and thus replace Islamic alms and tithes.

A third type of accommodation is where religious values or customs are rationalized, or explained by an appeal to 'modern' secular values. Thus prayer, or fasting during Ramazan, are said to be excellent for the health, to lead to regular exercise, to purge the body, and so on. Such explanations imply that Islamic wisdom long anticipated current scientific ideas, which serve to verify it.

This third type of accommodation can be reversed and people may declare that, in all important essentials, republicanism is close to Islam. Such an argument is hard to maintain because of problems of historical fact, such as Atatürk's known personal antipathy to Islam. None the less, these problems are ignored, almost as if Atatürk, to have achieved so much, must have been on God's side. So, for instance, stories from early republican local history label as 'atheists' (*dinsiz*) those who fought *against* Atatürk and *for* the Sultan–Caliph and traditional Ottoman–Islamic rule; or the townspeople explain that Atatürk was not originally against religion but when religious fanatics threatened the new Republic he was forced to turn to secularism.[12]

This latter gloss on republican history is not so much wrong as oversimplified. What is interesting about it is the way fanaticism is condemned. All townspeople (including the two dozen or so 'extremists') reject fanaticism, past or present. Traditional religious leaders are described as having been ignorant, while contemporary 'extremists', whether in Iran or from Turkish sects, are seen both as ridiculous, unthinking puppets manipulated by outsiders for political purposes, and as Machiavellian opportunists who would cheerfully sell heaven for their personal gain. It is important to realize that the same scorn and repugnance are also directed against political fanaticism of both right and left. Looked at the other way, the general notion of 'fanaticism' is a foil which makes both republicanism and Islam seem monolithic, moderate orthodoxies.

So far, we have described ways in which townspeople treat republican and Islamic ideologies as distinct and separate, if complementary, in those areas where they can make the type of accommodating arguments we have outlined. Such accommodating explanations are popular, unquestioned and used as evidence that neither Islam nor republicanism poses a serious threat to the other.

The notion that there is a balance between the two distinct ideologies and associated institutions is clearly evident where either balance or discreteness are felt to be at risk. For instance, people are well aware that since the 1980 military intervention there has been a considerable increase in republican propaganda, much of which focuses on Atatürk himself, resurrecting and perpetuating his example and image. Many see this propaganda as unnecessary and boring; as one man said: 'Even our Prophet Muhammad is dead and his bones in a box!'[13]

Finally, there are cases where people are aware that they are mixing religious and secular issues which ought, they feel, to be kept separate; but they do it anyway. So, for example, all important new enterprises (buying a new car, opening a shop, laying foundations of a new house, and so on) should be initiated with a sacrifice; but if one asks more about such sacrifices, people usually talk about custom and superstition (*bâtıl inanç*), and how such sacrifices have little or nothing to do with Islam. For example, in autumn 1984, the night after a new bulldozer was bought and inaugurated by the municipality, we chanced to see council workmen repairing two burst tyres by flashlight; shame-facedly, they explained that as there had been no sacrifice it might look as though the machine had been struck by the evil eye, so they very much wanted to avoid public comment.

JUXTAPOSITIONS AND HIDDEN ACCOMMODATIONS: A SINGLE IDEOLOGY?

Such types of accommodation townspeople recognize explicitly. In other areas, of which they seem unaware, republican and Islamic values and forms are juxtaposed in complex ways such that they can best be understood as parts of a single ideological structure. These areas range from the constant conversational references to God to the structural similarities between civic and Islamic rituals. We have mentioned how people give neither republican nor Islamic labels to explicit social values like 'humanity' and 'friendship' and a range of more basic concepts like respect, duty, purity and discipline. Similarly, the popular use of nearly identical aphorisms in different contexts confirms local belief in the separation of religion from the state while enhancing and multiplying the meanings of particular values. For example, the saying 'Find learning wherever you can' is attributed to Muhammad, while posters quote Atatürk's saying 'In life the surest guide is knowledge' (*hayatta en hakiki mürşit ilimdir*), the inscription on the façade of the Faculty of Letters in Ankara; and the Commando School has fashioned in huge letters on the mountainside above Eğirdir the slogan 'Knowledge is power' (*bilgi küvvettir*).

Examples of the juxtaposition of republican and Islamic concepts in Turkey are plentiful. For example, Mardin comments that republican laicism was a 'Janus-like affair' and, though the Caliphate had been eliminated in 1924, army training in the 1950s 'still culminated with the storming of a hill with cries of "Allah, Allah!"'[14] Norton describes contemporary Bektaşi ceremonies which have departed from the universalizing Sufism of the early twentieth century and have become nationalistic – Hacı Bektaş is treated as a sort of patron saint of Turkey who claimed that 'the Turkish nation was created to rule the world' and that even Muhammad and 'Ali were Turks.[15] Olson discusses ideological conflict conventionally in terms of 'Turkish nationalism versus Muslim identity' and 'secularism versus Islamic society', but with data on women's head coverings illustrating intrinsic relations between these different perspectives.[16] Gellner has observed that

the first generation of Kemalist modernisers embraced

secularism in an unwittingly Koranic, puritanical and uncompromising spirit. Professors would issue secularist *fatwas* through the press, confirming the legitimacy of a political coup. They still knew their Islam inside out, and also had to fight it in their own hearts, and unwittingly fought it in its own style and by its own rules. They were the *ulama* of Kemalism, and taught and thought like *ulama*. The next generation knew much less about Islam and had no need to fear it inwardly, and hence are far more willing to find accommodation with popular sentiment.[17]

Three broad areas where juxtaposition takes place indicate the centrality of the single ideology. The first concerns the pervasive, almost puritanical, work ethic to which townspeople subscribe and which has, without doubt, been an important element in their material prosperity. Hard work is a key republican virtue.[18] School-children promise twice daily in their oath of allegiance to work hard; and perhaps the most widely reproduced Atatürk saying of all (it appears under his bust on the main square and in innumerable other places) runs, 'Be proud, hard-working, confident' (*öğün, çalış, güven*). The value of hard work arises in quite different secular contexts as well: townspeople tend to see Kurds as potential arch-traitors to the state and they also assert that, unlike the hard-working Turks, Kurds are lazy and shiftless and make their women do the work.

But hard work is also part of the religious ethic. An individual's prosperity can be explained by phrases like 'God gives to the hard worker'. A well-known moral injunction runs: 'Prepare for death as if you will die tomorrow, but work as if you will live for ever.' In fact, people are keen to assert that Islam does not encourage fatalism but demands of Muslims hard work and self-improvement. There is even a category of 'deserving poor' (*gizli fakir*) to whom alms should be given. The work ethic is further fuelled by egalitarian ideals drawn from both republicanism and Islam. Ideally, the secular system is a meritocracy where a competitive, Western-type educational system reinforces individualistic capitalism. Parallel to this system is a path to personal salvation based on gaining merit (*sevab*) and cancelling sin (*günah*), which is a central goal of religious activity. It is essential to aspirations and choices in both systems that merits and faults can be and are given measurable values. In practice, of course, the intangible factors of influence and connection (*torpil*) are sources of inequality in the secular system, and the pursuit of religious merit is qualified by the notion of pious intention and the belief that salvation depends ultimately on God's unknowable will.

Secondly, there is a similar parallelism throughout the whole range of religious and civic rituals. Maurice Bloch has proposed (in discussion) two basic models of ways in which Muslims can contact the divine: in the *sacrifice* model the divine is brought into temporal life and associated with fertility and prosperity on earth; in the *funeral* model the divine is separated into the afterlife. This second model is salvationist, sometimes millennial in character. In this light, it is fascinating that in Eğirdir both religious and civic rituals use both models. Many civic rituals focus on the sacrifice of republican martyrs, and we were told that when the head of state travels around Turkey so many animals are sacrificed in front of his car that he leaves a bloody shambles in his wake; but townspeople agree that the most important civic ritual is that which commemorates Atatürk's death. Among religious rituals, the *mevlûd* is most frequently and movingly heard in the context of death; funerals are prominent among life-cycle rituals; yet townspeople agree that the most important event of the Islamic year is the feast of Sacrifice (*Kurban Bayramı*).

The question of ritual parallels is a vast one: here we can mention only one other thread. Throughout civic and religious rituals there is a juxtaposition of egalitarian and authoritarian values. There are, for instance, many occasions (for example, in communal prayers and in the processions on national holidays) when people act as equals and move and articulate in unison, and which emphasize some notion of the mechanical solidarity between individuals in the community, as well as other more explicit values such as self-discipline and will-power. But these rituals also express acceptance of a kind of authority (political or religious) which is hierarchical, and generated and imposed from the top down. It is surely not coincidence that the voice of authority in Turkish often sounds the same: the teacher addressing a class, the Imam giving a sermon, the local dignitary making a speech, the officer giving commands to a subordinate, all use the same style and intonation.

The third and most striking juxtaposition, yet one which

townspeople find quite unthinkable, involves the similarities that struck us in attitudes and behaviour towards Atatürk as founder of the Republic, on the one hand, and the Prophet Muhammad as founder of Islam, on the other. Both are 'Great Men'. Atatürk is spoken of as deathless and as a judge of all that goes on in Turkey today; his role in these respects is like that of Muhammad in heaven. Both men deserve the utmost honour for the legacy they have bequeathed ordinary people. In each case, moreover, this heritage was gained in battle. The military campaigns of Atatürk and Muhammad are the most widely known and understood parts of their respective biographies. In many ways the history of Atatürk's journey, from Samsun to Ankara and around the country until the expulsion of the Greek army from the mainland, replicates the Hejira, when Muhammad left Mecca for Medina whence he was later able to conquer Mecca by force. The similarities are manifest not only in biographical details, but in ritual as well. Islam forbids the depiction of the figure of Muhammad, and it is not illustrated in current Turkish iconography, while in the Hollywood-style biopic *The Messenger*, based on the life of the Prophet, which was shown to general approval on Turkish TV during Ramazan 1984, Muhammad was always present just off-camera. By contrast, pictures and statues of Atatürk are ubiquitous in private and public places; yet, in the tableau of the War of Independence presented to the town on the national holiday of 19 May, Atatürk was represented by a bust carried by soldiers. When we asked, in both cases, why no actor played the part of Muhammad or Atatürk, we were told, not surprisingly, that respect made such an idea unthinkable: 'What men could possibly play such parts?'

Though the association between Atatürk and Muhammad was vehemently denied by townspeople to whom we suggested it, it is reproduced in data from other sources. For instance, the text of the *mevlûd* bears comparison with Koopman's account of poems about Atatürk which have appeared in the Turkish press in Western Europe. In these poems a variety of honorifics with religious connotations are used for Atatürk, including 'the saviour' and 'the mighty Mustafa'; he is treated as if he were asleep and could rise up and cleanse the nation and restore order; in others there is the suggestion of his messianic second coming.[19] The complementary and supportive association we are suggesting may be further compared with Mardin's comments on the cult of Atatürk, Fallers' remarks on the cult of the beloved Prophet and Webster's early account of the quasi-deification of Atatürk.[20] The taboo on the explicit identification of Atatürk and Muhammad contrasts dramatically with Muhammad Riza Shah Pahlavi's deliberate strategy for managing the religious commitment of the Iranian people, by associating himself and his family with the supernatural and charismatic figures of Shi'ite Islam.[21]

CONTINUITY IN PHILOSOPHIES OF KNOWLEDGE AND EDUCATION

One particular area in which accommodations are made between the republican and Islamic ideologies in a way which is not explicitly recognized is that of education, and the underlying language and philosophy of knowledge. The English term 'knowledge' is ambiguous, covering two kinds of 'knowledge' that in most other languages (and philosophies) are kept terminologically and conceptually quite distinct: one is theoretical, scientific, analytical, learned from texts by memorization; the other is personal, practical and holistic, and comes from experience and intuition.

Thus, in the Islamic world (including Turkey) there has always been a clear dichotomy between *'ilm* and *ma'rifa*, both Arabic terms translated as 'knowledge'. Put simply, *'ilm*, the religious science of the Ulema, was institutionalized in the orthodox religious hierarchy and in formal education imparted by the preachers and teachers in the mosques and religious schools. The nature of this knowledge has been discussed extensively elsewhere.[22] The basis was the memorization and correct recitation of the Koran and other religious texts and commentaries. The method of teaching was direct instruction by the teacher, backed up by physically imposed discipline, with the aim of progress and achievement through the acquisition of increasing amounts of an extensive but limited body of 'known' facts. Argument and debate are conducted through the appropriate deployment of texts.[23]

Ma'rifa was the esoteric, personal knowledge gained from experience. For Morocco, Eickelman contrasts *'ilm* (religious sciences and knowledge) with *ma'rifa* (non-religious knowledge, for example craft skills). In Turkey, and elsewhere in the Islamic world, the connotations of *ma'rifa (marifet)* certainly do include expertise and skill, but principally the esoteric knowledge of the Sufi. Not surprisingly, craft guilds in Islamic towns and cities were usually organized in direct association with or imitation of Sufi orders. The objective of this form of knowledge is not learning, but understanding through experience: a journey along the Way (*tariqa*) under the guidance of a *murshid* or shaikh, towards the goal of the still centre of *haqiqa* – 'truth', and the loss of self in God. The student is not disciplined by the teacher according to set rules, but must discipline himself according to the whim of the Guide. Understanding does not come cumulatively, serially, logically, but all of a sudden, holistically and intuitively.

In Ottoman times, both these forms of knowledge were encompassed within the religious institutions: *'ilm* in the hierarchically organized 'orthodox' Sunni community under the Ulema, and *ma'rifa* in the Sufi tarikats guided by the shaikhs. The reforms culminating in the Kemalist revolution and the foundation of the Republic brought a period of confusion between the two. The new institutions of education and philosophies of knowledge that have come to dominate in twentieth-century Turkey have produced an interesting series of syntheses and accommodations – particularly interesting in the context of provincial towns such as Eğirdir.

Yalman shows how reformists in the Ottoman Empire, and the republican intellectuals who followed them, with blind adherence to their ideas of Western secularism and rationalism, failed to comprehend the nature of either the religion of the Ulema or that of the tarikats:

> these men wanted a 'reformation' in Islam, but since in many cases their faith in Islam was shaken, they failed to see that the 'reformation' they so fervently hoped to bring about was already in the traditions of Islam. In the mystic brotherhoods all that the reformers had hoped for had already been fulfilled.[24]

The philosophy of the new education system brought in by Mustafa Kemal was based on that of France. It stressed rational learning, but with religion completely replaced by science, civic studies and the inculcation of loyalty to the nation-state. The content of education was radically changed, and it became co-educational and compulsory for both sexes.[25] None the less, the continuities with the older, Koranic system of education were considerable, particularly in teaching methods and in the categories constituent of the discourse of education.

For example, the term *ilim* (*'ilm*) continued for long to be used for the scientific knowledge imparted in school, until, with the slow process of introducing 'pure Turkish' words and neologisms to replace Arabic and Persian words, it gave way to the phonetically very close *bilim*. Similarly, *ma'lûmat* (information, learning, knowledge) was replaced by *bilgi*. Although teachers are now officially known by the Turkish term *öğretmen*, they are still informally called *hoca*, the old term still also used informally for the imams of the mosques. There is still, in school, a major stress on memorization of texts (albeit very different ones) and on ritual and unison repetition of slogans and formulae, especially the sayings of Atatürk. There is a reduced, but still significant, emphasis on physical discipline (backed up in some primary schools with physical punishment): students learn to subject themselves to the rules of society, and to obey and respect age and authority. Hard work and application (*çalışkanlık*) are strongly valued as the key to academic success.

Clearly, these continuities of method and terminology, where they are perceived, are not felt to be as significant as the radical changes in the content and philosophy of education under the Republic. The reformers did their best to stress these changes; it is interesting that to help them in this they appear, again perhaps unwittingly, to have appropriated at least some of the vocabulary if not the philosophy of the other form of knowledge produced in Ottoman times, that of the Sufi brotherhoods which they otherwise so deprecated as ignorant superstition, empty ritual, and at the same time as dangerous to the state.

For instance, the general term for education and public instruction, in use for many years until replaced by the 'pure Turkish' *eğitim*, was *maarif*, with its esoteric connotations. One of Atatürk's most widely quoted sayings, already mentioned above, is *hayatta en hakiki mürşit ilimdir*, 'the surest [spiritual] Guide in life is [scientific] knowledge.' Andrew Mango has pointed out that both *mürşit* and *ilim* are terms with a primarily religious sense;[26]

so, for that matter, is *hakiki*; but surely the significance of the phrase is that it validates modern scientific knowledge by employing key terms from the traditions of both the Ulema (*'ilm*) and the Sufis (*hakiki, mürşit*).[27]

Republican changes should have made irrelevant some of the traditional stumbling-blocks for non-Arab Muslims such as the 'Arabic Koran', but ironically the translation of the Koran into Turkish and the use of Turkish in the call to prayer were received with widespread hostility. However, the fact that sermons and religious instruction in the mosques are now always given in Turkish is an important element in the juxtaposition of 'religious' and 'secular' values and practices. The same points could be made with regard to the use of the romanized Turkish script. In effect, the religious aesthetic has changed and become accessible to a wider public. Today, many well-educated Turks cannot distinguish between the words 'Allah' and 'Muhammad' in Arabic script, but of course they read these names in Romanized script constantly, on religious posters and in both religious and secular publications of all kinds. Atatürk, by introducing the new script and establishing the Turkish Language Foundation with responsibility for purifying Turkish and ridding it of all foreign (including Arabic) loanwords, sought to create, control and manage language in ways not unlike the founder-heroes of many other cultures.[28]

Parallels in attitudes to Atatürk as founder of the Republic and to Muhammad as founder of Islam were examined earlier. In the present context of education, one could also interpret Atatürk's role in republican Turkey as that of Sufi *mürşit*. Although much of the iconography presents him as the Great Leader, he is also said to have insisted that he merely showed the Way (*yol*). Many of his most remembered sayings are not didactic, but use the parables and paradoxes of the Sufi. Moreover, his language pre-dates the purges he initiated, employing a heavily arabized Ottoman vocabulary nearer to present-day Islamic discourse than contemporary republican politics – his sayings, as has often been pointed out, need translation for the youth of today.

In effect, with this construction of knowledge and of education, Atatürk and his followers largely succeeded in synthesizing the earlier distinct forms of knowledge, and in the process removed the central 'Islamic' element in them both. 'Islam' remains a highly ambiguous category in Turkey.

EDUCATION AND RELIGION IN EĞIRDIR

Some of the teachers in Eğirdir, particularly the older generation brought up in Atatürk's time and now retired, take the determinedly secular line of many older urban intellectuals. For these 'Republicans', 'religion', which includes both the controlled Islam of the mosque and the outlawed activities and beliefs of the Sufis, represents 'darkness' and 'reaction' and a threat to the integrity of the state, as against light and progress. These dichotomies slip very easily into others: traditional versus modern, ignorance versus knowledge, rightist versus leftist politics. 'Republicans' are strong in their reverence for Atatürk and his achievements, and scathing not only of his successors and their concessions to traditionalism and to the revival of Islamic observances, but of the modern official cult of Atatürk. They are themselves often from village backgrounds, and do not fit easily into the more conservative milieu of the older town élite, who none the less respect them for their experience and consistent devotion to the Republic.

Other, younger teachers, brought up since the Second World War, take the position of perhaps the majority of educated urban Turks. They compartmentalize their identity as spokespeople for the republican ideology and their own highly personal Islamic practices and beliefs. Many of these 'Liberals' are outsiders, from other regions of Turkey, but predominantly of urban or small town origins. Afraid of threats to the state from political extremism within and hostile neighbours without, the 'Liberals' strongly support the cult of Atatürk as the focus for national unity and identity, though they lack the historical experiences that make it both meaningful and ridiculous to the 'Republicans'. They take a neutral attitude towards the modern, rational, personal, ethical 'religion' taught now within the school system and oppose it to the rituals and 'ignorant superstitions' of the Sufis and various modern 'fundamentalist' movements.

The latter now include organizations such as the Nurcu, which is far removed in style from the traditional Sufism of personal ties to the spiritual Guide, being based on the contrary on the written works of the founder, which are devoted to explaining the message of the Koran to large audiences.[29] Thanks to a positive acceptance of the 'communications revolution', Nurculuk has spread with rapidity among provincial intellectuals: school teachers and officials. In the Eğirdir region there has been a history of involvement with the Nurcus; the founder of the sect, though of Kurdish origins, spent several years of enforced residence both in Eğirdir town itself and in the nearby sub-district of Barla, and recruited many local followers – as well as many enemies. Membership of the sect remains clandestine; several Eğirdir townspeople belong or are sympathetic, including a small number of teachers. These 'Fundamentalists' seem to experience a tension between the demands of their job for a strictly secularist treatment of religion in education, and their personal conviction that all true knowledge is founded on a modern interpretation of the Koran and that the greatest danger to the state (which they profess to support) is godlessness.

In their various ways, which we have barely been able to hint at here, each of these categories of teacher – the 'Republicans', the 'Liberals', and the 'Fundamentalists' – maintain their own versions of both types of knowledge: that of theory and science and that of experience and understanding; and they make different accommodations between them. The debate between these different versions of knowledge and reality is continuing and changing; it rarely if ever (during our fieldwork) surfaced as a public argument, but the positions of individuals were stated by them in the appropriate social contexts and were very well known and often commented on by others.

A 'FUNDAMENTALIST' IDEOLOGY?

The ideological structure apparently underlying both republican and Islamic values in Eğirdir is remarkably similar to the structure of Protestant fundamentalism as depicted by Barr.[30] Thus, the sayings of Atatürk, and certain details of his personal biography, are used in schools and elsewhere as *inerrant texts*. They are uncriticized, and presented as without precedent or wider social context. They are a central part of the mythology of the Turkish Republic, and have their ritual counterparts in the use of photographs, film and pageantry on television and in civic rituals. Similar treatment is given to the sayings of Muhammad and stories of the Prophet's life, especially in the *mevlûd*. The mediatory and personalizing roles of both Atatürk and Muhammad have many implications; here it is enough to say that in the use of their sayings and biographies as texts, there is an extreme formalization of language, which, as Bloch describes, can be further associated with traditional authority and social control.[31] Further, acceptance of the text can be used as a *test of faith*; but among believers the text is used *devotionally* and often becomes an invocation or icon itself.

Secondly, access to the central values of both the state and Islam are mediated by visionary generals. Of the utmost importance is the *salvationist* role which is ascribed to them both. Muhammad showed men a way of finding eternal salvation and gave Muslims all the privileges and responsibilities associated with their faith. So too, Atatürk saved the Turkish nation from being devoured by the Western powers at the end of the First World War; he gave the Turks an identity and the chance and duty to defend it against all-comers. (Indeed, Atatürk is presented as the last of the Ottoman Ghazis,[32] much as Muhammad was the 'seal of the Prophets'.) A pervasive theme to which townspeople return again and again is that only through constant effort and vigilance can they hope to maintain and protect their way of life and the promise of an afterlife against the forces of evil and the sources of sin.

As we have seen, there is a distinct *ahistoricity* in the present treatment of Ottoman and early republican history. In this respect, Atatürk is the source of values which should guide Turkey through all time: he is the 'eternal leader'. Political rhetoric in the town is almost invariably based on themes of returning to origins, that is, Atatürk's example, and is often about which party most truly follows the republican tradition. The same ahistoricity is seen in townspeople's approach to Islam: they constantly repeated to us how the messages of the Jewish and Christian prophets had been corrupted and that Muhammad's message had to introduce people to the word of God completely afresh. Moreover, in the practice of Islam in the town, one finds that, rather than some idea of returning to an Islamic Golden Age (which would bring with it embarrassing issues concerning the Caliphate and Ottoman relations with the Arabs), what seems to happen is that Muhammad's life is the focus of devotion, and in the *mevlûd* recitations it is made to seem as if he lived only yesterday.

Atatürk himself seems to have regarded Islam as a 'natural', *rational* religion;[33] and it seems clear that his early intention was to rid Islam of 'superstitions' and local customs, and to initiate a period of religious enlightenment, in Berkes' words to 'rationalize or Turkicize Islam' by such measures as translating the Koran into Turkish and insisting that sermons also be delivered in Turkish. Such aims are now central to the bureaucracy that controls religious teachers, Imams and other officials; they are also accepted without question by virtually all Eğirdir townspeople. It is interesting that those few Nurcus and Süleymancıs whom other townspeople regard as 'fanatics' are also those who go to extremes to show how modern science proves Islam right: yet their main texts, apart from the Koran, are the obscure writings of a twentieth-century Kurdish mystic.

CONCLUSIONS

We have argued elsewhere that both nationalist ideologies and the traditions of the Semitic religions have a general fundamentalist potential for exclusivity and opposition and that fundamentalisms might be linked to the experience of power in a nation-state.[34] In the Muslim world, nationalism, and particularly the degree of external threat perceived by a community, is an important factor in the appearance of fundamentalist religious ideologies. In large part, this response is a reaction to threats believed to be posed by Western and Soviet imperialisms; it is not inappropriate that Islamic fundamentalisms offer tight, authoritarian control over populations and at the same time encourage values and behaviours that are likely to lead to competence in economic, military and other technologies.[35]

Turkey, which is proudly nationalistic, seems, because of the explicit secularism of the state, to be an exception to our argument. The data from Eğirdir suggest, however, that an 'Islamic' fundamentalism does underwrite many contemporary values and activities and is an important covert prop of the state. But the townspeople are very reluctant to acknowledge any such connection. This taboo is due to republican teaching, and is certainly related to the fact that nationalism on a Western model could not have been created without shedding many imperial traditions and with them the hierarchical, tolerant Islam of the Caliphate. Nowadays, Turkish Islam has a definite 'Protestant' character, which parallels other establishment orthodoxies, yet appears discrete and separate from the secular state.[36]

By and large the people of Eğirdir are mild, tolerant and aware of and sensitive to international opinion and issues. Equally, it is a peaceful town. It differs in degree from other such towns in Turkey in two respects: it is relatively both prosperous and homogeneous. We agree with local opinion, that peace in the town stems directly from both these factors, and we suggest that the open, tolerant 'fundamentalism' that we found there also derived from them. Homogeneity means that threats to the community tend to be located outside; it also means that virtually the whole community participates in a prosperity that might be jeopardized by an extreme 'fundamentalism'. As they say themselves, 'we keep the hungry dog from our kitchen'. In Eğirdir the 'fundamentalist' ideology is not associated with extremes of political action. However, other towns in the province were not so quiet in the years before the 1980 intervention. Civil disturbances in towns such as Yalvaç or Senirkent, for example, took a variety of political and religious forms, but opponents of all shades were generically labelled 'fanatics', thus suggesting something of both the richness and centrality of the ideology itself and the need to explain extremist reactions in terms of their specific local context.

Can we generalize to the national level? Turkey was the first republican state with a predominantly Muslim population. For reasons of geography and because of its sophisticated imperial background, the Turkish state had an early start both in creating a cultural uniformity among its population and in offering them the possibility of Western-type prosperity.

To date, the development of the public rhetoric and civic rituals of the Turkish Republic remains obscure. It is not clear how, when and at what levels detailed policies relating to civic educational and military idioms, etiquette and ceremonial were formulated and established.[37] It is certainly the case, however, that by the mid-1930s celebrations of national holidays in the provincial capital of Isparta were at base similar to those of today. This suggests that such celebrations have drawn on sources closely related to the stability of the Turkish state and the people's commitment to it.

Many accounts have described how the state formally redefined Islam and determined its character, but the very fact of the state's determination to dominate religion makes it difficult to discern the subtle ways in which Islamic beliefs and practices have simultaneously determined the character of the state. Our hypothesis is that Turkish republicanism/nationalism and Turkish Islam today are both expressions of a single underlying ideology of social control. This ideology, which shows through in the ritual and symbolic parallels between the officially separate Islamic and republican ideologies as they are popularly perceived and articulated, is fundamentalist in character, though at present remote from the extreme 'fundamentalism' of the Western media. The fundamentalism of the ideology is best revealed by the shifts in emphasis which have followed a variety of internal and external threats over the sixty years of the Republic. Indeed, recent changes have led other observers to remark on the fundamentalist character of this establishment ideology.

Today Turks would risk a great deal if they adopted an extreme fundamentalism which transformed their relations with the West and with the Soviet empire. However, it is just those relations, and the threat seen to be posed by Kurds, Greeks and Armenians, which lie behind the degree of fundamentalism associated with the dominant ideology of the state. Dissidents of left and right who created the terror of the late 1970s were seen as agents of outside powers. And to vanquish them after the intervention of 1980, the state, with its Islamic props, moved at first to a rather more hardline, 'fundamentalist' nationalism.

NOTES

1. The argument and much of the material in this chapter were first published in our ' "Thank God we're secular!" Aspects of fundamentalism in a Turkish town', in Lionel Caplan, ed., *Aspects of Religious Fundamentalism*, London, Macmillan, 1987, pp. 51–78.
2. Lloyd Fallers, *The Social Anthropology of the Nation State*, Chicago, Aldine, 1974, pp. 94–5.
3. Fallers, *The Social Anthropology*, pp. 95–104. See also Paul Magnarella, *Tradition and Change in a Turkish Town*, New York, John Wiley, 1974, pp. 151ff.

4. Nur Yalman, 'Islamic reform and the mystic tradition in eastern Turkey', *European Journal of Sociology* 10, 1969, pp. 41–60.
5. Our fieldwork ended in 1984, and the present tense here refers to the early 1980s.
6. See the detailed local history of Eğirdir by Süleyman S. Yiğitbaşı, *Eğirdir-Felekabad Tarihi*, Istanbul, Çeltut, 1972; as well as the history of Isparta by B. Süleyman Sami, *Isparta Tarihi*, Istanbul, Serenler, 1983.
7. Cf. Şerif Mardin's comments on the expansion of medreses in Isparta at the end of the nineteenth century: *Religion and Social Change in Modern Turkey*, Albany, SUNY Press, 1989, pp. 151ff.
8. See Tapper and Tapper, ' "Thank God we're secular!" ', p. 74.
9. Cf. Yalman, 'Islamic reform'. Nur Yalman, 'The center and the periphery: the reform of religious institutions in Turkey', *Current Turkish Thought*, 38, 1979. Türker Alkan, 'The National Salvation Party in Turkey', in Metin Heper and Raphael Israeli, eds, *Islam and Politics in the Modern Middle East*, London, Croom Helm, 1984, pp. 79–102. See Şerif Mardin, 'Turkey, Islam and Westernization', in Carlo Caldarola, ed., *Religion and Societies: Asia and the Middle East*, Berlin, Mouton, 1982, pp. 187f., for a summary of some of the complexities of these associations for Turkey as a whole; and Mardin, *Religion and Social Change*, *passim*, for Nurcu associations with the Eğirdir region.
10. For this distinction between 'confirmatory' and 'piacular' rituals, see E. E. Evans-Pritchard, *Nuer Religion*, Oxford, Oxford University Press, 1956, pp. 198ff.
11. See Nancy Tapper and Richard Tapper, 'The birth of the Prophet: ritual and gender in Turkish Islam', *Man* (N.S.), 22, 1987, pp. 69–92.
12. See P. Xavier Jacob, *L'enseignement religieux dans la Turquie moderne*, Berlin, Klaus Schwarz, 1982, p. 84, note 155.
13. In the late 1980s the official cult of Atatürk has been toned down: for example, the annual national 'shut-down' on 10 December, the day of Atatürk's death, was officially abolished in 1988, the fiftieth anniversary.
14. Şerif Mardin, 'Ideology and religion in the Turkish revolution', *International Journal of Middle East Studies*, 2, 1971, p. 208.
15. John Norton, 'Bektashis in Turkey', in Denis MacEoin and Ahmed Al-Shahi, eds, *Islam in the Modern World*, London, Croom Helm, 1983, pp. 80f.
16. Emelie Olson, 'Muslim identity and secularism in contemporary Turkey: the headscarf dispute', *Anthropological Quarterly*, 58, 1985, p. 165.
17. Ernest Gellner, *Muslim Society*, Cambridge, Cambridge University Press, 1981, p. 60. See Fallers, *The Social Anthropology*, pp. 86–7.
18. See Webster's comment on the new motto, 'we work' (*çalışırız*), which replaced traditional phrases referring to fate; D. Webster, *The*

Turkey of Ataturk, Philadelphia, American Academy of Political and Social Science, 1939, p. 289.

19. Tapper and Tapper, 'The birth of the Prophet'. F. L. MacCallum, *The Mevlidi Sherif by Suleyman Chelebi*, London, John Murray, 1943. D. Koopman, 'Atatürk as seen by Turkish workers in Europe', *Anatolica*, 8, 1981, pp. 159–77.

20. Şerif Mardin, 'Turkey, Islam and Westernization', p. 181. Lloyd Fallers, 'Turkish Islam', unpublished paper given at University of Chicago, 1971, p. 12. Webster, *The Turkey of Ataturk*, pp. 146f., 196, 281.

21. See G. W. Braswell, 'A Mosaic of Mullahs and Mosques: Religion and Politics in Iranian Shiah Islam', unpublished PhD thesis, Chapel Hill, N.C., 1975, pp. 206f., 237.

22. For example, Dale F. Eickelman, 'The art of memory: Islamic education and its social reproduction', *Comparative Studies in Society and History*, 20, 1978, pp. 495–516; and idem, *Knowledge and Power in Morocco*, Princeton, Princeton University Press, 1985. Mardin, *Religion and Social Change*, pp. 118ff.

23. See Roy Mottahedeh, *The Mantle of the Prophet*, New York, Simon and Schuster, 1985.

24. Nur Yalman, 'Islamic reform', p. 47.

25. See Jacob, *L'enseignement religieux*.

26. Andrew Mango, 'Islam in Turkey', in Douglas Grant, *The Islamic Near East*, Toronto, 1960, pp. 198–209; quoted in Jacob, *L'enseignement religieux*, p. 82.

27. There is more possible word-play with Sufi concepts such as *zahir* and *bâtın*, the old 'outward–inward' distinction, which in modern Turkish can be understood as 'bright' versus (with one consonant change to *bâtıl*) 'empty' and 'ignorant'; while modern Turkish makes little or no phonetic distinction between *tarik(at)* (Sufi order, the Way) and *tarik* (dark) – all of which confirms the dogma that the Sufis' esoteric pretensions are superstitious.

28. Cf. S. J. Tambiah, 'The magical power of words', *Man* (N.S.), 3, 1968, pp. 182f.

29. Mardin, *Religion and Social Change*, p. 36.

30. James Barr, *Fundamentalism*, London, SCM Press, 1977; see further, Tapper and Tapper, ' "Thank God we're secular!" '.

31. Maurice Bloch, 'Symbol, song, dance and features of articulation. Is religion an extreme form of traditional authority?', *European Journal of Sociology* 15, 1974, pp. 44–81.

32. See Mardin, *Religion and Social Change*, p. 4.

33. Niyazi Berkes, *The Development of Secularism in Turkey*, Montreal, McGill University Press, 1964, p. 483.

34. ' "Thank God we're secular!" ', pp. 56–9.

35. See Ernest Gellner, 'Waiting for Imam', *The New Republic*, 3622, 18 June 1984.

36. Cf. Cornelia Sorabji's application of our argument in her discussion of religious versus state ideologies in the federalist system of

Yugoslavia, 'Muslim Identity and Islamic Faith in Sarajevo', unpublished PhD thesis, University of Cambridge, 1989, pp. 152f.
37. See Webster's chapters on propaganda and education: *The Turkey of Ataturk*, pp. 181f.

4

MOSQUE OR HEALTH CENTRE?:
A Dispute in a *Gecekondu*

Akile Gürsoy-Tezcan

INTRODUCTION

Turkey, in its present stage of development, claims to be able to make economic and social progress while remaining loyal to some of its traditional ways of living. The Japanese model of development is frequently referred to by leading statesmen as a successful example of this. The new position and shape of Islam in the Middle East, however, is another dimension that needs to be taken into consideration. The reforms of Mustafa Kemal Atatürk in the first half of the century are often seen among other considerations to be a guarantee that Turkey will not make any serious diversion from its path towards 'modernization'. When questions related to fundamentalism arise, these are viewed and discussed at an abstract historical and national level, often without referring to the individual or to the actual effects of religion as it shapes the life of individuals. In this chapter I shall discuss a particular incident that demonstrates the specific interaction of religion, politics and cultural norms of family and gender in the Turkish context.

Since 1986 I have been leading a research project in a *gecekondu* (squatter) settlement of Istanbul, with the objective of investigating the cultural causes of infant mortality and the state of child health.[1] Initially the research had no particular focus on, and no special interest in, the development of Islam in modern

Turkey. However, discoveries made during field research, and the nature of the ethnographic data collected, have necessitated an examination of the impact and ideological meaning of religion in the daily lives of the inhabitants. What began as research into the cultural causes of infant mortality and child health became partly diverted into an attempt to explain a particular configuration of the impact of religion at the local level.

INFANT MORTALITY: THE TURKISH PUZZLE

Infant mortality rate (IMR) – the number of newborn children dying before one year of expressed age per 1,000 live births – is a commonly cited criterion of development and has received increasing attention over the past twenty years.[2] In recent years, the World Health Organization and international public opinion have focused considerable attention on infant and child health and deaths. In 1982, James Grant, World Director of UNICEF, publicly stated that out of the 125 million children born that year 17 million would die before reaching their first birthday, and he called all countries to joint action against this state of affairs.[3] In 1979 the 32nd World Health Congress revised the Alma Ata Meeting decisions of the previous year, and the outlines of an international strategy were published under the title of 'Health for All by 2000'. Within this perspective, 12 global objectives were defined. One of these was directly related to IMR: 'Infant mortality rate will be less than 50 per thousand for each identifiable subculture in each country.'[4] Studies exist that look at the different IMR in different subcultures.[5]

It is assumed, and generally borne out in national statistics, that there is a negative relationship between a country's (or community's) level of economic well-being and IMR. Whereas developed countries have on average an IMR of 15 per thousand, underdeveloped countries have a rate of about 80 per thousand. This is not, however, simply a relationship between IMR and level of income. Turkey, with a GNP per capita of $1,160, between 3 and 5 times higher than that of Burma, Sri Lanka, Madagascar or Kenya, has a higher IMR than these countries.

According to available figures for 1985 on a total of 121

countries, there are 53 whose GNP per capita was higher than that of Turkey and whose IMR was lower: these include the Western, industrialized, 'developed' countries. Secondly, there are 43 countries with a lower GNP per capita and a higher IMR than Turkey: these countries have an average GNP per capita of only $260. Thirdly, however, there are 22 countries with a GNP per capita lower than or the same as Turkey, but with a lower IMR than Turkey: this group includes several Central and Latin American countries with a variety of economic problems yet an IMR nearly half that of Turkey, but also included are a number of African countries with GNP per capita less than a third that of Turkey, and some countries in Asia and the Pacific with very large populations. Finally, only two countries in the world have both GNP per capita and IMR higher than Turkey: these are both predominantly Muslim Middle Eastern countries – Oman, with a GNP per capita of $6,490 and IMR of 109 per thousand, and Libya, with a GNP per capita of $8,520 and IMR of 90 per thousand.[6]

In fact, nearly all Middle Eastern countries share the same problem that faces Turkey as regards its high IMR in relation to its GNP per capita. Countries like Syria, Iraq, Jordan and Egypt have IMR higher than nearly all other countries with similar GNP per capita. The United Arab Emirates and Kuwait are the two countries with the highest GNP per capita in the world, yet their IMRs are respectively only 47th and 32nd lowest in the world.

Turkey, at 84 per thousand, has a higher IMR than six African and Latin American countries that have a very similar GNP per capita to Turkey, between $1,100 and $1,200: Costa Rica (IMR 19 per thousand), Jamaica (20 per thousand), Mauritius (26 per thousand), Guatemala (65 per thousand), Equador (67 per thousand), Congo (77 per thousand). Furthermore, Turkey seems to have a higher IMR than all its neighbours: in 1985, the IMR in the Soviet Union was reported to be 54 per thousand, in Syria 54 per thousand, in Iraq 73 per thousand, in Greece 14 per thousand, and in Bulgaria 16 per thousand.[7]

In Turkey, as in most Middle Eastern countries, neither the GNP per capita nor other criteria of development seem to justify the high incidence of infant deaths. Countries with a mortality rate for adults and children over five similar to that of Turkey have a much lower IMR. The causes of the particularly high infant and child mortality rates in Turkey remain unexplained. It is not clear whether they are due to certain diseases or health conditions that uniquely affect Turkey, or malnutrition, or whether the health care practices that exist for adults do not exist to the same extent and at the same effectiveness for infants and children.[8]

While IMR seems to be a simple health statistic that reflects material culture and environmental conditions, it is also a silent but meaningful indicator of a country's (or community's) life-style, of the value given to different generations, age-groups and genders, and of many other unspoken balances of power that exist in that culture. The importance of conditions beyond the material and environmental has emerged in research such as that by Nancy Scheper-Hughes in a Brazilian shanty-town in 1982. Scheper-Hughes interviewed over 72 women aged between 19 and 71: out of 585 pregnancies (9.5 per woman) she found a total of 329 living children (4.5 per woman), a total of 16 stillbirths, 85 miscarriages and abortions (1.4 per woman), 251 child deaths (birth to 5 years: 3.5 per woman), and 5 childhood deaths (6 to 12 years). In the essay that won the 1985 Stirling Award, she points out that 'the so-called Brazilian Economic Miracle [which is] a policy of capital accumulation ... has increased ... the Gross National Product [but that] childhood mortality rate has been steadily rising throughout the nation since the late 1960s.' She mentions political party leaders advocating free distribution of children's coffins where necessary as election propaganda in the district.[9]

Generally, in developing and developed countries, research on infant and child deaths has concentrated on intermediate variables affecting child health. Studies have been carried out to measure the effects of nutrition, of breastfeeding and of morbidity.[10] The role of respiratory and intestinal diseases and infectious illnesses has been examined.[11] Socio-economic variables such as family income, mother's and father's level of education, environmental factors and level of technology have also been the focus of study. Generally, a significantly positive relationship has been found between the total number of pregnancies a woman has had, the total number of her children, the number of members of the household, and infant mortality. A significantly negative relationship has also been found between the amount of schooling the mother has had, the level of family income, and infant mortality.[12]

Scientists often try to explain mortality by stating the existence of a relationship between mortality figures and selected variables such as these. In fact, however, the manner in which these variables do affect mortality, and the way they are interconnected with national and global policies and ideologies, are left unexplained.[13]

Mosley and Chen have proposed a framework for research on child survival which shows how the causal linkages can be traced 'back' from death to health status, thence to a variety of intermediary factors, and finally to a layer of determinants which they place in one category called 'socio-economic'. It has been remarked that, even though they have received a great deal of research attention, the socio-economic determinants remain a black box to this day.[14]

RESEARCH IN AN ISTANBUL *GECEKONDU*

Our research has been aimed at the specific problem of explaining the higher than expected IMR in Turkey. With the above considerations in mind, we wanted to study both the implications of national policies and the local cultural factors operating together to determine child health in Turkey. In view of the rapid and increasing urbanization in the country, we chose an area which would be representative of this trend. Within our selected area, we have been comparing 100 families that have experienced infant mortality with 100 families that live in the same area and share similar socio-economic conditions but have not experienced infant mortality. By carrying out intensive in-depth interviews and observations on these two groups of families, and by conducting ethnographic field research in the area, we wanted to discover the family circumstances, proximate kin and cultural factors that lead to infant deaths. In other words, at a macro-level we wanted to see how national policies reflect on child health, and at a micro-level how local conditions and family life influence child care.

In order to determine the sample of 200 families, we carried out a preliminary survey in a *gecekondu* (squatter) settlement of Istanbul. We chose the area of Göçkent (a pseudonym) as our location of research because it had received migrants from nearly all parts of Turkey for the past 20 to 25 years, and we assumed this would be representative of many newly-settled *gecekondu* areas of Istanbul and probably of Turkey. These areas are populated mostly by members of the urban working class or unemployed and underemployed. Housing is generally of low prestige and durability. In Göçkent, some squatters own their own homes, some officially so, while others rent, making it a combination of squatter settlement and slum.[15]

In November and December 1986, information was collected from 1,025 households about household composition and size, age distribution and mortality. The objective of this preliminary study was to obtain relevant demographic data to enable us to select a sample for ongoing research on the cultural factors affecting infant mortality and child health among migrants in Istanbul.

Respondents were asked the number of people actually inhabiting the house, their ages and dates of birth, how they were related to each other, and whether there were any pregnant women at the time. Secondly, they were asked whether anyone had died the previous year (between November/December 1985 and November/December 1986), and, if so, their age, cause and date of death. The results of this study were used as a basis for finding and comparing similar households that had and had not experienced infant mortality, with a view towards determining the causes of a higher than expected IMR in Turkey.

Our sample of 1,025 households was distributed over 9 streets in an area randomly selected from the district municipality plan. The suburb is characterized by adjacent buildings or flats where tenants and landlords (who represent different economic and migration patterns) live next door to each other. Therefore, in selecting our sample, we chose a small but complete area and investigated every individual dwelling, rather than using a random sample of dwellings over a wider area; by so doing, we aimed to include all the different types of dwellers in the area concerned. Information was collected from nearly all the dwellings on these streets; those houses where no respondents were to be found were visited two more times in an attempt to get full coverage of the sample streets. The questionnaires were administered by social anthropology graduate students and the primary investigator.

The area we call Göçkent is situated in a densely populated area of Asian Istanbul. Although the mobility of the population and the large number of unregistered people make it difficult to get an exact population record, we can say that it is inhabited by a total of about 200,000 people, of whom nearly all are rural migrants, including a small group of gypsies who came to Istanbul in the last 10 to 20 years from Central and Eastern Turkey and the Black Sea Coast. Our household survey and the subsequent in-depth interviewing took place in a particular district within the official boundaries of the *muhtarlık* (local headman's jurisdiction), consisting of between about 28,000 and 30,000 inhabitants within the larger Göçkent suburb. This district has a main road with a number of groceries, markets, a few butchers, many furniture, electrical goods and kitchenware shops, construction material and carpentry shops, barbers, clothing and shoe shops, and a large number of private doctors' surgeries and pharmacies. The availability of shops selling items like furniture and electrical goods points to the presence of a consumer market in the district. Within the boundaries of the district there are three mosques, about 20 men's coffee-houses, and a couple of beer shops or billiard halls (which are all also local social and business centres) and a physical activity centre for men. During our research, one flat in the district was converted into a mosque, bringing the total number to four. The district has no school, however. In 1986, about 2,000 children of junior-school age were forced to enrol in a school in a neighbouring district. It was estimated that in 1987 this figure would rise to about 3,000.

The results of the preliminary survey showed that most of the demographic patterns – household size (a mean of 4.7 persons), age distribution (about 50 per cent under 20) and sex ratio (normal), ages and causes of adult mortality – were similar to figures and trends that characterize urban Turkey.

The same is true of household composition: 71 per cent of households are nuclear families, composed of husband, wife and children, a few of them including semi-permanent guests. Some sets of nuclear families living in the same block of flats might in fact be classified as semi-extended families, where one nuclear family includes the parents of a senior member of another, so that they eat most of their meals together, spend time together, and go to their individual flats only to sleep. Some of these families have been classified as 'extended families', depending on how the respondent actually described and named her type of family. Some researchers have distinguished 'temporary' from 'permanent' extended families, depending on who is the 'bread-winner' in the household. In our survey, however, the extended family is defined as a family unit consisting of at least two generations of adults, sharing housing and pooling economic resources. The traditional patriarchal model of the extended family consists of the father, mother, son, son's wife and their children. This form of the family unit undergoes various permutations according to the life-cycle of its members.[16] Thus, a total of 21 per cent of the households are patrilineally extended families, and 3 per cent are extended families where the wife's relatives are present. About 3 per cent were found to be broken homes, and 1 per cent were inhabited by single-dwellers (7 men and 5 women were middle-aged people living alone). In 3 households, the husband was a polygynist with two wives present in the same household.

When we come to infant mortality rates, however, we find that Göçkent has a higher rate than that usually given for Turkey: 97 per thousand. Out of 164 live births in the previous year, 16 babies died before completing their first year. The most frequent cause of infant death is described as involving 'high temperatures, infantile convulsions and sudden death'. Nearly half these babies died before completing their first month.

EXPLAINING INFANT MORTALITY IN GÖÇKENT

The IMR for the Middle East in general in 1985 was stated to be 86 per thousand, and that for Turkey was 84 per thousand.[17] One might have expected the rate to be lower in our suburb in 1986. The higher IMR in Göçkent might be explained by the general conviction that actual IMR is usually higher than the official statistics in Turkey, and that the reliability of present official data is questionable,[18] or by a more significant statement that child health is deteriorating in at least some urban areas.

An interesting difference becomes apparent in the family structures of households which experienced infant mortality in the previous year. Extended patrilineal families constitute only 22 per cent of all households where there is a married woman of reproductive age (that is, between 15 and 45), but 38 per cent of households which experienced infant mortality live in extended patrilineal families. There is evidence from the Middle East and elsewhere to suggest that the relationship between extended household structure and higher IMR is not unique to Göçkent. In her research on the relation between household structure and child morbidity in low-income areas in Amman, Deeb found that the presence of another woman (usually mother-in-law) was associated with a high childhood mortality, despite the fact that these extended households were characterized by a higher total income than nuclear-family households. A similar finding was reported by Caldwell among Nigerian women, where it was found that children living in extended households experienced higher mortality than those living in nuclear households. 'Caldwell argues this is because mothers in extended households are restricted in their decision-making by traditional beliefs imposed by the in-laws. In contrast to this, a study in Malaysia . . . found that the presence of grandparents was associated with lower infant mortality.'[19]

It is questionable whether traditional beliefs and practices imposed by the older generation would be more conducive to poor child health in Göçkent. Therefore two hypotheses come to mind which might explain the influence of family and household structure on child health and mortality. Either adverse economic conditions may force families to live with extended kin, and these adverse conditions may also cause insufficient care of the infant; or the dynamics of extended patrilineal family life may somehow be detrimental to the health care of the infant. Our current research is in part an attempt to test these hypotheses.

In trying to explain the significantly higher incidence of infant mortality among patrilineally extended families in Göçkent, we are led to an array of disputes over the conceptualization of households, and the meaning attributed to different types of family structures. It is also at this point, in attempting to enter the 'black box' of family life and relationships, that an analysis of the impact of Islam on daily life becomes a crucially important part of the investigation.

Research evidence suggests that in rural areas of countries like Turkey, extended families tend to be associated with larger landholdings. Peasants with sufficient land and capital resources can form and sustain extended households, and continue to call on the labour of grown and married children.[20] Extended families have thus been associated with patriarchal authority and economic prosperity, while households with little or no land are, demographically speaking, of nuclear composition. Furthermore, in family enterprises with activities outside agriculture, nuclear family units may reside autonomously, but these households (which have been called 'separate cauldron, common income') are functionally connected and may display even greater evidence of patriarchal control over the younger generation. This is true regardless of the structural composition of those living under the same roof in any given family unit. Kandiyoti suggests that not only the presence or absence of household property, but also the various forms it takes (land versus capital) have a direct bearing on the demographic and authority structures of the household.[21]

Therefore, in an urban community of recently settled migrants, our ultimate definition of a household has tended to be a selective combination of the demographic approach, which defines households according to the demographic composition of those living under the same roof; the sentiments approach, which takes into consideration the attitudes and expectations of family members towards each other; and the household economics approach, which makes definitions according to the subsistence strategies according to which different members are deployed.[22] Again, the base of these family relationships, and the patterns by which they relate to each other, are closely intertwined with beliefs and a world view which are in part conceptualized and expressed as 'religion'.

Our concern over the causes of infant deaths and the socioeconomic factors influencing child health has led us to observe the dynamics of interactions within the family. It has been remarked that 'the level which best reflects the workings of culture and ideology may be found in the internal distribution of resources within the household'. In fact, a household with limited resources at its disposal may not necessarily tell us how these resources will be distributed. 'For instance, scarce food may be distributed fairly equitably among household members, or distribution may take a particularly hierarchized form.' We are cautioned against the pitfalls inherent 'in treating households as representing a unity of interests, where all members' needs and interests coincide'.[23] In other words, cultural expectations, especially as regards the sexual division of labour and gender differences, are particularly relevant when it comes to researching child health, both at the level of health-related behaviour and in the distribution of resources that affect infant health.

THE DISPUTE

In view of the fact that not all the research data have been analysed, at this stage we have to pose more questions than we can provide answers for as regards the internal dynamics of family life in our research area. However, one local incident has forced us to reflect on the impact of Islam on infant and child mortality in Göçkent. An intense local dispute was discovered in the district over whether a particular site should continue as a Health Centre, or whether a mosque should be built in its place. The following is a summary of the developments leading to the dispute, which remains unresolved.

In 1967 a group of leading men of the district donated a plot of land to the Treasury, to be used for the public good, and the Ministry of Health began to use the plot for a dispensary. A prefabricated two-room building was erected, and two nurses and two doctors began to function in the centre. In May 1980, the Muhtar (headman) of the district, together with other leading officials, handed a petition to the Ministry of Health, to the effect that the two-room building was too small to carry out mother–child health, gynaecological and internal-illness services. Commenting on the fact that this was the only Health Centre for a population of about 200,000 inhabitants, they asked for the construction of another floor. The request was granted; however, once the health staff were withdrawn in order to allow construction work to begin, one room of the prefabricated building began to be used by local men for prayer, and the other became a storage place for Kızılay (the Turkish Red Crescent). Shortly afterwards, foundations for the construction of a mosque were laid on the same site, right next to the Health Centre.

A bust of Atatürk, originally placed near the Health Centre by the Kaymakamlık (District Office), was removed by persons unknown, and relocated on that part of the site where construction was in progress, probably in order to foil any attempt to demolish the mosque, since it is illegal to remove or damage a bust of Atatürk. In any case, even without the protection of such an untouchable symbol, once the construction of a mosque began, a decision to demolish it would be difficult in view of the intense emotions such a move would arouse.

The local Muhtar, who came to office by election in 1982, and who is in favour of having the Health Centre re-established, has been to the Ministry of Health in Ankara on many occasions to make his case. He has done this at considerable personal and political expense to himself, since the political party to which he belongs has made election promises to have a mosque installed on this site, and since the Governor of Istanbul has refused support for the re-establishment of the Health Centre. In conversation, he always emphasizes that he himself is a believer, a Muslim, and that he has nothing against the building of mosques, but that this is a different matter. He has argued before the Governor and in Ankara that in his district (with about 30,000 inhabitants) there are already four mosques, but no primary schools, and that the Health Centre in question was the only one to serve a population of about 200,000. For this reason, he argued, the site should not be allowed to be taken over by those wishing to build yet another mosque.

Those building the mosque (who were believed to be from the Süleymancı sect and to have obtained financial support for their project through German channels) offered to have one section of the ground floor available as a Health Centre. However, in March 1987, despite the Muhtar's efforts, the Ministry of Health issued an official statement to the effect that the mosque construction had already made considerable progress, that the Governor also supported the endeavour, and that it was not advisable to have a health centre so close to a mosque, since the separate and different nature of each could cause conflicts in the days to follow. Although it is common practice in some parts of the Middle East to have health centres adjacent to or integrated with mosques, this is not the case in Turkey, which has adopted a secular pattern where all health and educational services are expected to be independent of religion.

The Ministry has decided that, as the matter stands now, separate support should be given to the suggestion of the Muhtar that he himself set up a health centre, using his personal resources. In fact, the Muhtar does not at present have immediate access to sufficient funds to establish such a centre, but he felt that after his and his family's considerable personal investment in the issue he was in honour bound to offer such a thing. Land is in short supply and expensive in the area, and no site has so far been found for the building of a new health centre.

In 1988 five district Muhtars collectively signed and submitted a petition asking for the use of another plot in the area, with the intention of building a health centre and a school. Since then, surprisingly, this plot has been rented to a contractor in Istanbul, so the district still lacks the land for establishing a health centre and school. During this period, Turkish state television has been urging Muhtars throughout the country to support the government's local family planning and child health centres and programmes, quoting Turkey's very high IMR as the reason for the appeal.

When no satisfactory results could be obtained from the Ministry of Health with regard to the Health Centre in Göçkent, a group of local families and the Muhtar of the district made one final effort. In May 1987, when a leading Turkish statesman made a visit to a nearby lycée, the Muhtar's daughter presented a petition to him in person, asking his help in having their Health Centre re-opened. In the envelope, which she had great difficulty in handing to him because of the efforts of both the statesman's bodyguards and the builders of the mosque to stop her, she included a summary of the preliminary results of our research, a survey which showed that infant mortality in the district was 97 per thousand in 1986, much higher than in most countries of the world, even those, such as Burma, Sri Lanka, Madagascar or Kenya, which have per capita income much lower than Turkey.

The incident of the Muhtar's daughter submitting a petition to the statesman appeared in the Turkish national press, where it was commented that the girl, a student at lycée night-courses, had presented the petition as a last effort to save the district's former Health Centre. In the following days, the Muhtar's daughter was threatened anonymously, and told to keep silent and stay at home. The local papers, however, made no mention whatsoever of the petition or of the Health Centre, and instead expressed approval of the progress made in the construction of the mosque. Some 'left-wing' journals and periodicals too have not found this incident worth reporting; they said they were after more 'political' news.

When the petition received no response, in autumn 1987 two bus-loads of local women went to protest and make a plea to the Governor of Istanbul and also to the Central Office of the Motherland Party (ANAP). The women, accompanied by their children and babies, voiced their protest at the take-over of their only Health Centre. They expressed the importance of having a health centre within walking distance of their homes, and pointed out that they used to have a free or very inexpensive health service. The party officials and officials in the Governor's office viewed the women with astonishment, and said they would look into the matter. The mosque construction, however, was continuing six months later.

One final incident deserves attention for its symbolic significance. On 10 November 1987, the anniversary of Atatürk's death, during a period when construction of the mosque was temporarily halted by order of the government while the issue was under consideration, the bust of Atatürk which had been moved to the construction site was thrown to the ground at some distance from its pedestal. Yet local women also quote Atatürk as the leader of progress in Turkey and as the founder of an overall change that also encompasses and stands for their rights. I think it is in this ambivalence and in the local-level resistance that we find the uniqueness of the Turkish situation as regards Islam.

CONCLUSIONS: HEALTH, EDUCATION AND RELIGION

The frequency of such disputes is naturally a point of interest for those concerned about the extent and nature of fundamentalist activities. There are sporadic reports in the national press, indicating that incidents such as the one described above are not uncommon. Thus, the centrist *Milliyet* on 15 February 1987 reported an incident in a village in western Turkey where a group of Süleymancı (a recent offshoot of the Nakşibendi) was forcing the opening of a second mosque. The paper commented that it was against the law for a village to have more than one mosque, and related the story of how the local inhabitants made a petition to the state leaders, asking them to intervene and restore law and order in the village. In a case similar to that of the Health Centre, it was reported in *Milliyet* on 26 September 1988 that the Ministry of Industry and Trade had decided to demolish a kindergarten (which was opened for service in May 1988 by the Minister himself) in order to build a mosque 'open to the public' instead. On 31 July 1988 *Hürriyet*, the most popular daily newspaper in Turkey, reported the construction of a spectacular new mosque in a small village in central Anatolia. The mosque cost 100 million TL (about £40,000), but the village had only 50 houses, and only 30 men used the mosque regularly for prayer.

The weekly satirical magazine *Limon*, on the other hand, published a cartoon in May 1987 making fun of the inflation in the number of mosques in Turkey, as did *Milliyet* on 15 September 1988. On 12 September 1988, *Cumhuriyet*, a left-of-centre paper, ran the following front-page headline: 'In the past three years, the number of mosques in Istanbul has increased by 306 from 1490 to 1796. No figures are given for mosques whose construction is under way, which are not yet open for service. . . . The number of school buildings entering service in the past three years was only 205.' The following day, the leading article in *Cumhuriyet* dwelt on this issue and asked the reader to question whether we were becoming a nation more concerned with the other world than with this, and to ask where the finance for the construction of these mosques was coming from, and whether these priorities would help us enter the ranks of the 'developed' world. Muhammad Zakariya, an American citizen converted to Islam, commented in an interview published on 28 May 1988 in *Cumhuriyet* that Turkey appeared to be more Islamic than any other Muslim country that he had visited, and that there was no country with more mosques than Turkey.

The large number of mosques in Turkey may not of itself be an important indicator of religious activity and involvement. Other facts may have greater significance. Reed, for instance, in an article on Islam and education in Turkey, points out that according to the 1985 Turkish Statistical Yearbook and related data issued by the Ministry of Education, Youth and Sport, in 1976 there were 927 regular lycées and 73 Imam–Hatip schools, while eight years later, in 1984, the former numbered 1,190 (an increase of some 28 per cent) and the latter 374 (an increase of over 500 per cent). Analysing 1985 data on Technical and Vocational Schools, Reed comments that, in contrast to the 220,001 students enrolled in the 374 Imam–Hatip lycées, there were only 18,144 enrolled in the 91 Health Care Schools, and only 2,640 in the 23 Agricultural Schools.[24]

It is not the intention of this chapter to discuss the intricacies of state policies, or to make an evaluation of relevant press reports. Our field research, based on the question of the cultural causes of infant mortality and child health in Turkey, allows us to comment on one particular area only. The example which emerged during our research, of the dispute concerning the Health Centre versus the mosque, illustrates the varied and complex reactions of local inhabitants on the one hand, and the political parties, the Ministry, the local administration, and the heads of state on the other. The silence and *laissez-faire* attitude of the latter with regard to this issue seem to be in direct contradiction with the open public support given to immunization, family planning campaigns, and the reforms of Atatürk as regards improving the position of women. Furthermore, the incident and the way it was reported in the press seem evidence of fundamental conflicts between local and national interests: conflicts between secular and religious power bases, and between male and female needs and interests that reflect the cultural construction of Turkish family life. The issues which are emerging in our research are at the heart of contradictions between traditional and modern, culture and politics, local and national, and male and female interests, both in Turkey and also in other parts of the world.

NOTES

1. I would like to express my gratitude to the Turkish Economy Research Centre, to the Research Foundation of the University of Marmara, and to Middle East Awards for supporting and funding this research.
2. K. Sümbüloğlu, *Sağlık Alanına Özel İstatistiksel Yöntemler*, Ankara, TTB Ankara Tabib Odası Yayını, no.4, 1982, p. 236. W. H. Mosley, 'Child survival: research and policy', in W. H. Mosley and L. C. Chen, eds, *Child Survival, Strategies for Research*, Supplement to *Population Development Review*, 10, 1984, pp. 3–48. OECD, *Social*

Sciences in Policy Making, Paris, Organization for Economic Co-operation and Development, 1979–1983. R. L. Sivard, *Women: A World Survey*, Washington, World Priorities, 1985. *1983 World Statistics*, New York, UNICEF. *World Bank Development Report, 1980*, Oxford University Press, The International Bank.

3. J. P. Grant, *The State of the World's Children 1981–1982*, New York, UNICEF, 1982.

4. WHO, *Global Strategy for Health for All by the Year 2000*, Geneva, World Health Organization, 1981.

5. See Bozkurt Güvenç, *İnsan ve Kültür*, Istanbul, Remzi Kitabevi, 1974, pp. 104, 116, 130. H. F. Reading, *A Dictionary of the Social Sciences*, London, Routledge and Kegan Paul, 1977, p. 204. L. A. Sawchuk, D. A. Herring and L. R. Waks, 'Evidence of a Jewish advantage: a study of infant mortality in Gibraltar, 1870–1959', *American Anthropologist*, 87, 1985, pp. 616–25.

6. J. P. Grant, *The State of the World's Children 1987*, Oxford University Press, UNICEF, 1987, pp. 90–1.

7. Ibid. There are no figures for Iran for the last few years.

8. F. C. Shorter and M. Macura, *Türkiye'de Nüfus Artışı (1935–1975)*, Ankara, Yurt Yayıncılık, 1983, p. 21.

9. Nancy Scheper-Hughes, 'Culture, scarcity and maternal thinking: maternal detachment and infant survival in a Brazilian shantytown', *Ethos*, 13 (4), 1985, p. 292.

10. K. H. Brown, 'Measurement of dietary intake', in Mosley and Chen, eds, *Child Survival*, pp. 69–92. Carol Delaney, 'Symbolism of procreation and implications for education and population planning', unpublished MS, 1983. S. L. Hoffman and B. B. Lamphere, 'Breastfeeding performance and child development', in Mosley and Chen, eds, *Child Survival*, pp. 93–118. W. Martorell and T. J. Ho, 'Malnutrition, morbidity and mortality', in ibid., pp. 49–68. S. Tezcan, *Türkiye'de Bebek ve Çocuk Ölümleri*, Ankara, Hacettepe Üniversitesi, Tıp Fakültesi Halk Sağlığı Anabilim Dalı, Yayın no. 26, 1985.

11. R. E. Black, 'Diarrhoeal diseases and child mortality and morbidity', in Mosley and Chen, eds, *Child Survival*, pp. 141–62. D. J. Bradley and A. Keyme, 'Parasitic diseases: measurement and mortality impact', in ibid., pp. 163–90. G. M. Foster and B. G. Anderson, *Medical Anthropology*, New York, John Wiley, 1978.

12. A. Adlakha, *A Study of Infant Mortality in Turkey*, Ann Arbor, University Microfilms, 1970. J. Briscoe, 'Technology and child survival: the example of sanitary engineering', in Mosley and Chen, eds, *Child Survival*, pp. 237–56. Delaney, 'Symbolism of procreation'. Akile Gürsoy-Tezcan, 'Türkiye'de bebek ölümleri ve düşündürdükleri', *Türk Ekonomisi ve Türk Ekonomi İlmi*, Istanbul, Türkiye Ekonomisi Araştırma Merkezi Yayını, 1986, pp. 211–31. Deniz Kandiyoti, 'Sex roles and social change: comparative appraisal of Turkey's women', *Signs* 3 (1), 1977, pp. 57–73. T. P. Schultz, 'Studying the impact of household economics and community

variables on child mortality', in Mosley and Chen, eds, *Child Survival*, pp. 215–36. *1985 World Statistics*, New York, UNICEF, 1985. H. Ware, 'Effects of maternal education, women's roles and child care on child mortality', in Mosley and Chen, eds, *Child Survival*, pp. 191–214.

13. Mosley, 'Child survival', p. 25. Scheper-Hughes, 'Culture, scarcity and maternal thinking'.

14. Mosley and Chen, eds, *Child Survival*. F. C. Shorter, 'The production of health in [Cairo] households', unpublished paper presented at 'Assessment of health interventions', Middle East Awards workshop in Aswan, October 1987, p. 1.

15. Cf. D. G. Epstein, 'The genesis and function of squatter settlements in Brazilia', in J. Fried and N. J. Chisman, eds, *City Ways*, New York, Crowell Company, 1975, pp. 261–2.

16. S. Timur, 'Türkiye'de aile yapısının belirleyicileri', in N. Abadan-Unat, ed., *Türk Toplumunda Kadın*, Ankara, Turkish Social Science Association, 1979, pp. 117–32.

17. Sivard, *Women: A World Survey*, p. 38. Grant, *State*, 1987, p. 90.

18. Adlakha, *Infant Mortality*. J. Blacker and W. Brass, 'Experience of retrospective demographic enquiries to determine vital rates. The recall method in social surveys', in Louis Moss et al., eds, *The Recall Method in Social Surveys*, University of London, Institute of Education, 1979. D. S. Casley and D. A. Lury, *Data Collection in Developing Countries*, Oxford, Clarendon Press, 1981. Gürsoy-Tezcan, 'Türkiye'de bebek ölümleri'. Tezcan, *Türkiye'de Bebek*. M. Tolon, 'İstatistik, tavşan avcılığı ve diş hekimliği', *Güneş*, Istanbul, 1986.

19. M. E. Deeb, 'Household Structure as Related to Childhood Mortality and Morbidity among Low Income Areas in Amman', PhD thesis, Baltimore, Johns Hopkins University, 1987, p. 152. J. C. Caldwell, 'Education as factor in mortality decline: an examination of Nigerian data', *Population Studies*, 33 (3), 1979, pp. 395–413. W. P. Butz, J. Davanzo and J. P. Habicht, *Biological and Behavioural Influence on the Mortality of Malaysian Infants*, Rand Corporation, N–1638–AID, 1982.

20. Deniz Kandiyoti, 'Continuity and change in the family', in Türköz Erder, ed., *Family in Turkish Society*, Ankara, Turkish Social Science Association, 1985, p. 33.

21. Kandiyoti, 'Continuity and change', p. 34.

22. Idem, 'Continuity and change', p. 33.

23. Ibid.

24. Howard A. Reed, 'Islam and education in Turkey: their roles in national development', *Turkish Studies Association Bulletin*, 12 (1), 1988, pp. 2-4.

5

ETHNIC ISLAM AND NATIONALISM AMONG THE KURDS IN TURKEY

Lâle Yalçın-Heckmann

INTRODUCTION

This chapter considers a theoretical problem and attempts a critical assessment of its various dimensions. The problem is the relation between ethnic and national identities and more universalist and religious commitments; more specifically, it concerns ethnicity, nationalism, Islam and social movements among the largest minority group in Turkey, the Kurds of eastern and southeastern Anatolia. In order to discuss the relevant issues in this sociological problem, I use field materials collected in Hakkari province, and various historical, sociological and political studies of Kurdish movements within the Ottoman and more recent political formations, namely the Turkish Republic and surrounding states. I intend first to identify unsatisfactory elements in the models that have been used to analyse Kurdish social movements, and secondly to ask the relevant questions and suggest more suitable methods of answering them. My aim is to clarify some of the concepts and the models that have been used and to suggest further areas of research which would enable a more satisfactory understanding of ethnicity and Islam among the Kurds.

My interest in Kurdish ethnicity and nationalism is older than my interest in Islam among Kurds. In my doctoral work I discussed various aspects of Islam, but mostly as secondary issues.

Here I reconsider my material in the light of evaluations and impressions drawn from more recent visits to Hakkari.

Lately there has been much general political discussion of 're-Islamization' in Turkey, especially as it concerns the Kurds. Sociologists and political scientists have shown an interest in this development and have been studying the new Islamic organizations and their publications.[1] The Turkish press reports frequently on the activities of Islamic organizations and militant or secret groups in different parts of the country, and some recent publications suggest that areas with a Kurdish majority are becoming more susceptible to militant Islamic influences than other areas.[2] The number of Islamic or fundamentalist movements which can be identified is still not clear. However, if there is sufficient evidence that such activities are strong and significant among the Kurdish people, the following question arises: is there a special and significant relation between Kurdish ethnicity and Islamic militancy or fundamentalism? If there is, at what level (village, region or wider) and from what aspect (ideology, recruitment, leadership or organization) should we analyse this relation?

RELIGION AND NATIONALISM: THE ŞEYH SAIT UPRISING

Looking at analyses of various Kurdish uprisings around the time of the First World War and the early years of the Republic, one sees a curious mixture of religious and nationalist motivations. The extent to which these movements were religious or ethnic-nationalist is disputed by historians and social scientists.[3] The Şeyh Sait rebellion in 1925 is a case in point. This uprising, which affected three or four provinces in eastern and southeastern Turkey, when allegedly between 30,000 and 40,000 people (soldiers, rebels and civilians) were killed, had many serious political implications in those early years of the Republic; it continues to influence Kurdish and Turkish politics, and is often referred to, especially in Turkish sources, as a religious fundamentalist (*dinî* or *hilafetci*) uprising.[4] The press at the time used words like 'bandits', 'religious fanatics', 'enemies of the Republic', or 'irredentists' (*irtica*), especially for the leaders.[5] The most obvious reason for these names is of course that the Nakşibendi tarikat provided the organization and communication network for the uprising, while the leader Şeyh Sait was a very influential shaikh of this order. Shaikhs were leading tribal and non-tribal groups in the uprising, their followers (*mürid*) were prominent agents of the organization, and the shaikhs' religious reputation and influence were a major impetus for the uprising. Hence for many observers it was essentially a fundamentalist, even a messianic uprising, a reaction to the abolition of the Caliphate by the new secular regime of Mustafa Kemal.

The fullest political, sociological and historical analysis of the uprising has been published by the Dutch anthropologist Martin van Bruinessen in his book *Agha, Shaikh and State*. His analysis is particularly rich and reliable, because he not only used the few written sources by Kurdish nationalists and Turkish authors but also interviewed some prominent participants, tribal leaders and Kurdish intellectuals who had survived or escaped, and are now living in Syria. He takes into account the major international and local political events and their influences, the formal political organization and groups among the Kurdish nationalists at the time, the tribal structure and the base of the movement, as well as the Nakşibendi religious order, its restricted hierarchical structure, and the role shaikhs played between feuding tribes. He compares the organization of the Nakşibendi shaikhs and tarikat in this uprising to those of the Sanusi shaikhs in Cyrenaica studied by Evans-Pritchard in the 1940s. He points out that the Sanusi were more hierarchically organized and thus had a wider base, whereas the Kurdish shaikhs had a more satellite-like organization where the communication and influence were often broken and discontinuous.[6]

Van Bruinessen makes the following points about the base of the movement and its primary interests:

> Outside the central area where the revolt had a mass character, participation or non-participation or even opposition of tribes to the revolt was apparently determined to a large extent by the same kind of considerations that had for centuries determined tribal politics and policies vis-à-vis the state. Motivation of the commoners – be it religious or nationalist – played no part worth mentioning yet. Chieftains joined or opposed according to what seemed the

advantageous thing to do and to what their rivals did; the commoners simply followed the chieftains.[7]

Thus, according to van Bruinessen, for some tribes it was basically a game of chiefly politics, where chiefs made alliances or feuds according to *their* assessment of the strong or weak parties in the conflict. The majority of the tribes participating in the uprising were Sunni Muslims, and van Bruinessen notes that tribal feuds and traditional rivalries were not responsible alone for some Alevi tribes' staying out of the rebellion:

> It was the orthodox sunni, anti-shi'i ideology that had always been the justification of [Sunni] discrimination and oppression [of Alevis] ... Mustafa Kemal's Turkey was a secular republic; for the first time Alevis had officially equal rights, and law protected them. An independent Kurdistan, under authority of sunni shaikhs, could only be to their disadvantage.[8]

Religion then seems in this case to be *the* factor determining participation in a basically Sunni movement. Van Bruinessen's analysis shows on the one hand the complexity of such an uprising, the way interests are intermingled and yet discernible and identifiable, and on the other hand the importance of the leadership and organization of the movement for success or defeat. As for the question whether the revolt was religious or nationalist in character, he points out that it was 'neither a purely religious nor a purely nationalist one. The nationalist motivation of *those who planned* it is beyond doubt, but even among them many were also emotionally affected by the abolition of the Caliphate.'[9] Şeyh Sait, then, was clearly a very pious man and the movement was called a jihad, but van Bruinessen insists that 'the *primary* aim of both Şêx Seîd and the Azadî [the political organization of the revolt] leaders was the establishment of an independent Kurdistan.'[10]

Before proceeding to draw some conclusions and discuss some of the issues raised by van Bruinessen's analysis of the Şeyh Sait revolt, I want to refer to a later study by him, where he looks at the political career of the Kurdish tribal leader Simko, who led various smaller revolts along the Turco-Iranian border between

1910 and 1920. In this paper, van Bruinessen focuses on the strategies employed by Simko, the way he played the political interests of the surrounding Great Powers against one another, and the way he manipulated tribal conflicts and tried to overcome them by either paying his supporters well, making marriage alliances with influential religious leaders, or using nationalist rhetoric.

Like Şeyh Sait, Simko's motivations were also complex: 'nationalist and private ambitions went together in him and cannot be separated'. His supporters, on the other hand, were mostly Kurdish soldiers, 'either simply deserters or people with nationalist motivations; others, mercenaries attracted by the high pay and the fact that Simko gave them wives'. Van Bruinessen adds that most of Simko's followers were 'motivated more by pay and loot than by nationalist sentiment or personal loyalty'. Nationalism for them 'was at best an additional motive'.[11]

Thus, van Bruinessen's analysis of the nationalist as opposed to other sentiments of the leaders and followers of a social movement shows that these motives and sentiments are often mixed and inseparable. This observation has some implications for analysing social movements, which I deal with in the following section.

ANALYSING SOCIAL MOVEMENTS

Problems related to the analysis of social movements will be discussed under two headings. The first group of problems pertains to the sociological model used and its basic assumptions. The second group concerns the relation between the model, together with its assumptions, and the social 'reality', that is, the 'real' behaviour and ideology of the social actors, and how these do or do not fit the initial sociological model.

Under the first heading I look specifically at 'Islam' and 'nationalism' as two sources of organizational and ideological constructs which are assumed to give rise to various social movements. To begin with, most theoretical discussions of Islam, especially because of its role in revivalist or protest movements, emphasize its 'orthodox' framework and present it in terms of an 'ideal model': official Islamic discourse is unitarian, defines its community on the basis of shared beliefs and practices and not on ethnic, linguistic, racial or other lines. Because belief and practice are the crucial criteria for membership of this Islamic community, loyalties to other social organizational systems outside Islam, such as tribe, nation or secular states, are discouraged. This 'ideal model' assumes that primordial and higher levels of loyalty have to give way to Islamic concerns: unity should be sought not against a rival tribe or nation, but against the heathen non-believers and non-Muslims. Following such a model, a religious, messianic or fundamentalist movement would unite all those people who are religiously motivated; it would be a movement where ethnic, national, tribal or other divisions are secondary or even unimportant.

The 'ideal model' suggests that, compared to the universalism of Islam, ethnic and nationalist movements are particularist, perhaps of a middle order. Where Islam as an ideology demands loyalty to a large community of Muslims, ethnic and nationalist ideologies demand loyalty to, and common action with, a group larger than a primary group but smaller than a religious (here Islamic) community. Thus, these ideal models not only assume homogeneity and consistency on the part of the ideology, but they also have a socio-psychological aspect to them, where individuals and groups (of varying sizes) are thought to be bound by various forms and degrees of loyalty.[12] Moreover, these sentiments and loyalties, especially when they are directed to different groups, are thought to be in conflict with one another.

The conflict of loyalties is to be observed at several levels, from that of the individual to that of the social movement itself. To the degree that the individual is located at the centre of concentric circles of loyalty groups (with the innermost and smallest primary group demanding the highest loyalty, and the outermost and most comprehensive ethnic group demanding the least) he is bound to find himself in situations where his interests and sentiments contradict each other. Moreover, the success or failure of a social movement are seen to be determined by the degree to which it entails groups and individuals with varying loyalties and hence an inbuilt tendency for conflict. Van Bruinessen appears to depend on such an 'ideal model' and its assumptions in his evaluations and discussions of 'endemic conflicting loyalties', 'nationalist movements suffering from tribal divisions', or 'messianic movements having particularist elements in them'.[13]

The second group of problems, relating to the correspondence between the ideal model and the social reality, points up the complexity of the social reality as well as the difficulty of working with ahistorical and non-contextual models. Where it is hoped somehow to measure and standardize 'loyalty' and 'the political action as its consequence', the model acquires mechanical qualities. For instance, leaders and followers of a social movement are examined separately in terms of how dedicated they are to an 'ideology' and how they distinguish between their different levels of social commitment and the interests involved in them. A further step of theoretical accommodation would then be necessary to account for the behaviour of a specific leader or follower. If a leader goes against the nationalist principle – for instance by attacking members of his own nation/ethnic group, as Simko did – then one assumes either an underdeveloped or divided loyalty or a tactical move in order to maximize self-interest or the interest of a particular group. Here, underlying assumptions about individual or group behaviour involve the problem of rationality. Rational behaviour is attributed, for instance, to leaders as they maximize their interests by employing various strategies and adhere to certain ideologies; but irrational behaviour is assumed on the part of the mass of followers, who lack awareness of their own interests and blindly follow this or that leader.

I do not argue that the concept of strategy should not assume a degree of rational behaviour (even if necessarily a 'relative' or 'contextual' rationality) but the fact that groups and individuals can change from being tribal particularists here to religious fundamentalists there does not on its own explain how this change occurs, what people themselves think about, and what *their* concepts of these groups, their solidarity and fission are. In other words, we are left with a tautological description of various followers joining together in a movement, but for different reasons, and because there are such different reasons and interests the movement runs into problems.

The problems of depicting social reality are indeed not limited to how it fits a sociological model. In many cases social reality is not fully depictable, especially if it pertains to past events. Hence, in the analysis of social movements, a focus on the behaviour and ideology of leaders may be the only possibility, where the rest of the participants form the large but silent majority. Obviously, we do not have access to knowledge of all the motivations, meanings, ideologies and interests involved in a social movement, but it is important to try to understand whether the contradictions thought to exist between these ideologies at a theoretical level are also contradictions for the people themselves. If not, why not? When do people start expressing their economic, social and political differences as being due to ethnic, national or religious differences? And why do they express their differences in an ethnic, national or religious discourse? Should we expect that, once there is a 'clearer' discourse of these different ideologies, they will also become clearer to the people, and that people will choose one of the ideologies as subjectively the most important? In other words, would a nation-building process such as happened in Turkey necessarily create a *dominant* nationalist ideology? If not, if these various loyalties and identities continue to co-exist with varying degrees of importance, where should we look, as social scientists, in order to depict the main trends of a movement, or to predict a nationalist instead of an Islamic uprising?

These questions form the focus of my attention, and as my concern here is with how people construct their ethnicity or Islamic community, rather than how leaders lead them, I shall return to the community I know best and try to analyse *their* views on Islam and ethnicity.

ISLAM IN HAKKARI

The area I worked in is rather appropriate for this mental exercise. Hakkari, the extreme southeastern province of Turkey, bordering Iran and Iraq, experienced various nationalist and religious uprisings around the end of the Ottoman period and in the early republican years. A prominent local Sayyid family produced influential Nakşibendi shaikhs as well as a member of the Ottoman senate who was later hanged for his alleged involvement in Şeyh Seit's uprising. More recently, of course, Hakkari has been one of the major arenas for nationalist Kurdish guerrillas as well as propagandists for the Ayatollahs in Iran, especially Hizb-ul-Islam.[14] The Iraqi Kurdish revolution, that is the Barzani movement, and the war of the Kurds against the Iraqi government in the early 1970s, had a major influence on local people's concepts of their own Kurdishness and on matters of nationalism. Such a historical and political background makes Hakkari a suitable and interesting area for researching local concepts of ethnicity, nationalism and Islam. Let us look at the local constructs one by one.

To begin with, Islam is intimately linked with local culture. Islamic practices and beliefs, and the teachings of Islam, form a fundamental, if not the most important, part of the local cultural discourse. Consciously or unconsciously, many daily activities are moulded by Islamic prescriptions. The semi-formal speech forms for greeting, wishing farewell, inquiring after health and family, consist primarily of Islamic formulations: wishing peace from Allah, Allah's protection and generosity, and so on. The language is most elaborate and full of such Islamic expressions in the village and tribal context, and it loses its richness and meaning with more educated and urban people. Educated Kurds, for instance, in such situations use either more Turkish, or Iraqi Kurdish, and fewer Islamic formulations.

Concepts of time and calendar, especially within the village, again follow Islamic usage. The working day is divided according to prayer-times, and meals follow suit. Friday is for rest and socializing; other days of the week are similarly classified according to religious criteria; certain days are good for washing, others for working outdoors; certain hours of the day should not be used for cleaning, and so on. These practices are striking compared with western parts of Turkey, especially with urban life. In Hakkari, villagers are aware of the 'unorthodoxy' of some of their beliefs, such as being 'moonstruck' or afflicted by the evil eye, but they see such beliefs as their own mixture of 'old wives' tales' and Islamic practices, which in effect serve to draw a boundary between villagers and people of urban origins.

What is perhaps more significant is the dominance of Islam as a source of moral and ethical values. Someone who has moral virtues is *ahlaklı* (they use the Turkish) and a religious person should be *ahlaklı*. The virtues of justice, fairness, modesty, helpfulness, hard work, love for one's family, generosity, are all parts of this construct, and a good Muslim will strive for these qualities. Muslims who do not have these high virtues are held simply to be either bad Muslims or not real Muslims at all. Someone who is not a Muslim, however, or who is consciously and deliberately irreligious, can hardly be thought to have all the fundamental moral virtues. Practising Christians, in the eyes of the villagers, have the possibility of learning and maintaining some of these virtues, but their belief is thought to be misguided in certain respects, so they cannot really be *ahlaklı* either.

In order to support their arguments, villagers give examples from hadiths or other Islamic oral and written sources. Adducing precedents from the Prophet's sayings is like invoking the ultimate authority on moral issues. The lives and sayings of the prophets are often the starting or concluding points of debates on justice and proper behaviour. Knowing the Word, the Koran, is on its own a merit, and the actual practice and experience of reading it, especially by heart, independent of whether you understand the text or not, is thought to be meritorious and religiously creditable. Consequently, the local religious personnel have significant roles in villagers' lives. The village imam (*mela*) is the person who is most often consulted on matters of health, misfortune, religious practices and life-cycle rituals. The status of the mela requires a minimal respect for the position, as well as payments in kind or cash for his services. His prestige can increase remarkably, however, depending on the level and length of his religious education, on the reputation of his teachers, on the languages he can speak, as well as on his personal qualities of wisdom, behaviour or style of life.

Religious personnel, who have an important role in shaping people's religious concepts, do in fact represent different sources of religious authority, and perform different functions. In this area they can be classified into five types. The first three are all called mela. The first is the ministry-appointed mela, paid by central government; usually an outsider to the region, whose success and popularity within his community depend considerably on his ethnic and social background and the languages he speaks, in addition to his personal qualities. He is, however, most often identified with the 'religion of the state', and treated accordingly. For instance, such melas would have difficulty asking the villagers for the special payment (usually expressed as *zekat*) for their living expenses. Together with the school teacher, they would usually be expected to mediate when necessary between villagers and state officials and the military.

The second type, probably equally widespread, is the locally employed mela, usually trained in clandestine medreses in Turkey or Iraq, and often of Kurdish or Arab origin. This type of mela is found in many villages, and they are often part of the village community through their ethnic background as well as style of life: they may own small plots of land, engage in pastoral production, stay in summer camps, and marry within the village community.

The third type come from respected and holy lineages of melas (*mela-zade*); of all types of melas, these are accorded the highest religious respect. Members of mela lineages do not automatically become functioning melas, as the status is primarily acquired and needs a certain training: learning as well as esoteric knowledge (*marifet*). They would usually be consulted in cases of Sharia application, or for matters of higher religious and social importance, such as the interpretation of which goods are liable to *zekat* tax, or cases where a marriage could be nullified.

The other two types of religious personnel are shaikhs and sayyids, whose roles are fundamentally different from those of melas. Shaikhs are basically leaders of tarikat orders, and acquire this status through membership and training in an order, and after being appointed by a khalifa. They hold their position clandestinely for the most part, though their fame may be known to many, sometimes across international or regional borders, and not only to one particular ethnic group. In a way, such famous shaikhs and sayyids symbolize the universalism of Islam for the local people. In general, villagers consult shaikhs on matters of ultimate religious importance and complexity; among their most frequent patients are infertile women and men and the mentally ill. They are also called on to resolve disputes involving the possible application of Sharia laws. Their judgement, however, is disputable, and not absolutely binding. In Weberian terms they are more like charismatic leaders than religious functionaries.

Sayyids, finally, are members of holy lineages claiming descent from the Prophet himself or his close family. Being a member of these patrilineages is in itself enough to command the respect of all, but this respect or recognition is more for the history and reputation of the lineage than for the specific person. Some sayyids, of course, can gain a personal reputation for being especially learned, talented, or gifted by Allah in healing, mastering good and evil spirits or forseeing future events.

What is the significance of having all these different types of religious personnel and leaders in the community? To begin with, the religious personnel could be said to form the cornerstone of the religious authority structure for the villagers. They are people who can be consulted for help according to their prestige and the severity of the problem. Just as important, however, is the place of religious personnel in the overall system of meanings for the people. They are not simply functionaries fulfilling certain roles, they are also symbols of the omnipresence of a religious system of thought, reinforcing many concepts held in this system by their presence, or challenging some of those concepts by their failure.

The existence of such religious experts and holy persons, in other words, contributes to the wider concept of Islam, where the meaning and significance of the cosmic and worldly order are maintained and reproduced. Islam is also a source of moral values and judgements: gender roles, class differences, age differences, existing or expected injustices and misfortunes, as well as prosperity, are explained by reference to its teachings. It is not only a source of justification for certain existing gender and class relations, but also a means to challenge the differences. Women, for instance, gain a special status by overt piety, mastery of religious practices or being able to recite the Koran by heart. Van Bruinessen notes that among the oppressed and the poor, joining a tarikat and becoming the follower of a powerful and influential shaikh are a means of gaining some status, however precarious.[15] Because material wealth has an ambiguous aspect to it, the rich are susceptible to accusations about their moral qualities and integrity, and the poor can accept material poverty in this world while expecting a better deal in the next one. Thus, the teachings of Islam can be used to argue both for and against the existence of differences in social status and prosperity.

Finally, Islam also provides universalistic meanings and aspects to people's lives. Believers feel they share the values, meanings and beliefs of millions of people in the world. The Hajjis' account of seeing thousands of other Muslims from many different countries, their experience of sharing the same beliefs, are related and heard with reverence and genuine interest; they compare their own types of practices, understandings and interpretations of Islam with those of other ethnic groups, and discuss, for instance, whether Turks are more religious, or Laz are less religious, and so on.

Islam thus creates a social arena for them, where they both define themselves as an ethnic group and at the same time trace binding ties to other groups and cultures.

For Kurdish villagers in Hakkari, ethnicity and Islam come together in a special relationship. Their particular type of 'ethnic Islam' is not an unitarian or homogeneous construct. It sets up neither 'Kurdishness' nor 'Islam' as the unique or fundamental part of their identity. Local concepts of ethnic identity are based on language, customs, history, place of residence and kinship, and none of these criteria on its own is sufficient or necessary for identity as Kurdish. Islam, on the other hand, is a system which connects them to other similar groups of people. These two dimensions of 'ethnic Islam' are equally important and indispensable. Nevertheless, there are instances where ethnic differences within the larger Islamic community are given special attention. For instance, ordinary Kurdish villagers, who hold rather modest views of their own piety and understanding of Islam, seem to see a correspondence between the position of Kurds within the international community and their superficial adherence to Islam. The villagers told me a joke in which their ethnic identity is ironically related to their religiosity:

> As the story goes, all the nations of the world were present at the Prophet Muhammad's court, and he was hearing the requests of each group. The Arabs approached him in the most respectful terms, saying 'ya Rasulullah, ya Rahmetullah, what can we do to be in your service?' and the Prophet presented them with all the Holy Land and all the oil. The Turks were next to approach the Prophet, and they too addressed him with reverence and due respect, 'ya Muhammad, ya Peyghambar, what can we do for your service?' and they were given their own country, Anatolia. The Kurds addressed the Prophet in their typical familiar way, and said, '*halo Muhammad, çi dikey, çowani?*' which means 'hallo, uncle Muhammad, how are you these days?' The Prophet was angry at this impudence and threw the Kurds out of his court saying, 'I don't care where you go, you don't have any country!'

The story is full of irony and could be seen as reflecting the

Kurds' self-deprecating views, but it also shows that they feel secure enough about their ethnic identity that they can joke about it. The message from such stories is rather the acknowledgement of differences between various ethnic and national groups among the international community of Islam. It also shows how people relate their 'national faith' to a 'faith' which has been somehow predetermined, so that nations can also be significant for the Cosmic Order and Divine Justice.

There is no easy, clear-cut answer to the question whether religious practices and personnel have any ethnic significance attached to them. On the one hand, religious practices such as reading the *mevlûd* in Kurdish,[16] or consulting the Kurdish shaikhs and *mela-zade* for medical treatment and advice, could be seen as enhancing ethnic identity and solidarity; villagers trust and believe in the practices and the personnel because of their Kurdishness *and* religious effectiveness. On the other hand, the practices, the personnel, and the belief in them are touched by rival concepts of modernity versus tradition, rural versus urban, and female versus male. Vergin has argued in the case of a north Anatolian town for an interpretation of 're-Islamization' not as a new phenomenon but as a new understanding of the old, being due to the need to 'express' the social change which has occurred and to react to it; adherence to Islamic practices could express different social statuses and attitudes towards the state and modernization. Vergin shows that Islam could be re-discovered, so to speak, not because of a desire to return to an old tradition and sever ties with the new society, but in order to deal more efficiently and thoroughly with the immense and rapid changes in an industrializing town.[17] Similarly in Hakkari, giving alms in order to fight evil spirits, or consulting tarikat shaikhs, could be seen as an old-fashioned and rural tradition by young townsmen without necessarily endangering any aspect of their Kurdish identity, whereas the same practices may be carried out by villagers specifically because of their 'Kurdishness'.

CONCLUSION: ETHNICITY AND ISLAM IN HAKKARI

Coming back to the initial problem, that is, how to understand *where* ethnic interests are conceived to clash with the universalistic principles of Islam, and *why* people start seeing these interests as contradictory, I have some preliminary and tentative propositions.

First, seen from local people's point of view, at the level of the Turkish state and polity there is no clear disjunction between ethnic differences and Islam. The discourse of the Turkish state (which comes from the administrators, the military and especially the political parties) includes Islamic discourse as well. For many village men, for instance, the army and military conscription are the source of their knowledge about the spread of Islam in Turkey and its wide practice, even in the army. Village men see members of other ethnic groups, city-dwellers and rural villagers practising Islam, and have a means of comparing different attitudes to Islam by the different sectors of the military. Thus, there is hardly any ground for villagers to think that their ethnic group is in some opposition to a non-believing, non-practising state apparatus.

The state is more fragmented and heterogeneous on the issue of Islam than it is on the issue of ethnic differences. The political discourse is more relaxed and flexible about the use of Islamic concepts and terminology than it is about ethnic terms and concepts, which imply minority–majority relations and differences. To what degree this is a new development needs separate consideration. None the less, at least at one level of state and military apparatus, the use of Islamic rhetoric is no longer taboo, as can be observed in propaganda against the Kurdish nationalists. The attack on the 'irredentists' and 'reactionaries' of the 1925 revolt seems very dated when one reads the government's call for Islamic unity and brotherhood against the 'infidel' Kurdish guerrillas of Marxist-Leninist orientation. The military distributed leaflets in Hakkari in 1987, calling local people to support the government's measures against the guerrillas, and, as also appeared in the press, the Kurdish guerrillas, especially those belonging to the PKK (Kurdish Workers Party), were accused of co-operation with the 'infidel' Armenians and Greeks. During my fieldwork, I witnessed various cases where the local gendarmerie asked the villagers to swear on the Koran that they did not possess arms or know where fugitives were hiding. This was an effective method most of the time, as the villagers tried to avoid taking the oath if they feared giving false testimony.

Secondly, from local people's point of view, ethnic interests and universalistic Islam *do* seem to contradict each other at the level of

Kurdish ethnic–nationalist organization which is currently being propagated. These nationalist organizations within Turkey are primarily left wing and have promulgated (as they did especially in earlier times) anti-religious views. More recently this anti-religious attitude seems to have become covert or even to have changed. There is some evidence that the religious feelings and beliefs as well as the tribal bonds of the local people are coming to be seen as a source of possible ideological and organizational potential, rather than just a threat to Kurdish nationalism. In the 1980s, the PKK carried out various political and guerrilla activities in Hakkari, and, compared to pre-1980 Kurdish left-wing politics, their attitude towards religion and the tribes seems to have softened. The politically active youngsters before 1980 used to draw hostile reactions from the local people by their refusal to fast during Ramazan and by smoking in public when others were fasting. The more recent activists emphasize their Kurdishness in dress and language, and their anti-religious political ideology does not seem to come into discussions with the commoners. In their publications, although tribal and religious loyalties are presented as backward and as obstacles to political and ideological development, there is also concern to form close contact with the local people, and caution against the direct contradiction of people's beliefs, especially at first contact.

Thirdly, although Islam is a prevailing element in local culture, it is not the only source of cultural identity. Tribal and kinship ties, regional loyalties, educational and class differences provide the local people with alternative and complementary sources of identity and culture networks. Islamic or nationalist discourses might become more dominant, and overtly contradict each other, if these alternative frameworks of identity and reference were to become inconsistent, weak or irrelevant. If the 'cultivated and shared disposition'[18] ceases to be heterogeneous, that is, if the mixture of strong kinship ideology, tribalism and fluid ethnic identity loses its significance, then the Islamic discourse, because it is so all-encompassing, *or* the nationalist discourse, because of its increased application (by both the Kurds and the Turkish state) may replace the convertible and fluid qualities of these discourses. An immediate crisis situation can force people to show their allegiance clearly (by taking up arms and fighting against the separatists, or facing the danger of being shot by them) and can cause a sharpening of subjective perceptions of a conflict between universalist and particularist principles.

Finally, the discussion here has focused on the meaning and possible sources of ethnic and religious identification of the common people, who are expected to and do take part in nationalist and/or fundamentalist/sectarian struggles. The emphasis has been on subjective perceptions and meanings, in order to criticize approaches which give prominence to the leaders and the 'official ideology and rhetoric'. I do not advocate that the latter be left aside, but that the analysis of a social movement should examine the multiplicity of rhetoric, the fragmentation or homogeneity of discourse, the co-existence under certain circumstances of apparently incompatible ideologies. A Geertzian type of analysis,[19] where analysis of the historical background, modernization processes, social structure and action complement the analysis of meaning, is more fruitful as well as more interesting. Although my material does not allow generalization for all Kurds, as far as Hakkari's ordinary tribesmen and peasants are concerned the above discussion has suggested that ethnicity and Islamic loyalties are parts of a continuum rather than of an opposition, and they are not necessarily or naturally in an endemic situation of ideological conflict, so long as both of these constructs continue to maintain their heterogeneity and fulfil certain roles in power strategies and political processes.

NOTES

1. See, for example, chapters by Acar, Ayata, Güneş-Ayata and Saktanber in this volume.
2. See *2000'e Doğru*, 17 (17.4.1988). Martin van Bruinessen discusses various periods of close ideological and organizational ties between Kurdish Islam and nationalism in his *Agha, Shaikh and State: On the Social and Political Organisation of Kurdistan*, private, Utrecht, 1978 see especially chapter V. Nur Yalman ('Islamic reform and the mystic tradition in eastern Turkey', *European Journal of Sociology*, 10, 1969, pp. 41–60) points out the different meaning of Islam in eastern Turkey, especially the different attitudes towards

'official Islam' promoted by the republican and secularist state and the 'unofficial/ unorthodox' Islam and its functionaries in eastern Turkey. Yalman sees the flourishing of unorthodox medreses and medrese teachers in eastern Turkey as a reaction to the state's harsh approach and attempt to 'secularize' Islam. He does not, however, elaborate on this 'unorthodoxy' as being specifically 'Kurdish' or 'ethnic'.

3. See, for instance, M. Tunçay, *Türkiye Cumhuriyeti'nde Tek-Parti Yönetimi'nin Kurulması (1923–1931)*, Ankara, Yurt Yayınları, 1981. İsmail Beşikçi, *Doğu Anadolu'nun Düzeni*, Ankara, E. Yayınları, 1970. B. N. Şimşir, *İngiliz Belgeleriyle Türkiye'de 'Kürt Sorunu' (1924–1938)*, Ankara, Dışişleri Bakanlığı Basımevi, 1975. Ş. Vedat, *Türkiye'de Kürtçülük Hareketleri ve Isyanlar*, Ankara, Kon Yayınları, 1980. I. Parmaksızoğlu, *Tarih Boyunda Kürttürkleri ve Türkmenler*, Ankara Türk Kültürünü Araştırma Enstitüsü, 1983.

4. See Parkmaksızoğlu *Tarih Boyunda Kürttürkleri*, pp. 85–6. Vedat *Türkiye'de Kürtçülük Hareketleri*, pp. 70–7. Beşikçi *Doğu Anadolu'nun Düzeni*, p. 313.

5. See van Bruinessen, *Agha, Shaikh and State*, pp. 388–96, for a review of the Turkish press on the Şeyh Sait rebellion.

6. Ibid. E. E. Evans-Pritchard, *The Sanusi of Cyrenaica*, Oxford, Clarendon Press, 1949.

7. Van Bruinessen, *Agha, Shaikh and State*, p. 398.

8. Ibid., p. 399.

9. Ibid., pp. 404–5.

10. Ibid., p. 405.

11. M. van Bruinessen, 'Kurdish tribes and the state of Iran: the case of Simko's revolt', in R. Tapper, ed., *The Conflict of Tribe and State in Iran and Afghanistan*, London, Croom Helm, 1983, pp. 384, 385, 390, 392.

12. According to E. Kamenka, 'the concept of the nation and the nation-state as the *ideal, natural* or *normal* form of international political organization, as the focus of men's loyalties and the indispensable framework for all social, cultural and economic activities became widespread only at a specific historical period': 'Political nationalism – the evolution of the idea', in E. Kamenka, ed. *Nationalism*, London, Edwin Arnold, 1976, p. 6 (emphasis given).

13. Van Bruinessen, *Agha, Shaikh and State*, pp. 397–406.

14. Hizb-ul Islam is an illegal political organization which strives for an Islamic revolution of the Iranian kind in Turkey. The organization is claimed to recruit followers especially in eastern Turkey.

15. Ibid., p. 261.

16. The *mevlûd* is a poem about the birth and life of the Prophet Muhammad; the Kurdish *mevlûd* was written by Melayê Batê, a native of Hakkari.

17. N. Vergin, 'Toplumsal değişme ve dinsellikte artış', *Toplum ve Bilim*, 29–30, 1985, pp. 9–28.

18. P. Bourdieu, *Outline of a Theory of Practice*, Cambridge, Cambridge University Press, 1977.
19. C. Geertz, *The Interpretation of Cultures*, New York, Basic Books, 1973.

6

THE NAKŞIBENDI ORDER IN TURKISH HISTORY

Şerif Mardin

INTRODUCTION: THE NEED FOR A LONG-TERM VIEW

Among the received ideas propagated by ideologues of official secularism in Turkey, none is as common as that of the threat posed to the republican regime by the Sufi orders, the tarikat. Among the tarikat, none has acquired as flamboyant an image of subversion as the Nakşibendi.

No doubt evidence can be marshalled to support the thesis of Nakşibendi treasonable activities. Were one to go back to the earliest roots of modern secular Turkey, namely to the policies of the Young Turks, one could make a strong case for the dangers posed by religious fanaticism to their admittedly ambiguous and limited secularizing policies. One may then focus on the so-called 'Incident of 31 March 1909', a rebellion of privates and non-commissioned officers directed against the purported atheism of Young Turk officers.

The rebellion appears to have taken shape in the wake of fiery propaganda emanating from a newspaper, the *Volkan*. This paper had organic links with a political party that styled itself 'The Party of the Prophet Muhammad'.[1] The editor of the *Volkan*, 'Dervish' Vahdeti, was a Nakşibendi.[2] The rebellion was quelled, Vahdeti was hanged and various sentences were passed on 10,000 privates. But the threat of a split in the armed forces remained suspended over the grand project of the Young Turks, namely accelerated

121

modernization, partly through the fracture of existing Ottoman social institutions so as to make Turkey a state with the necessary clout in the concert of Europe.

The Turkish Republic which emerged in 1923, following the disintegration of the Ottoman Empire at the end of the First World War, had also reason to feel apprehensive about the Nakşibendi, for it was shortly after the new state's foundation that a dangerous threat to its existence emerged from this quarter. In 1925 a rebellion led by a Nakşibendi shaikh surfaced in Eastern Anatolia, a region honeycombed by Nakşibendi networks. This Kurdish rebellion was suppressed and its leaders were executed or sent into internal exile. All tarikat were thereafter banned in Turkey. A third Nakşibendi outbreak which figures in the ideological panoply of Turkish secularists was the Menemen incident of 1930 when, in a provincial town close to Izmir, a shadowy Nakşibendi figure called Muslims to rally around the green flag and destroy the impious republican regime.

Recent writing on the Nakşibendi has painted an image of this order which underscores features diametrically opposed to those evoked by the secularists. Hamid Algar and Irfan Gündüz provide good examples of this genre,[3] which has attempted to show that the Nakşibendi are basically non-political and that individual Nakşibendi – whose primary aim was to keep Islam alive in the Turkish community of believers – were ruthlessly persecuted in the Turkish Republic. These writings claim that a retrospective glance covering the last three centuries of Nakşibendi activity would show them to have been primarily interested in keeping Islam in orthodox channels and combating the dilution of faith among the Muslims.

Of these two assessments of Nakşibendi influences, the first is grounded on a conspiracy theory of history which is often what passes for a philosophy of history in contemporary Turkey. Nakşibendi have, no doubt, been involved in movements contesting what they saw as an impious regime, but the unidimensional portrayal of their activities is no help to deeper sociological understanding. The second, positive estimate of the Nakşibendi takes a similarly simplistic view of their activities. The fact that this interpretation of their behaviour has originated among Muslims highly sensitive to the integrity of their cultural inheritance reminds one of a characteristic of writings that strive to recuperate Islam for the modern world: namely the absence of any internal critique, which transforms even the most scholarly assessment into a species of whitewash.

I shall try to show that, for the purposes of analysis, it is more satisfactory to see the Nakşibendi order as propelled by its own internal dynamics, which both these theories ignore. I claim that there *was* and *is* a Nakşibendi involvement in politics, although the pattern of this involvement is not immediately obvious, and also that the mode of involvement has changed with time.

I would phrase my theory as one which also takes Nakşibendi *longue durée* as a datum that cannot be ignored in an account of Turkish history. There are in this *longue durée* a number of watersheds, profound changes in strategy, which show an extraordinary sensitivity to ambient conditions, and this quality also emerges as one of the most striking characteristics of Nakşibendi history.

An important preliminary distinction to make at this point is to try to blot out some of the qualities that the term Sufi connotes in popular usage. The Nakşibendi are usually described as a Sufi order, but this account does not fasten on their most characteristic internal spring. If Sufi means mystic, Islamic mysticism, whether ecstatic, spiritual, poetic or cosmic, whether induced by rules of mortification or framed by theosophical speculation, does not fit well with the sober, inwoven, inwrought, disciplined spiritual practices of this order, which also have had a major role to play in its viability. What in the case of the Protestant ethic seems to have worked for capitalism, in the case of the Nakşibendi worked for the social mobilization of Muslims. This sobriety also provided an important key to the earliest history of the Nakşibendi, as well as to its role in Ottoman Turkey.

NAKŞIBENDI ORIGINS AND EARLY HISTORY

Very early in its history, the order acquired its characteristic tonality, its inward-looking attitude, which shunned 'show or distracting rites'.[4] The Nakşibendi were enjoined to remember that at every moment a divine presence gave content to the phenomenal world and that one could see its imprint on the most minute aspects of daily life. Life thus became a silent celebration of this divine mark, mysticism was focused on the 'heart' or the 'breast'. In one author's words, 'the Nakshibendi sufis accomplish by their strict observance of the divine law and the normative example of the prophet Muhammad what other sufis attain by means of various spiritual exercises.'[5] It is this technique for turning an outward enthusiasm inward which to students of the order explains the influence that the Nakşibendi were to have among the Turks of Central Asia. The externalized religious enthusiasm which characterized the practices of the pre-Islamic central Asian Turks could now be deflected to an internal focus. This bridge between the religion of Central Asian Turks and the total 'package' offered by the Nakşibendi assured the 'attachment of Turkic people to the Sunni tradition'.[6] In view of our limited knowledge of the type of religion practised by pre-Islamic Turks, this is still conjecture.[7] The theory, however, seems to fit well with what we do know about the 'shamanistic' aspects of Turkmen practice.[8] In what follows, the Nakşibendi devotion to one's spiritual guide will also be seen to have provided a structure homologous to the leadership pattern found among the Turkmen.

From the fifteenth century onward, two lines of development shaped the Nakşibendi order, and both have to be followed to understand its influences in Turkey. The earlier one is the furrow the order opened in Ottoman religious history at the time of the foundation of the Ottoman Empire. The second is the movement of spiritual renewal which took shape in the Moghul setting in the seventeenth century and which became influential in Anatolia in the nineteenth. The Moghul setting has been studied in detail; Ottoman developments, however, have only recently been reconstituted by scholars such as Butrus Abu-Manneh, Hamid Algar and Irfan Gündüz.

I shall take up the Indian tradition first.

SIRHINDI AND THE MUJEDDIDI TRADITION

The Nakşibendi tradition in India was shaped by Ahmad Faruqi al-Sirhindi (1563–1624), who came forth to combat the religious eclecticism of the Mughal Emperor Akbar. Sirhindi felt that the tolerance of Akbar for Indian civilization and religion was sweeping away the distinguishing characteristics of Islam, that it was duping Muslims into becoming idol-worshippers and destroying the central Muslim belief in the unicity of God. To counter this dilution he promoted a movement of spiritual renewal which became known as 'renewalist' or Mujeddidi.

Sirhindi's self-appointed role as the renewer took its force from a Muslim tradition that God would 'send to his community on the eve of every century a man to renew its *din* [religion]'.[9] Thus a reformed spiritual tradition came into existence 'which played a prominent role in keeping the threads of the community together in the political and social chaos that followed the decay of Mughal power'.[10]

The relation of the Nakşibendi order to the centre of political power in the period antedating Sirhindi had been complex. Bahaeddin Naqshband (1317–1384), an eponymous figure among the founders, is said to have

> kept his distance from the court of the rulers because power enmeshes the heart in the affairs of the world and turns it away from God. In his early life he had certain experiences of public affairs but [later] . . . turned away from the things of the world.[11]

The legends relating to Bahaeddin's meeting with a Turkish dervish and his association with him until the latter became Sultan Khalil of Transoxiana (1340) give us another insight into the willingness of Nakşibendi to influence rulers.

A similar picture of Ubaidullah Ahrar (1404–1490), a companion of Nakshband and an important Nakşibendi personality, is painted by Jo-Ann Gross in her doctoral thesis on Ahrar.[12] The uses of power held no mystery for him. The populistic, anti-intellectual character of Ahrar's religiosity has also been underlined.

Yohanan Friedmann's book on Sirhindi is the most detailed attempt to study the Nakşibendi sage's political involvement, but the study minimizes his political role. Friedmann's appraisal stems from a literalistic Western understanding of the term 'political' which, he should have known, cannot apply to Muslim society. Sirhindi's involvement in politics seems clear if we simply remember the extent to which he provided the Nakşibendi order with a novel mobilizational thrust and recollect his conflictual relation with Mughal rulers.[13] Three elements play a central role in Sirhindi's views. The first relates to his critique of some forms of Sufism that were current in his time, which also included the Sufi attempt to transcend everyday worldly experience. For Sirhindi, dissolving one's earthly moorings through the quest for union with God is an incomplete, and therefore harmful, exercise. The true believer has to return to earth and come to grips with the realities of the world – and this world is one where one's task is to establish the reign of Sunni morality. From this derives Sirhindi's belief that the theosophical speculations of the mystic Ibn al-'Arabi – a most influential Muslim thinker – should not be understood as ends in themselves but as guidelines to a deeper understanding of the religious law and orthodox practice.

A third contribution of Sirhindi, more directly related to an activation of the Muslim community, is his theory of the two *mims* (Arabic letter 'M'). It appears from what we can follow in Sirhindi's correspondence, the *Mektubat*, that the Prophet Muhammad had

in his lifetime two individuations (*ta'ayyun*) the bodily–human and the spiritual–angelic. These two individuations were symbolized by the loops of the two *mims* in his name. The bodily individuation guaranteed the uninterrupted relationship between the Prophet and his community and consequently ensured its spiritual well-being. The spiritual one, on the other hand, directed itself towards the Divine and received the continuous flow of inspiration emanating from that source. A proper balance was thus maintained between the worldly and the spiritual aspects of Muhammad's personality, and the Islamic community was under guidance both prophetic and divine. Since the prophet's death, however, his human individuation has been gradually weakening while the spiritual one has been steadily gaining strength. Within a thousand years the human individuation disappeared altogether. Its symbol, the first *mim* of Muhammad, disappeared along with it and was replaced by an *alif* standing for divinity (*uluhiyat*). Muhammad came to be Ahmad. He was transformed into a purely spiritual being, no longer interested in the affairs of the world ... [this, however, had] an adverse impact on his community which lost the light of prophetic guidance emanating from Muhammad's human aspect. . . . Sirhindi . . . agrees that the ideal prophetic period was followed by a gradual decline caused by the growing imbalance in the performance of the two prophetic tasks.[14]

Sirhindi's self-appointed task was to revive the existing straight path of prophetic guidance. The Nakşibendi order which follows his tradition is thereafter known as Mujeddidi, or 'renewalist'.

A spiritual successor of Sirhindi, Shah Wali Allah of Delhi (1703–1762), was to take over this task of revitalizing the inner spring of Islam. He attacked 'the social and economic injustices prevailing in society, criticized the heavy tax to which the peasantry was subjected and called upon the Muslims to build a territorial state which might be integrated into an international Muslim super-state'.[15] This India-based Nakşibendi activism of the eighteenth century was the fountainhead of an Indo-Muslim revivalistic movement which bore fruit during the nineteenth century and which in the various forms it took over time was also to affect the Ottoman Empire.[16]

We now have to cast a backward glance at Anatolia to follow the path of Nakşibendi influence as it formed in the Ottoman Empire.

THE NAKŞIBENDI IN THE OTTOMAN EMPIRE

Thirteenth-, fourteenth- and later fifteenth-century Anatolia was the theatre of successive waves of disruptive social change. The Mongol invasions which put an end to the rule of the Seljuks, the large-scale westward migration of Turkmen tribal elements, the later disintegration of Mongol administration, millenarian rebellion spearheaded by Turkmen charismatic leaders, were all part of this picture of turbulence.

In the fourteenth century, the period during which the Ottoman principality was acquiring clearer outlines as an autonomous Sultanate, the first Sultans could not but support the so-called colonizing dervishes who accompanied the Turkmen tribesmen and who directed their settlement in Anatolia. The appeal of these forceful leaders to their following depended not so much on their religious learning as on their charisma, which in turn followed from their purported ability to communicate with the world of spirits, and from their control of magic.[17]

Turkmen solidarity groups established on this basis, such as the Babai, were a thorn in the side of Seljuk rulers and subsequently gave rise to social movements reverberating throughout Anatolia. Later Anatolian millenarism bears the mark of this ethnic composition and quasi-religious leadership pattern. One of the most important of these endemic outbreaks occurred a decade after the Ottoman Sultanate had already received the hardest blow of its formative years, namely the defeat of Sultan Bayezid I (r. 1389–1402) by Tamerlane. The defection of Turkmen tribesmen played an important role in the defeat. The later rebellion which took shape in 1416 was led by Shaikh Bedreddin of Samona (present-day Greece), who had occupied an important position as Kadi (magistrate) in the emerging Ottoman religious establishment. He had been demoted before his rebellion, but his earlier religious status does not seem to have deterred him from organizing a movement which reflected the model of the earlier Babai outbreaks: his loyalty went to Turkmen groups and their plight rather than to the new religious institution.[18] I shall now try to show that this choice was one connected with a watershed in Ottoman history.

The lessons to be drawn from Turkmen rebelliousness, and the ability of charismatic shaikhs and solidarity groups like the mystic brotherhood of the Kalender to incite rebellion, were not lost on the Ottoman rulers. The earlier, frontier role of dervishes as colonizers in Anatolia was now superseded. To Ottoman rulers the reconstruction of their realm, which had fissioned after the defeat of Bayezid, seemed to depend on a firm foundation of Sunni orthodoxy, a foundation which would quell Turkmen turbulence by linking orthodoxy to a new principle of citizenship: *bedeviyet* or loyalty to the lineage was to be replaced by *medeniyet* or loyalty to the city or Sultan.[19] This, in practice, meant the creation of a network of medreses whose graduates, while serving as quasi-employees of the state, would also, as 'clerics', propagate the doctrine of the straight Sunni path and enable the centre to control dubious tarikat or mystic fraternities.[20]

The Nakşibendis, who had established privileged relations with the Timurid dynasty,[21] had come to Anatolia with the armies of Timur. Their orthodoxy seems to have impressed the Ottomans, who soon established links with them. The son-in-law of Bayezid I, the celebrated mystic Emir Sultan (1368–1429),[22] was himself the son of Seyyid Emir Kulal, a disciple of Bahaeddin Nakshband. Sultan Mehmed II (r. 1451–1481) invited a number of prominent Nakşibendi to Istanbul. Molla Ilahî (d. 1490–1491), an inhabitant of the town of Simav, may have been propelled by a desire to bolster the *medeni* reputation of this town when he started on a journey which ended in Central Asia and his initiation into the Nakşibendi order. Back in the Ottoman Empire, he established the first Nakşibendi *tekke* (lodge) of any importance, first in his home town and then in Istanbul.[23] The Nakşibendi thereafter acquired a central position in Turkish religious life, which they kept despite rivalries with the Halveti and Mevlevi orders.[24]

Incidentally, Irène Mélikoff's thesis, that the Bektaşi also served the same pacifying and integrating purposes as the Nakşibendi but were subverted by the heterodox groups they had the task of bringing back onto the straight path, shows some of the difficulties encountered by even the most sincere champions of orthodoxy.[25]

The Ottoman link-up with Mujeddidi currents acquires more precise outlines with Shaikh Muhammad Murad Bukhari (d. 1729), who travelled to India where he was initiated into the Mujeddidi branch by Muhammad Ma'sum, one of Sirhindi's sons. After India, he embarked on a series of travels which enabled him to graft Mujeddidi ideas in Syria and Anatolia. The increased influence of the Mujeddidi branches in the Ottoman Empire can be followed in the Turkish translation of Sirhindi's *Mektubat* by Müstakimzâde Süleyman Saadettin in 1787.[26]

THE HALIDI AND THE PERIOD OF OTTOMAN REFORM

The most important propellant of Mujeddidi ideas, however, was no doubt that which took shape in the circle of Mevlâna Halid/Khalid, known as Mevlâna Halid Baghdadi (1776–1827). Born in the district of Shahrizur in present-day Iraq, he met a lieutenant (*khalifa*) of the celebrated Mujeddidi Shaikh Abdullah Dihlavi, who convinced him he should study with Dihlavi in

Delhi. He left India in 1810–11, returned to Süleymaniye, feuded with the Shaikh of the Kadiri order, went to Baghdad and established the first Halidi lodge in that city in 1813. From there his order spread to Süleymaniye and then, by his own account, to Jerusalem, Aleppo, Basra, Kirkuk, Erbil, Diyarbakir, Cizre, Mardin, Urfa, Gaziantep and Konya.[27] The Halidi now emerged with a mobilizational, proselytizing stance. Their spiritual fathers had already embarked on a project of mobilization which had international dimensions: in the Caucasus in the 1790s Mujeddidi Nakşibendi had fought the Russian invasion and had attempted to unite various tribes; then, from the mid-1830s to 1859, Shaikh Shamil resumed the same struggle.[28] Mevlâna Halid appears to have given instructions to his appointed lieutenant in Istanbul, Abdulfettah al-Ukari, to propagate the mobilizational activities and proselytizing stance in the 1820s. These instructions have the clear outlines of a historical project that one may, without fear of anachronism, describe as Pan-Islamic. They mentioned North Africa, Bukhara, Egypt, Medina, India and the Far East as areas to be brought under Halidi control. The rules which Halid's lieutenants were to follow – including constant communication with Halid at the centre of the order in Damascus – would have the approval of any present-day international agitator.[29]

The Halidi branch of the Nakşibendi was also influential in government circles in Istanbul. Butrus Abu-Manneh's description of the influence of the Mujeddidis in the early nineteenth century in the Ottoman capital shows that at this particular time both 'progressives' and 'conservatives' in Ottoman official circles could fit under the Nakşibendi ideological umbrella. This was due to to the Nakşibendi support of the idea that the central powers, the bureaucrats in Istanbul, should refurbish the apparatus of state and rejuvenate Ottoman might in the face of Western military and administrative superiority. We are thus alerted to the fact that in the 1820s an option existed for Ottoman reform to proceed in an Islamic mode. We may describe this project as that of the then most powerful Islamic state, the Ottoman Empire, taking upon itself the rallying of its Muslim citizens around the common goal of strength through unity in belief. This unity was to be promoted by strictly following prophetic usage (*sunna*), 'checking bad innovations' and making rulers and their appointed delegates responsible for keeping to this line.[30]

Such a Muslim option for Ottoman reform disappeared – temporarily as we shall see – from the formulas promoted by bureaucrats when the officials staffing the chancery complex of the Porte came to the conclusion that there existed a better 'flag' than religion around which to gather the Ottomans. The new reformist mode of the 1840s was that of Western enlightened despotism, where citizens were made useful to the state by facilitating their economic pursuits and raising their educational level. The early Nakşibendi model seems to have been presented to Ottomans once more in the 1880s and 1890s by the Muslim reformer, Jamal al-Din al-Afghani. To Ottoman officials it must have seemed a reheated version of an option they had avoided much earlier.

The Halidis also established a set of seminaries in the Hizan-Van region of Eastern Anatolia, which were to be the fountainhead of a later movement, the Nur, which we shall take up in a moment. Sultan Mahmud II's prescience of the Halidis' transformational role as agitators rather than religious guides was to be justified two decades after his death when the first movement against the reformist policies of the Tanzimat was to be led by a Nakşibendi, Shaikh Ahmed of Süleymaniye (1859). The Turkish historian, Cevdet Pasha, mentions how the conspirators in this event could not be condemned to death because of the gap in the criminal code, and had to be jailed.

The general climate of the 1860s in the Ottoman Empire was not conducive to the promotion of Nakşibendi opposition to the reforms of the Tanzimat. In these years, part of the energy of the Muslim conservative opposition to secularizing reforms was drawn into a collaboration with the constitutionalist–liberal team of intellectuals and bureaucrats known as Young Ottomans.[31] Nakşibendi activities therefore presumably operated with less visibility than did the contemporary alliance of some clerics with the Young Ottomans, but did surface during the Russo-Turkish war of 1877–8, when Nakşibendi shaikhs volunteered for military service. Süleyman Efendi, a Nakşibendi of the Özbek tekke in Istanbul, also kept communication links – possibly a sort of intelligence service – with Central Asian Muslims.[32]

The most important nineteenth-century Halidi leader in Turkey was Ziyaeddin Gümüşhanevi (d. 1893).[33] Presumably wary of Shaikh Ahmed's experience, his moves were stealthy and gradual. He established his centre in a ruined mosque which was

nevertheless close to the Sublime Porte. Piqued by the establishment of an Ottoman Bank, he founded a community chest for his
lodge (*dergâh*). The initial capital was to be made up from
donations by rich disciples. It was to be used for loans to small
businesses and for the support of the destitute. Part of the capital
was used to set up a printing plant and part to establish libraries
in Istanbul and the provinces. A pedagogic innovation was
Gümüşhanevi's 'streaming' of disciples according to their varying
abilities. An attempt to muscle into two weekly prayer-gatherings
in a popular, well-attended mosque drew a warning from the
government. In the 1860s the Grand Viziers Âli Pasha and Kıbrıslı
Mehmed Pasha wanted him exiled, but Sultan Abdülhamid II
seems to have been more tolerant and to have used Gümüşhanevi
for his own purposes. It seems natural that Sultan Abdülhamid,
who had entrusted Shaikh Abulhuda with the mission of eliciting
support for the Sultanic administration in Syria (hoping Abulhuda's Rifa'i Sufi connections would contribute to this goal)
would also support Gümüşhanevi.[34]

Gümüşhanevi's main published works were a collection of
books concerning moral precepts (*Levami ul-Ukul*, 1877), pre-
ceded by a book on ethics (*Ahlak*, 1832, 1858).[35] In this respect
he was competing with many of his contemporaries, other sincere
reformers but with an eye to the West, who had also penned their
own versions of the social ethics suitable for a reformed Turkey.

MODERN NAKŞIBENDI FIGURES: SAID NURSI AND KOTKU

The 1890s, which saw the intrusion of an increasingly Western
pattern of everyday life among the bureaucratic upper classes in
Istanbul, was a time when the few instances of a publicly
manifested intention to recapture one's Islamic past abated. The
last serious sign of such an attempt had been Ahmet Cevdet
Pasha's protest against the Ottoman cabinet's plan to adopt the
Napoleonic Civil Code (1868). Possibly also Sultan Abdülhamid's
Pan-Islamic policies of the 1880s and 1890s had deflected the
energies of Muslim fundamentalists. We do not therefore see a
successor worthy of Gümüşhanevi at the helm in Istanbul for
more than four decades, although there is some indication that a
Halidi shaikh who set out for Turkistan in the 1920s went with

the approval of none other than Kemal Atatürk himself.[36] It is only in the 1930s that Shaikh Abdulhakim Arvasi emerges as an influential sage. At that time, Arvasi becomes the spiritual guide of the eminent Turkish poet Necip Fazıl Kısakürek. It is to this influence that we owe the publication by Kısakürek in 1943 of the periodical *Büyük Doğu,* which took up the defence of Islamic values at a time when this represented a real danger to the publisher.

The interlude between the 1920s and the 1930s is also marked by a remarkable phenomenon emerging outside the capital, which is also of Nakşibendi origin: Bediüzzaman Said Nursi (1876–1960), who was trained in the Halidi–Nakşibendi seminaries of Eastern Turkey, took up the Mujeddidi torch in the Bitlis–Hizan region of Anatolia. The 'peripheral' source of this movement is interesting in that it replicates similar developments in the margins of the Islamic world at that time. Clearly what we have here is an aspect of the 'mobilization of the periphery',[37] which appears to be an important dimension of the revitalization of Islam in the nineteenth and twentieth centuries.[38]

Said Nursi was to establish relations with the Young Turks in a mode which shows him to have been fascinated by politics. Only in the 1920s did he shift this stance and start a campaign of mobilization which rejected the political option. He now relied on religious mobilization, from which he expected political consequences to flow naturally. His influence spread through the dissemination of a series of brochures which aimed at enlightening the Muslims of middling social status about Islam.

A parallel influence was that of the Halidi Shaikh, Mehmed Zahid Kotku. Kotku witnessed the closing of the religious orders in 1925, the time of his youth. After studies in Istanbul he returned to his home in Bursa, where he was a village imam for fifteen years. Thereafter he was appointed imam of the Uftade mosque in Bursa by the Republican Directorate of Religious Affairs. In 1952 he was called to succeed Abdulaziz Bekkine, who had taken over the secret leadership of the Nakşibendi in Istanbul. Kotku's new official position – most probably through the acquiescence of the Directorate of Religious Affairs – was that of Imam of the Ümmügülsum Mosque. In 1958 he was transferred to the Iskenderpaşa Mosque, where he remained until his death in 1980.

A number of features of Kotku's strategies are clearly a continuation of the Halidi social stance. First, he gathered a circle of persons around him who later, in the 1970s and 1980s, played a key role in politics. Among them we may mention Dr Necmettin Erbakan, the founder of the first Turkish clerical party; Korkut Özal, brother of the present Prime Minister of Turkey; and Mehmet Şevket Eygi, publisher of the most influential Islamic daily *Zaman* (briefly in 1988). Kotku encouraged and contributed financially to two remarkable developments. First, he convinced Dr Erbakan that he should establish a model Islamic industrial plant, and this led to the founding of a factory making irrigation pumps. Second, he influenced the founding in 1968 of *Sabah*, a daily which was to take up the Islamic cause. His influence has yet to be studied seriously. His extraordinary sensitivity to modernity stands out when one recalls his selection as son-in-law of a man who is now Professor at the Faculty of Theology of Ankara, Esat Coşan, who is also his successor in the order. Professor Coşan is at the head of an organization which publishes three periodicals with an Islamic ideology, one of which, entitled *İlim ve Sanat* (Science and Art), makes profitable reading as an informative magazine when compared to its secular counterparts. I do not know of a similar success in capturing the discourse of secular intellectuals in any other Muslim society.

Another Nakşibendi organization of note is that of the Süleymancı, which came out of the Balkans and has had an immense success in organizing Turkish workers in Germany.

REASONS FOR NAKŞIBENDI POLITICAL SUCCESS

Seen in the perspective of the last century, the course of Nakşibendi history seems truly remarkable. While its success in populistic mobilization may bring to mind Shi'i parallels, there is in fact no connection. I have already dwelt on the strong Sunni cast of Nakşibendi thought; beyond this, the Nakşibendi do not seem ever to have questioned the legitimacy or the integrity of the Ottoman Sultanic position. Not only has the prominent role of the Nakşibendi order in the Ottoman Empire survived, but it has been able in our own time to capture and to use the connotations of prestige that the secular intellectualistic discourse evoked in modern Turkey. But our purpose here is not to celebrate the liveliness of this organization, rather to devise an explanation for this success.

First, it would appear that authors such as Algar are not justified in denying that the Nakşibendi have a bent for the uses of power.[39] Throughout its history, the Nakşibendi order has always been on the alert for opportunities to use power for what it considered the higher interests of Muslims.

Second, the particularly influential role of tarikat in the Turkish setting has a link with the role of mystic fraternities in Central Asia, of which the Kalender are the best example. The perpetuation of these fraternities in a continuously changing frame provides the setting for the secret-society aspect of tarikat which may be the Ottoman equivalent of Freemasonry and which certainly helped the Halidi order in its activities during the nineteenth century.

Third, Nakşibendi collaboration with the state acquired a sour note in the nineteenth century, and the Halidiye attained a new autonomy at that time. The twentieth century has seen an increasing amount of fission *within* the order. It has been been argued that the ability to establish branches without the consent of the *pir* or leader is, in itself, an organizational plus for the Nakşibendi, and that this may be one reason for their long-term success.[40]

Fourth, from the sixteenth century onward the Nakşibendi elaborated ideological instruments which, with time, became increasingly focused on mobilizational methods. But the success of the order was not simply an outcome of these organizational features. After all, its direct influence on followers was through the effectiveness of a discourse. This discourse was based on such elements of self-discipline as 'awareness in breathing' (*hūsh dar dam*), 'watching one's step' (*nazar bar qadam*), 'internal mystical journey' (*safar dar watan*), 'solitude in the crowd' (*khalwat dar anjuman*), 'recollection' (*yād kard*), 'restraining one's thoughts' (*bāz gard*), 'watching one's thoughts' (*nigah dāsht*), and 'concentrating upon God' (*yād dāsht*).

What kind of correlation is there then between the force of this esoteric discourse and the power of the Nakşibendi as an organization?

I think, in a preliminary estimate, which is the only one we can make at the moment, we have to invoke two types of features in trying to solve this problem: one which we may call 'boundary conditions', and the other 'cultural constants'. The difficulty of this approach lies in that both of these frames also change with time.

By 'boundary conditions' I mean the general state of the ambient world. One set of these conditions promoted the rise of the order in tandem with that of the Ottoman Empire. While Sirhindi's activism was limited by the boundary conditions of his own time, the later, more systematic mobilizational doctrines of Shah Wali Allah of Delhi (1703–1762), whom we have already encountered as a spiritual successor of Sirhindi, and those of Mevlâna Halid, seem to me to be related to the perception of the dangers encountered by Islamic society in relation to the expansion of the West. My guess would be that a set of interrelated factors which we know as the 'Modern World', that is, the geographical discoveries of the early Renaissance, the change in trade routes, the world capitalist system and the growth of the modern nation-state, impinged on the consciousness of Muslims somewhat earlier than we realize. This was a diffuse feeling, a sense of anxiety linked with the realization that the dynamism of Islam was on the wane.

Later, we encounter a further change related to the communications revolution of the nineteenth century. At that time, the Halidis take it upon themselves to work for the mobilization of the periphery, the centre having eluded their grasp. But 'mobilization' is only sufficient to accentuate the workings of a network in a macro-perspective; it does not tell us which aspect of mobilization allows the individual to be taken into its net. To elucidate this aspect of Halidi success we have to remember that, with some notable exceptions, in the late nineteenth and early twentieth centuries Halidis sought support among persons who were left outside the stream of cultural modernization. This meant that few of their clients had the education which would enable them to acquire élite status, since after the onset of the reforms of the Tanzimat a secular education became increasingly necessary for access to the political or cultural élite. There already existed an Ottoman cultural package going back many centuries which could be used to appeal to those individuals who had been left by the wayside. In the Ottoman Empire, persons who were on the outer

margins of the 'Great Tradition' of the literati were interlinked by
the loose network of their own popular culture. They may also be
thought of as constituting a potential team for concerted action in
society. A characteristic of this quasi-group[41] was that it was
made up of persons who, to a greater or lesser extent, took their
value cues from, and organized their daily strategies around,
religious law, that is, the Sharia. This 'virtual' group had a
collective identity which may be described as that of the 'just',
since they adhered to the values of justice and equity stemming
from the Sharia. The Sharia played an important, active role in the
strategies of the just, in the sense that it ensured the protection of
the basic rights of common citizens, including life and property, in
a way that was not true for the sultanic team. The Sharia therefore
constituted a shield behind which popular resistance could take
shape.

What gave the just an even more delineated identity was the fact
that they confronted another team – the team of the unjust –
which took its own values from sultanic practice (Weber)[42] or, in
a starker characterization, from 'Oriental despotism', and which
operated just outside the boundaries of the Sharia. As has recently
been underlined by Cornell Fleischer, the connotations attached to
this term were known to Ottoman Ulema and common citizens
long before it appeared in the West.[43] The boundaries of these
two groups were the very product of Ottoman social organization,
in the sense that the team of the just was also the group that paid
taxes while the unjust were exempt from taxes. We may thus
understand why the sultanic team could often be seen as the team
of the unjust to which ordinary citizens gave habitual, but no
doubt frequently grudging, obeisance.

Two characteristics of the team of the just need to be
underlined. First, the élite of this team, the Ulema, had often led
the masses in movements that protested against the practices of
the unjust.[44] Second, a more common form of protest against the
unjust was the set of adversary, underground strategies aimed at
deflecting and subverting the burdens generated by sultanic
policies. A tactic clearly directed against the 'Great Tradition' –
the culture of the unjust – was the discourse of the central
character in the Turkish shadow-play, Karagöz.[45]

The secret, often semi-conscious and collective manoeuvres I
have mentioned have been studied in a more general frame by

Michel de Certeau, who has highlighted the ways in which the totality of such popular stratagems subvert the canon of the powerful, and has called the field where this subversion takes place 'the everyday' (*le quotidien*).[46] In a sense, the Halidi acquired their clientele – the just – because they could refer to the place occupied by Islam in the 'everyday' of the just. They could also transform it and set it within a new frame, that of the external constraints of modernity. The ultimate bonus of this tactic was the transmutation of the values of the just into those of a populistic ideology, an Islamic equivalent of democratization which itself now became the basis of legitimation.

CONCLUSION: THE 'DISCOURSE' OF RENEWAL

It is of particular interest that, in the specific case of the Ottoman Empire, 'renewalist' social movements took shape among men of religion somewhat earlier than they did among Ottoman statesmen. The explanation may well be that the topology of the Ottoman bureaucratic mind was concentrated for a long time on saving traditional Ottoman state mechanisms. When they decided to follow the West, it was by methods culled from enlightened despotism, and in this scheme ordinary citizens were meant to become good citizens by the state's encouragement of their economic bent. Wide-ranging participation in the Tanzimat was to be achieved through the blasting of traditional Ottoman constraints on the economy. But the Ulema, by contrast, had a historical role which potentially suited them to mobilization through what we may loosely describe as 'discourse' rather than mobilization by the creation of economic opportunities. Changes in the 'boundary conditions' during the nineteenth century gradually unfolded this potential. By discourse I mean, as I already stated, a form of life and a language for life, a set of structured concepts for grasping and manipulating the phenomenal world, which is the way I see the culture of Sharia, *adab* (cultural norms that regulate the behaviour of a cultivated Muslim) and *ahlak* (ethical norms and conduct). There is here a large unexplored area, that of the cultural dimension of Islamic discourse, which deserves further research. The concept of a culturally-framed 'imaginaire', in the sense used by Gaston Bachelard and developed by Castoriadis, may also be of use at this point.[47] Because of this continuity of imaginary worlds, the Ulema had a hold over the élite of educated Muslims as well as the common citizens which had deeper resonance than the secularists' proposals for reform. At the other end of the spectrum, the Ulema had greater potential for the development of an ideology to be used as a 'flag' for the Muslim community than was at the disposal of Muslim Westernizers. The Ulema were also closer than the governmental class to social forces which have been central in modern societies, namely mass movements and the mobilization of the periphery. But Naksibendi had still another weapon, namely the opportunity to influence Turkish Muslims as individuals, and this time in the psyche of these individuals. Even a phenomenon as close to our time as the formation of a circle around Zahid Efendi in the 1960s shows that the disorientation of individuals, at the time when traditional Ottoman Islamic bonds were dissolving and being replaced by new institutions, created a fertile field for religious influence at the individual level. This disarray of individuals is highlighted by the large numbers of books on practical ethics which appeared in the nineteenth century at a time when the secular institutional reforms of the Tanzimat were proceeding apace.

And here, once more, 'discourse', as a means of coming to grips with reality, legitimating social bonds and transforming the world, emerges with a primordial role: the individual and his disorientation appear on one side of the coin, the disorder to which he reacts on the other.

In short, the Nakşibendi case leads us to think of Islam as the primary, ideological anchor, the matrix for thinking and action which has the most basic ideological role to play, and of Muslim political activism, as well as diffuse democratization, as something generated in the interstices of faith. In that sense, the Nakşibendi contention that one should not establish too close a relation with politicians is a sincere Islamic cry of the heart based on the correct conviction that Islamic faith will by itself put one on the political warpath without any abrupt transition from faith to ideology.

It is indeed unfortunate that in attempting to provide an explanation for modern Islamic revivalism, Islamic studies have insisted on concentrating on the differences in the role of religion as between 'Western' and 'Eastern' societies taken as polar opposites – a trap which also caught Max Weber – instead of trying to recapture the internal spring of Islamic social structuring as a dynamic process. I would propose that this has to be done by looking at three levels of social structuring, namely the interaction of a culturally constructed 'imaginaire' and its practices, a given world of social relations, and changing 'boundary conditions'. The workings of Islamic culture as an 'imaginaire' is the most fascinating of the three areas of analysis I have proposed, but it is also the most difficult.

NOTES

1. Tarık Zafer Tunaya, *Türkiye'de Siyasî Partiler*, 2nd ed., Istanbul, Hürriyet, 1985, I, p. 183.
2. Sina Akşin, *100 Seneda Jön Türkler*, Istanbul, Gerçek Yayinevi, 1980, p. 115.
3. Hamid Algar, 'Der Nakşibendi Orden in der republikanischen Türkei', in Jochen Bläschke and Martin van Bruinessen, eds, *Jahrbuch zur Geschichte und Gesellschaft des Vorderen und Mittleren Orient*, Berlin, Express, 1985; Irfan Gündüz, *Gümüşhanevî Ahmet Ziyaüddin*, Ankara, Seha Neşriyet, 1984.
4. J. Spencer Trimingham, *The Sufi Orders in Islam*, London, Oxford University Press, 1973, p. 63.
5. Johann G. J. ter Harr, 'The Naashbandi tradition in the eyes of Ahmad Sirhindi', in *Naashbandis*, proceedings of the Sévres Round Table, ed. Marc Gaboriau et al., Istanbul 1990, pp. 83–94.
6. Trimingham, *Sufi Orders*, p. 63.
7. Ahmet Yaşar Ocak, *Bektaşi Menakibnâmelerinde Islam Öncesi Inanç Motifleri*, Istanbul, Enderun, 1983, pp. 35–6, 63, 68. One aspect of the transmutation from the religion of pre-Islamic 'Turks' to Islam would seem to be simply that the diversity of religions which Turkic groups tapped before Islamization was replaced by one single religion, Islam; see Gregory Frumkin, *Archaeology in Soviet Central Asia*, Leiden/Cologne, Brill, 1970, p. 79.
8. Mehmed Fuad Köprülüzade, *Influence du Chamanisme Turco-Mongol sur les Ordres Mystiques Musulmans*, Istanbul, 1929.
9. Yohanan Friedmann, *Shaykh Ahmad Sirhindi*, London and Montreal, McGill/Queens University Press, 1971, p. 13.
10. Fazlur Rahman, 'Revival and reform in Islam', in P. M. Holt, Ann K. S. Lambton and Bernard Lewis, eds, *The Cambridge History of Islam*, Volume 2, Cambridge, Cambridge University Press, 1977, pp. 632–56; cf. Annemarie Schimmel, *And Muhammad is His Messenger*, Chapel Hill, University of North Carolina Press, 1985, pp. 216f.; Friedmann, *Shaykh Ahmad*, p. 74.
11. Albert Hourani, 'Shaikh Khalid and the Naqshbandi Order', in S. M. Stern, A. Hourani and V. Brown, eds, *Islamic Philosophy and the Classical Tradition*, London, Cassirer, 1972, p. 91.

12. Jo-Ann Gross, 'Khoja Ahrar: A Study of the Perception of Religious Power and Prestige in the Late Timurid Period', unpublished PhD Dissertation, New York University, 1982.
13. Schimmel, *And Muhammad*, p. 217.
14. Friedmann, *Shaykh Ahmad*, pp. 15–16.
15. Fazlur Rahman, 'Revival and reform', pp. 638–9.
16. Schimmel, *And Muhammad*, pp. 219–21.
17. Ömer Lûtfi Barkan, 'Les derviches colonisateurs turcs de l'époque de la conquête et la zaviye', *Vakıflar Dergisi*, 2, 1942, pp. 279–386; Emel Esin, '"Eren". Les derviš hétérodoxes Turcs d'asie centrale et le peintre surnommé "Siyāh ḳalam"', *Turcica*, 17, 1985, pp. 7–41.
18. A more idealistic explanation of his decision to collaborate with the promoters of the rebellion is given by J. H. Kissling in *Encyclopedia of Islam*, Leiden, Brill; London, Luzac. 2nd edn, 1, p. 869.
19. The Sultans and their advisers were rather clever at disinterring the genealogical principle when it suited them, but this happened at their own discretion.
20. This seems to have occurred in two stages, the first in the reign of Murad II (1421–1451) and the second at the time of Sultan Mehmet II (1451–1481); see Cahid Baltacı, *XV–XVI Asırlar Osmanlı Medreseleri*, Istanbul, Irfan, 1976, pp. 46–7.
21. Gündüz, *Gümüşhanevî*, p. 40.
22. *Encyclopedia of Islam* 2, p. 697.
23. Algar, 'Der Naqshbendi Orden', pp. 168–9.
24. Cornell Fleischer, *Bureaucrat and Intellectual in the Ottoman Empire*, Princeton, Princeton University Press, 1986, pp. 17, 57.
25. Irène Mélikoff, 'Un ordre de derviches colonisateurs, les Bektachis', in *Memorial Ömer Lûtfi Barkan*, Bibliothèque de l'Institut Français d'Études Anatoliennes d'Istanbul, Paris, Maisonneuve, 1980, pp. 149–57.
26. Gündüz, *Gümüşhanevî*, p. 62.
27. Gündüz, *Gümüşhanevî*, pp. 240–3; Butrus Abu-Manneh, 'The Naqshbandiyya–Mujaddidiya in the Ottoman lands in the early 19th century', *Die Welt des Islam* (N.S.), 22, 1984, p. 6.
28. Trimingham, *Sufi Orders*, p. 127. The order penetrated into Indonesia in the 1840s and propelled resistance movements against the Dutch.
29. Gündüz, *Gümüşhanevi*, pp. 31, 36–7.
30. Abu-Manneh, 'Naqshbandiyya', p. 13.
31. Şerif Mardin, *The Genesis of Young Ottoman Thought*, Princeton, Princeton University Press, 1962 *passim*.
32. Gökhan Çetinsaya, 'II Abdülhamid döneminin ilk yıllarında "Islam birliği" hareketi (1876–1878)', unpublished MA thesis, Ankara University, 1988.
33. There was also a number of minor Mujeddidi personalities who took an important part in Ottoman social life in these years. Shaikh Ibrahim Ethem Efendi of the Özbek (Sultantepe) lodge played an important role in the development of industrial schools; see Grace

Martin Smith, 'The Özbek tekkes of Istanbul', *Der Islam*, 57, 1980, p. 136.

34. Gündüz, *Gümüşhanevi*, pp. 51, 53–4, 67.
35. Ibid., pp. 96, 106.
36. Smith, 'Özbek tekkes', p. 137.
37. For this concept see William J. Foltz, 'Modernization and nation-building', in Richard L. Meritt and Bruce Russett, eds, *From National Development to Global Community: Essays in Honor of Karl W. Deutsch*, London, Allen and Unwin, 1981, pp. 22–45.
38. John D. Voll, 'The Sudanese Mahdi: frontier fundamentalist', *International Journal of Middle East Studies*, 10, 1979, pp. 145–66.
39. Algar, 'Der Naqshbendi Orden'.
40. Martin van Bruinessen, *Agha, Shaikh and State: On the Social and Political Organisation of Kurdistan*, private, Utrecht, 1978.
41. R. Dahrendorf, *Class and Class Conflict in Industrial Society*, Stanford, Stanford University Press, 1959.
42. See Max Weber, *Economy and Society*, transl. and ed. G. Roth and C. Wittich, New York, Bedminster Press, 1968, p. 232.
43. Cornell Fleischer, unpublished lecture, Istanbul, October 1987.
44. What we should remember is that 'élite' refers to leadership by a 'lower clergy' quite often of impoverished status. For this mean social status, see Haim Gerber, *Economy and Society in an Ottoman City: Bursa, 1600–1700*, University of Jerusalem, Institute of Asian and African Studies, 1988, pp. 167–88.
45. For a recent study, see Walter G. Andrews and Irene Markoff, 'Poetry, the arts and group ethos in the ideology of the Ottoman Empire', *Edebiyat* (N.S.), 1, 1987, pp. 28–70.
46. Michel de Certeau, *The Practice of Everyday Life*, transl. Steven F. Rendall, Berkeley, University of California Press, 1984.
47. Cornelius Castoriadis, *The Imaginary Institutions of Society*, transl. Kathleen Blamey, Cambridge, Polity Press, 1987.

Part II

TURKISH MUSLIM INTELLECTUALS AND THE PRODUCTION OF ISLAMIC KNOWLEDGE

7

ISLAMIC EDUCATION IN TURKEY:
Medrese Reform in Late Ottoman Times and Imam–Hatip Schools in the Republic[1]

Bahattin Akşit

INTRODUCTION

The question of how the Islamic intelligentsia, Ulema and religious functionaries (imams, hatips, vaiz and so on) should be educated has been hotly debated in late Ottoman and Republican Turkey, reaching its highest intensity during the last quarter of the nineteenth century and the first quarter of the twentieth. These debates and discussions set the stage for both the Young Turk reform of the medreses in the 1910s and the Kemalist solution in 1924 of the Unification of Education Law (Tevhid-i Tedrisat). The problem, it seems, was forced underground, to re-emerge with the transition to a multi-party political system in the 1940s and 1950s, and to reach a new intensity during the late 1970s and the 1980s with the unprecedented growth in the publication of Islamic journals and books on Islamic education.

The increasing numbers of Imam–Hatip schools, with their swelling enrolment lists, have been hailed by some Islamic groups, orders and neo-orders as channels for the recruitment of new members and as a cradle for a new Islamic Ulema. Others have violently opposed them as extensions of the secular nation-state's apparatus of control. Secular circles too have divided opinions on Islamic education. Some welcome it as a source of scientifically-minded and enlightened men of religion (*aydın dîn adamı*); others forcefully oppose it as a breeding-ground for a radical–militant

Islam which might put an end to the secular state and to democratic pluralism. There are still other observers who see Imam–Hatip schools as alternative channels of upward mobility for the children of conservative and religious-minded rural and urban petty-commodity producers. This chapter develops and illustrates these themes.

IMAM–HATIP SCHOOLS DURING THE MULTI-PARTY REPUBLICAN ERA

Before discussing the formation of opposing debates and discourses on the Ulema and religious education in Ottoman and Republican Turkey, I shall present some statistical data on the development of Imam–Hatip schools since the 1950s. This, I hope, will set the stage for an understanding of contemporary debates and also the reasons why they should be studied in their social and historical contexts.

Between 1946 and 1949, twenty-five years after the abolition of the medreses, in the atmosphere of transition to multi-party politics, the Republican People's Party started a discussion of the education of imams (prayer-leaders) and hatips (preachers). In 1949, after some debate as to whether Imam–Hatip schools or short-term courses should be established, and whether these should be under the jurisdiction of the Directorate of Religious Affairs or the Ministry of Education, ten Imam–Hatip courses were opened in various provincial capitals, as well as a Faculty of Theology in Ankara.[2] In the academic year 1951–2, a year after the Democrat Party's accession to power, seven middle-level and lycée-level Imam–Hatip schools had been opened under the jurisdiction of the Ministry of Education. By 1958 their number had increased to 18, with 2,476 students, and in 1961, with the opening of a Higher Islamic Institute, the Department of Religious Education was established within the Ministry of Education. In the years between 1965 and 1969, when the Justice Party was in power, three more Higher Islamic Institutes and 40 more middle-level Imam–Hatip schools were established.[3] In the academic year 1969–70 there were 71 middle-level and 30 lycée-level Imam–Hatip schools, with a total of 42,443 enrolled students. In 1974–5, when the Islamicist National Salvation Party was in a coalition government with the secular Republican People's Party, the number of middle-level Imam–Hatip schools reached 101, and lycée-level 73, with 49,000 students. In the 1977–8 academic year, when the Justice Party, National Salvation Party and National Action Party were in a coalition government, the number of middle-level Imam–Hatip schools jumped to 334, and lycée-level to 103, with a total of 134,517 students. In 1987–8 there were 376 middle-level and 341 lycée-level Imam–Hatip schools, with approximately 240,000 students. In the academic year 1985–6, there were 4,400 official, secular, general middle-level schools and 1,206 lycées, with approximately 2.4 million enrolled students.[4] The ratio of Imam–Hatip school students to official general secondary-school students reached the level of one to ten in the academic year 1985–6, from the ratio of one to 37 in the academic year 1965–6.

Since the 1960s, Imam–Hatip schools have been transformed from vocational–religious schools, producing religious function-aries such as imams, hatips and candidates for recruitment into Higher Islamic Institutes and Faculties of Theology, into an alternative educational system whose graduates have entered various departments of national universities and become employed as civil servants as well as by the Directorate of Religious Affairs as imams and hatips. They are also among the consumers as well as producers of the radical Islamic journals and newspapers that have mushroomed during the 1980s.

The planners in the State Planning Organization, while writing the section on Imam–Hatip schools in the Third Five-Year Plan in 1973, were alarmed that when the academic years 1963–4 and 1971–2 were compared, the growth in the number of Imam–Hatip school students was 611 per cent, while it was only 127 per cent for all other technical and non-technical vocational schools.[5] Despite the planners' wishes and recommendations, the subse-quent fifteen years saw a 500 per cent increase in the numbers of Imam–Hatip school students.

It seems to me that this phenomenal growth has taken place on both 'supply' and 'demand' sides, so to speak. That is, politicians have supplied the schools and teachers in exchange for ideological allegiance and votes, and to meet demand from certain sections of the population. The latter have supplied students by sending their children, because the 'demand' for these students exists in the form of schools, teachers and scholarship opportunities. They hoped there would be continued opportunities beyond the Imam–Hatip schools, in the universities, among the professionals, intelligentsia and civil servants and perhaps also in the civil private sector as religious administrators, for example. In a recent Exhibition of Islamic Books, held in the grounds of the newly opened Kocatepe Mosque in Ankara, there were 50 Islamic publishing houses, which needed writers, distributors, salesmen and readers. Imam–Hatip schools have grown since the 1950s on the same soil that produced the old Sunni Sufi orders, the tarikats and their offshoots, the neo-orders. The only difference is that the growth of Imam–Hatip schools has taken place as an extension of the 'ideological' apparatus of the Turkish nation-state.

The question to be asked at this point, however, is which sectors of the population have supplied students for the Imam–Hatip schools? We can give only partial answers to this question, because we have little information on the family, class and ideological backgrounds of the students.

One partial answer I obtained by estimating the number of Imam–Hatip school students per 1,000 population in each province and calculating the correlation coefficient between this variable and others such as the degree of urbanization and industrialization, voting patterns and the proportion of urban and rural petty-commodity producers in each province.[6] The data used in the study were official statistics from the early 1970s, just before Imam–Hatip schools became a mass phenomenon.

The provinces with higher Imam–Hatip Schooling Rates (IHSR) were the following: Aydın, Bolu, Isparta, Burdur, Uşak, Kayseri, Çorum, Konya, Amasya, Adana, Denizli, Sakarya, Elazığ, Afyon; while the provinces with lowest IHSR were the following: Tunceli, Hakkâri, Bingöl, Artvin, Ağrı, İzmir, Mardin, Istanbul, Muğla, Urfa, İçel, Kars, Zonguldak, Hatay.[7] Both groups of provinces are rather heterogeneous, and clear patterns are not visible. However, when the degree of urbanization is taken into consideration, one finds that the second group (lowest IHSR) includes the provinces with both the highest and the lowest degrees of urbanization; while the first group includes the provinces with average and above average urbanization.

Justice Party votes in 1969 were high in most of the provinces with high IHSR. Another variable that correlated strongly with

IHSR was the proportion of urban and rural petty-commodity producers – the self-employed: the higher the proportion of self-employed, the higher the IHSR. It seems that provinces with high proportions of urban craftsmen and traders (*zanaatkâr* and *esnaf*) and rural farmer-peasants were more responsive to Imam–Hatip schools. In another study it was found that the same variable, both at the province level and at the level of the neighbourhood (*mahalle*), was predictive of National Salvation Party votes in 1973.[8] One observation to be added to this discussion is that the provinces with very low IHSR, apart from the two metropolitan cities İstanbul and İzmir, were mostly in eastern Anatolia; while most of the provinces with high IHSR were in western and central Anatolia. A similar East–West pattern was observed in a previous study on officially sponsored Koran courses scattered throughout Turkey.[9]

I can find no straightforward explanations of these findings; however some speculative hypotheses can be advanced.

The low rates of Imam–Hatip schooling and Koran courses in eastern and southeastern Turkey can be explained by the fact that these regions are less integrated with the centre and its institutions, and have their own local institutions of Islamic education such as shaikhs and informal and unofficial medreses.[10] In the rural and urban communities of these regions, Imam–Hatip schools and/or Koran courses are not perceived as channels of upward mobility, whereas in central Anatolia and western Turkey they clearly are. Officially recognized Koran course graduates, mostly from rural backgrounds, might become imams, and graduates of Imam–Hatip schools have graduated from different departments of various universities and have entered the professions.[11]

The blend of education offered in Imam–Hatip schools, half Islamic and half secular, seems to have an affinity with the values and ideology of such provinces as Adana, Denizli, Kayseri, Konya and Aydın, which have been undergoing rapid industrialization and urbanization; but not with those of İstanbul, İzmir and Ankara, provinces which have urbanized, industrialized and modernized over a longer period, and have larger metropolitan centres. This gives only qualified support to the hypothesis that secularization is a corollary of urbanization and industrialization.

The other hypothesis suggested by the findings is that provinces with high concentrations of civil servants, professionals and wage-workers have an affinity with general secular lycée and technical–vocational lycée education, while the provinces with high concentrations of urban and rural petty-commodity producers – craftsmen (*zanaatkâr*), traders (*esnaf*) and farmers – have an affinity with Imam–Hatip school education.

Further examination and discussion of these hypotheses require data at the level of households and individuals. In a study conducted in 1982, a survey questionnaire was administered to a nationwide representative sample of students from four different lycée-level educational systems: general secular, private secular, technical–vocational and Imam–Hatip.[12] In this study it was reported that the fathers of Imam–Hatip lycée students are predominantly rural farmers, farm workers, urban small traders, craftsmen and civil servants. At the other extreme are private lycée students whose fathers are predominantly urban professionals, big merchant-industrialists and civil servants. Technical–vocational lycée students' fathers are very similiar to Imam–Hatip students, except that urban factory and workshop wage-workers were predominant among them. The fathers of general lycée students, the largest and the most comprehensive secondary-education group in Turkey, are fairly evenly distributed among the occupations and professions, with a greater frequency of civil servants than others.[13]

The predominance of children of rural farmers and farm workers in Imam–Hatip lycées is evidence of a curious historical continuity. Discussing medreses in the middle of the nineteenth century, Berkes made the interesting observation that they 'became the refuge of the impoverished peasantry'.[14] The fathers of Imam–Hatip lycée students cannot be said to be impoverished, but they are not located at higher or even middle positions in the Turkish occupational hierarchy, rather they are mostly in lower-middle-class occupations and wish their children to climb the occupational ladder. As a matter of fact, in the study cited above, Imam–Hatip lycée students expressed the opinion that their parents wanted them to enter the medical or teaching professions, and most students agreed with their parents, although some 24 per cent preferred the religious professions.[15]

But why then do these students and parents choose Imam–Hatip schools, rather than general lycées or technical-vocational lycées?

Clearly, the chances of upward mobility are not less but more in general lycées than in Imam–Hatip schools, and about equal in technical–vocational lycées. This is a cultural–ideological question that requires qualitative anthropological research for a satisfactory answer. However in my own study carried out in the academic year 1977–8 in an Ankara Imam–Hatip school, some tendencies were indicated in response to open-ended questions.[16]

Most of the students stated that they had 'chosen' the Imam–Hatip school with their parents and that they were very happy to be in such a school, because they were learning spiritual and material 'sciences' at the same time. They believed that neither 'Western material sciences' nor 'Eastern spiritual sciences' were conducive to development and happiness. They disliked such courses as biology and philosophy, but the list of unpopular courses also included Islamic law (*fıkh*) and Islamic theology (*kelâm*). The list of preferred courses was headed by the Koran, but it also included mathematics, physics, literature, English and Arabic. Most students hoped and intended to enter one of the modern Turkish universities, preferring such subjects as engineering and medicine. However there were also those who preferred social science faculties such as public administration, law and theology. There were also a few who planned to become imams and hatips after graduation from school.

Most students articulated conservative and traditional attitudes towards gender roles and relationships. Approximately 25 per cent conceded that 'women should be educated' and 'must work', but only 8 per cent accepted that 'women can travel alone'. Approximately 60 per cent believed that 'positive sciences cannot solve all the problems of life', implying that some 40 per cent had greater faith in science. However, only 10 per cent agreed that 'there can be good men without religious faith'.[17]

As I reviewed essays written by the students, I observed that they conceptualized Imam–Hatip schools in terms of such oppositions as 'spiritual–Islamic sciences' versus 'material–Western sciences', the faithful versus unbelievers, immoral society in crisis versus moral society at peace. These are the elements of discourses on Imam–Hatip schools constructed from within. There are also those discourses from without that take an oppositional position, namely that these schools are a continuation of medrese scholasticism, that they are partisan in their outlook and militants of certain radical rightist movements, that they challenge the Kemalist Unity of Education, and so on.

These discourses from within and without, of praise and condemnation, are not at all new. They emerged with the crisis of medrese education towards the end of the nineteenth century, and with efforts at the reform of the medreses during the Young Turk revolution and at their abolition and/or transformation into Imam–Hatip schools during the early years of the Turkish Republic; the debate was silenced at the height of secularist zeal during the 1930s, but re-emerged in the 1950s. For a better understanding of Imam–Hatip schools, Islamic education and the Ulema, it is necessary to give a brief review of earlier developments, especially during the last hundred years.

MEDRESE REFORM AND THE EMERGENCE OF IMAM–HATIP SCHOOLS

By the time that the Ottoman Empire was established, economic dynamism, trade, philosophy and science had already shifted to the Western Mediterranean.[18] It is no accident that critical responses to the assimilation of philosophy and science into theology and law in core Islamic areas came from Ibn Rüşd and Ibn Khaldun as representatives of western Mediterranean Islam. It might be that invasions of pastoral nomads from Central and Eastern Asia helped to precipitate the deterioration of rational thinking, science and technology in the Islamic medrese system.[19] It is also true that, by the fourteenth century, nation-states were being formed in Europe ready to embark on economic, political, geographic, scientific and technological expansion.[20] However, these and other exogenous factors could not have been as influential as they were without the internal transformations that radically altered the status of philosophy and science in Islamic thought systems, states and medreses.

It seems to me that, by the fourteenth century, Islamic thought, philosophy and sciences had been transformed and routinized in the direction of traditionalization rather than rationalization in the Weberian sense. That is why the Islamic 'sciences' of Koranic interpretation (*tefsir*), Islamic law and Islamic theology had come to prevail over the rational and observational 'sciences' such as philosophy, mathematics and medicine. Ottoman dynamism and expansion, and the establishment of great medrese systems during the fifteenth and sixteenth centuries, could have reversed this trend by giving some kind of autonomy to reason and science.

The victory of the scholastic Ulema over rational philosophers and observational scientists was signalled by the demolition in 1580 of Taqi al-Din's observatory in Istanbul.[21] This was the time when Galileo was being tried and Tycho de Brahe was being burned in the West. In the West, however, something different had taken place and the dualities of spirit versus matter, mind versus body, faith versus reason, revelation versus observation, had assumed a form of Cartesian split and equality of status, whereby the former terms of the oppositions had been relegated to religion/church while the latter had been left to science/universities. Mysticism constituted a third element, co-operating with either science or religion as a source of inspiration and innovation.[22] Eventually, various sects and denominations in Christianity accepted subordination to science, as science became embodied in national universities, nation-state bureaucracies and capitalist–industrialist production systems.[23]

In Ottoman society, the Ulema of Islamic law and theology, in alliance with the central bureaucracy and the janissaries, had turned the medrese system into an expanded scholastic hierarchy and had subsumed philosophy, science and mystical inspiration under its hegemony. With the decline of the Sipahi system, the provincial land revenue administration and military organization, the Ulema hierarchy had expanded.[24] Critical voices had been raised by some followers of Ibn Khaldun, such as Katip Çelebi, Koçi Bey and Naima, against the scholastic consolidation and loss of dynamism in the Ottoman Empire. These criticisms had been reinforced convincingly and forcefully through the Ottoman defeats in Europe. From then on, the Ottoman Empire entered a process of peripheralization[25] in relation to the European core economies, technologies, and armies, thus urgently necessitating the introduction of a new organization of the Ottoman army, and the adoption of new technologies. The Greco-Islamic rational and observational sciences that had migrated to the West returned to the Ottoman Empire and Egypt in much-developed, Westernized and secularized forms. The Ulema had allowed these innovations only on condition that their authority was not challenged in the areas of Islamic theology, law, the family and the education of children.[26]

From the middle of the nineteenth century, it can be observed that the dualism of secular military state schools on the one hand and Islamic Vakıf (religious endowment) medreses on the other had been supplemented and, perhaps, challenged by the establishment of civilian state schools at the primary and secondary levels and the establishment of a law school (*hukuk mektebi*) external to and parallel with the medreses. These developments peripheralized the medreses further by taking from them the education of children and the administration of Islamic law. The new civil–religious law (*mecelle*) had been master-minded by Cevdet Paşa, who, as a forerunner of Ziya Gökalp, tried to synthesize Islamic and secular laws into a whole, leaving family, marriage, status of women and other 'personal' areas uncodified. The division of labour seemed to be such that commercial and official problems were to be handled by the graduates of law schools, while uncodified social relationships were left to the graduates of medreses.[27]

By the 1880s, the Ottoman education system displayed an unparalleled degree of pluralism: military state schools, civilian state schools, medreses, private Ottoman schools, private foreign schools and the religious as well as secular schools of all minorities in the Ottoman Empire.[28] From the point of view of this chapter, some of the private Ottoman schools opened in this period are particularly interesting, because in their curricula modern and Islamic sciences were combined and the official dress rules of the state schools were not observed. Reading about these schools suggested the possibility that there might be some similarities between them and the expanding Imam–Hatip schools of the 1960s: the middle-class İstanbul families of the 1880s and the rural or urban provincial families of the 1960s might have some affinities. This is a speculation, but what is beyond doubt is that the real forerunners of the Imam–Hatip schools, the reformed medreses of the 1910s, adopted a curriculum which differed little from that of some of these private schools of the 1880s.

By 1912, four years after the Young Turk Revolution of the Committee of Union and Progress, Ottoman educational pluralism seemed to be in a state of chaos and crisis. Even the Committee of Union and Progress had its own private school at the time. However, as the Committee had risen above its partisan interests and aspired to engineer a revolution from above, with some pluralistic support from below, many social, political, economic, cultural, ideological and educational issues were debated to produce proposals for the reorganization and reconstitution of many spheres of life in Ottoman society. At the macro-sociological level the issues were: centralization versus decentralization, unification versus pluralism, state initiative versus private initiative, state-level reforms descending to the family versus family-level reforms ascending to the state.

In the history of Turkish sociology, it can be stated that the former terms of the oppositions were forcefully articulated by Ziya Gökalp, the Durkheimian founder of sociology in Turkey, while the latter were defended by Prens Sabahattin, a follower of Le Play.[29] In educational reform, one of the interesting debates took place between Ziya Gökalp and Satı Bey.[30] What was to be done with the Ottoman education? Should it be left religiously and ethnically pluralistic, or should it be organized under state control? Should the reform start from above with higher education and proceed down to primary education, or should it start from primary education and proceed upward? In order to educate people you need educators; but how are the educators to be educated?

In the free and pluralistic atmosphere of the early years of the Young Turk Revolution, many educational theories and policies emerged along with the public figure of the pedagogue.[31] Because the Young Turk era was so brief, ending with the war, and because its leaders lacked experience, it did not perhaps bring lasting revolutionary transformations in economic, political and social spheres, but it certainly ushered in a pluralistic cultural 'revolution', in the sense that all the different ideas, policies and discourses were being developed in opposition to each other and in terms of antinomies of the period.

Ziya Gökalp and Satı Bey emerged in this atmosphere of cultural crisis, struggle and revolution to transcend the divisive currents of Islamism, modernism and nationalism and offer a viable educational policy for the multi-ethnic, multi-religious Ottoman society. At the time of the debate, both could be said to be Ottomanist, although eventually one became a theorist of Turkish nationalism, the other of Arab nationalism.

For Gökalp, the late-nineteenth- and early-twentieth-century educational pluralism of Westernist Tanzimat schools, Islamist medreses, separatist minority schools and foreign missionary schools were a breeding ground for moral crisis and Durkheimian anomie. He proposed a statist, centrist, collectivist and culturalist reorganization of the educational system by making a conceptual distinction between civilization and culture.[32] Islam and Western modernity have both represented relevant civilizations for the Turkish people, the emphasis shifting from the first to the second. However, for the people to constitute a nation, civilization is not enough: a national culture is needed. Turkish national culture has been both Turkish and Islamic. Since Islam is a rationalist religion, it could bridge rationalist Western civilization and Turkish culture. Hence the educational system has to be modernist, nationalist and Islamicist. A modernist educational system organized along statist and nationalist lines must be complemented by Islamic education. Primary, secondary and higher education should be under the control, co-ordination and guidance of the Ministry of Education, whereas religious education should be under the office of the Şeyhülislam. Therefore, the curriculum of the medreses should be modernized and transferred from the Ministry of Evkaf (religious endowments) to the Office of the Şeyhülislam (the chief authority, at the capital, of the religious hierarchy extending to the provinces), where there should be a special department of medreses, along with the departments of mosques and Sufi *tekkes* (lodges). The department of medreses was not only to carry out a reform programme for the medreses but also to establish higher-level educational institutions, as well as more occupationally specialized schools to train imams, hatips and other religious personnel.[33]

Satı Bey reacted to this position as culturally specific, short-sightedly nationalistic, and heavily centrist, killing individual initiative and creativity and, furthermore, as parochial and thus to the detriment of the universalist potential of humanity. As a social and political ideologist of the Committee of Union and Progress, trying to govern, reform and develop a pluralist society like the Ottoman Empire, Ziya Gökalp was invited to be more Ottomanist, which was possible, according to Satı Bey, by becoming more universalist, liberal, individualistic and developmentalist. Satı Bey was adopting natural science methods of developmental and educational psychology and was trying to devise a universalist Ottoman educational system which would balance reason with emotion, initiative with sincerity, idealism with pragmatism, irrespective of religion, ethnicity or class. Hence, for Satı Bey, religious educational institutions were to be closed and replaced by universalist–modernist institutions.[34]

This debate is interesting not only because it exemplifies one of the heated discussions of the period, but also because it has relevance for medrese reform and the emergence of the idea of Imam–Hatip schools. Now the problem with Satı Bey's universalism was that, once the idea of supranational and/or international Ottoman unity had proved to be non-viable, it collapsed into Westernism and/or Arab nationalism. Presumably, medrese reform and Islamic education were not on the agenda for Satı Bey in any possible position for him except Arab nationalism, given the assumption that Islam must be considered a component of the latter.

The problem with Gökalp's synthesis of modernism, Islamism and Turkism had been its tendency to disintegrate into a dualism of Islamist Turkism or modernist–secularist Turkism. The history of religious schools during the twentieth century, the attempts at medrese reform during the 1910s, their transformation and eventual extinction from the 1920s until the late 1940s and their reopening and proliferation after the 1960s suggest to me that these movements were oscillations between secularist nationalism and Islamist nationalism which failed to achieve Gökalp's golden synthesis of modernism, Islamism and nationalism. It seems to me, however, that, in the years between 1910 and 1916, an approximation to modernist Islam had been accomplished in the context of the medrese reform and the emergence of new secondary- and higher-level medreses, where both Ziya Gökalp and Satı Bey taught the sciences of society and education.[35]

The introduction of modern sciences such as mathematics, physics, chemistry, biology, rationalist philosophy, sociology, psychology and education into the curriculum of the medreses, and their transformation into modern Islamic educational institutions, had been intensely debated in the years between 1908 and 1914. There had been so many expressions of opinion, criticisms and counter-criticisms in the journals and newspapers of the period that some journals contained regular pages for discussions on medrese reform.[36] Some Westernists like Abdullah Cevdet had openly blamed medreses for the decline of the Ottoman Empire and argued for their abolition. Most of those who expressed their opinions, however, were in agreement with Namık Kemal, Cevdet Paşa, Ziya Gökalp and other Islamist modernists that modernism and Islam could be reconciled and that the new reformed medreses should be embodiments of their reconciliation. Yet nobody was sure how this process was to be accomplished, or what modifications should be made in modern sciences for them to be compatible with revealed knowledge and faith. Of course some Islamists may have just been mocking these efforts with the conviction that modernist Islam was not possible; however, there might also have been some among them who were contemplating the encompassment of modern sciences within Islam.[37] Medrese students especially were desperately exclaiming in the pages of journals and newspapers that they were in a deplorable and disgraceful situation, so the sooner the medreses were modernized the better.

An initial answer to these calls came in 1910 with a new regulation pertaining to medreses. This was an eclectic attempt at reform which introduced mathematics, geography, chemistry and philosophy into the existing curriculum, without any indication of how the two different approaches, methodologies and mentalities of modern 'sciences' and Islamic 'sciences' were to be reconciled. Furthermore, article 13 read 'when a *müderris* [medrese professor] dies, his post is to be given to his most industrious and steady son',[38] in the hope, perhaps, that this rule would exclude lazy and wayward sons! The regulation also specified that the müderris must be specialized in one of the following groups of 'sciences': Arabic literature, natural and mathematical sciences, logic, discussion and debate, Islamic theology, Islamic law, Koranic interpretation, Islamic traditions (*hadith*), history of Islam and history of the Ottoman Empire. Philosophy was also included in the curriculum, but it was not constituted as a field of specialization for the müderris.[39]

A year later, in 1911, M. Şevketi, a müderris in one of the İstanbul medreses, published a book on medrese reform, including a very comprehensive curriculum. Şevketi, being educated in both Islamic and modern sciences, was zealously arguing for the teaching of modern positive sciences such as mathematics, physics, chemistry, mechanics, biology and agriculture. He also supported the teaching of philosophy, psychology, logic and Western languages in addition to Turkish, Arabic, Persian and all of the

Islamic sciences.[40] Şevketi's curriculum in 1911 was as rich as the curriculum of contemporary Imam–Hatip schools; it seems to me, however, that he too failed to address the question of reconciling modern and Islamic sciences.

In 1912, Şevketi was one of a number of müderris who published an open letter entitled 'Confessions and Eyewitness', arguing for medrese reform. In a dialogue between this group and M. Şemsettin Günaltay, it was revealed that the Ulema were to be not the guardians of tradition but the upholders of reason.[41] Modern civilization and culture and Islamic civilization and culture were to be reconciled with each other, with reason implicit in both of them. But who was going to employ reason to achieve this collossal task? Modernists and Islamists were using their own logic and reasoning and were claiming incompatibility. The professors in the new reformed medreses were supposed to accomplish a synthesis and teach both modern and Islamic subjects without detrimental conflict and tension for the students. There were very few philosophers, scientists or Ulema like Ziya Gökalp, however, who knew both modern as well as Islamic sciences. So, how was it possible to find scientists, Ulema, professors or müderris who could achieve the synthesis and teach its methods and results to students in medreses?

A partial answer came in 1912 from Emrullah Efendi, the Minister of Education, with his establishment of the Faculty of Islamic Sciences in Darülfünun (the first modern university, later to become the University of Istanbul), and his Tuba-tree theory of education. The Tuba tree in Islamic paradise is supposed to be upside down, delivering its fruit to all inhabitants in their dwellings. Similarly the Young Turk educational reform was supposed to proceed from the top down, from the university to the secondary schools, eventually reaching primary education.[42] For Emrullah Efendi the education of educators had priority. Hence, the University in Istanbul was to be transformed from a timid Darülfünun subordinated to the Sultan, to an Ottoman University venturing innovation and producing new knowledge and policies.

Emrullah Efendi's idea seemed to be upheld in medrese reform as well, by the opening in March 1914 of a higher educational Medrese of Specialists, Medresetül Mütehassisin. The Şeyhülislam and Minister of Evkaf, Mustafa Hayri Efendi, was not a great believer in Tuba-tree theory, and hence, without waiting for the fruits of the Medrese of Specialists, he launched a comprehensive reform in September 1914 with the Medrese Reform Law, Islahi Medaris Nizamnamesi. With this law, all the medreses in Istanbul were organized into junior and senior secondary levels and undergraduate and graduate higher-educational levels under the name of Darül-Hilafetil Aliyye Medresesi. The curricula of the various levels of this medrese complex seem to balance the number of mathematical, natural and social sciences on the one hand and the number of Islamic sciences on the other, more or less replicating Şevketi's proposal.

During the First World War, between 1916 and 1917 the medrese reform was continued by the new Şeyhülislam Kazım Efendi, who included all of the medreses outside İstanbul under the new complex in the capital. Meanwhile, more occupational medreses, such as those for imams and hatips (Medresetül Eimme vel-Hutaba) and preachers (Medresetül-vaizin) had been opened, to be reorganized under Medresetül-Irşad.[43]

All these reforms of the years between 1910 and 1918 were carried out without a successful genuine programme of reconciliation between modernity and Islam, despite the ceaseless efforts of Gökalp, who was a professor of sociology in one of these reformed medrese complexes. This was an experiment in cultural revolution, but without the emergence and consolidation of a viable programme. Whether a genuine cultural, ideological and scientific programme has emerged and been consolidated during the republican era is a debatable question. There have perhaps been some beginnings, experiments and innovations here and there, but only an optimist would claim there has been consolidation and establishment of synthesis, cultural autonomy and creativity.

During the First World War and the War of Independence, the reformed medreses in the Anatolian provinces seemed to disintegrate. In response to various letters demanding the restoration of the medreses, in 1921 the Grand National Assembly in Ankara issued a regulation on Islamic Medreses, Medarisi İlmiye Nizamnamesi, to be complemented the following year with another.[44] From these two regulations it becomes clear that the revolutionary government in Ankara had conceived two types of medreses: those pre-dating the Young Turk reforms, with no courses on modern subjects in the curriculum, and the reformed medreses with half modern and half traditional subjects. Clearly, this is an indication of uncertainty and/or postponement of judgment on Islam and Islamic education. As a matter of fact, in 1923 there was a serious discussion as to whether the medreses should be converted from Medreses of the Caliphate into 'Medreses of Sovereignty'.[45] One year later, it was clear that the medreses, together with the Ministry of Evkaf, the Sharia and the Caliphate, were to be abolished, and modernist–nationalist republicanism firmly established. The Unification of Education law was not only a rejection of the traditionalism of the medreses, but it also put an end to the pluralism of minority schools, missionary schools and foreign schools and thereby asserted a centralist, modernist, national educational system under the guidance of rationalism and scientism, to establish a new nation with a new identity, and a new unified morality.

The break with the past and with Islam was not absolute; the same law that abolished medreses opened the new vocational Imam–Hatip schools to train enlightened (*aydın*) imams, hatips and other religious functionaries. In the same year the Faculty of Theology, closed in 1919, was re-opened in Istanbul Darülfünun, to educate modern-Islamic, enlightened Ulema. By 1932, however, when Atatürk was experimenting 'from above' with the call to prayer and recitation of the Koran in Turkish, the Imam–Hatip schools were extinct, and in 1933 the Faculty of Theology was abolished together with the Darülfünun.[46] During the 1930s and the first half of the 1940s there were intense efforts to engrain and encode secularist nationalism in the educational system. These revolutionary attempts[47] to constitute a secular Turkish republicanism from above were to be relaxed during the second half of the 1940s along with the transition to a multi-party political system. In 1949 a Faculty of Theology in Ankara University and a number of Imam–Hatip courses in several provinces were opened, to be followed, in 1951, by the opening and proliferation of Imam–Hatip schools, as discussed above.

ISLAMIC EDUCATION IN SOME CONTEMPORARY BOOKS AND RELIGIOUS JOURNALS

In the final main section of this chapter, we shall examine the discourses on Islamic education encountered in some contemporary Islamic books and journals.[48] First we shall review five books, two of which are publications of the Directorate of Religious Affairs, the others being by faculty members of three university-level theological faculties or institutes. In all these books, Islam and modern sciences are brought together in the context of Atatürkism, the official ideology of the modern–secular Turkish nation-state. The degree of synthesis and compartmentalization[49] in the 'bringing together' of Islam and modern sciences varies from book to book and position to position. We shall then briefly review two contemporary Turkish Islamic journals, to see how they discuss Islamic education, the Ulema and Imam–Hatip school graduates.[50]

The first book, *Atatürk and Religious Education*, was written by a faculty member of the Konya Islamic Institute and published in 1982 by the Directorate of Religious Affairs.[51] In this book, which has run to a fourth edition, it is argued that the inclusion of a compulsory course on Islam in the curriculum of all elementary and secondary schools in Turkey is against neither Atatürkism nor secularism as practised in Turkey, hence the new constitution (which was then in preparation) need not make religious instruction 'elective' as in the 1961 constitution; and because an elective course on religion breeds confusion and anarchy, such a course should preferably be compulsory, but if optional it should be made elective by asking parents to say if they do *not* wish their children to take it.[52] In the book, Atatürk is quoted as saying 'Islam should be taught in schools'. With numerous other quotations from Atatürk it is argued that he believed Islam to be the last and most perfect religion and that whatever was rational, scientific and to the benefit of the people cannot be against Islam. Western thinkers are also quoted extensively, to argue that modern sciences confirm the Koran. The Koran as the word of the God cannot be contradictory with sciences that reveal the laws of God's creation. If there appear to be contradictions, they are transitory, because science has not yet given its final word on those issues.[53]

The second book, *Education and Instruction in Islam*, was written for the International Youth Year in 1985 by a retired member of the Higher Religious Council of the Directorate of Religious Affairs, with a recent second edition.[54] The message given in this book is that Islam and positive sciences are not antithetical to each other because in the period between the ninth and fourteenth centuries Islam produced institutions of higher learning where a great number of scientists, the Ulema, carried out research in the fields of astronomy, medicine, mathematics, physics, biology, geography, history, and so on. The bulk of this pamplet-size book is devoted to lists of the names of Ulema and their works in these fields.

The third book is the publication of a symposium on religious education organized in 1981, the one hundreth anniversary of Atatürk's birth.[55] There are some sixty papers in the book, on problems of Islamic education in primary schools, secondary schools, Imam–Hatip schools, Islamic institutes, faculties of theology, radio and television, mosques, Koran courses, the family, and so on. In these papers, Islamic education is discussed in relation to secularism, modern sciences, development, the formation of morally responsible personalities and psychological health. Although there are a few papers constructing arguments from a strictly secularist perspective, and some others with a strictly Islamist perspective, most of the papers are Atatürkist–secularist and Islamist. One pole of most of the arguments is represented by statements such as that 'there is no need for the secular state to provide religious education, because religious faith is a part of the private life of each individual'. The opposite pole is constituted by the existence of those Islamic movements which challenge official Islamic education and offer their own underground educational alternatives. In some of the papers these externalized oppositional boundary arguments are used against each other to justify the existence and further development of Islamic education through the institutions of the secular nation-state. On Imam–Hatip schools, for example, the arguments are constructed in such a way that their opening and proliferation do not contradict unified education (Tevhid-i Tedrisat); on the contrary, they are furthering its aims by providing consensus and homogenization against divisiveness, anarchism and terrorism.[56]

The fourth book, entitled *Introduction to Education and the Values Islam Contributes to Education*, written by the head of an Islamic Institute, is eclectic in the sense that Western sociological and psychological theories of education and Islamic Turkish theories of education are brought together in a compartmentalized

way. The only hint of going beyond compartmentalization is the
implication that Islam has always embraced science and technology, and also that modern theories of education recognize a place
for moral and religious education, hence the teaching of Islam and
modern sciences in schools does not involve a conflict.[57]

The fifth book, however, *Education in Islam, with a Comparison with the Western System of Education*, by a member of
the Faculty of Theology at Marmara University, goes beyond
eclecticism and proclaims the superiority of the Islamic conception
and practice of education.[58] After reviewing Western theories of
education, the author expresses the opinion that the West does not
have a coherent theory, whereas Islam encompasses all the
positive contributions of all Western theories of education and
goes beyond, because the Islamic conception of education,
together with information on the nature of human beings, is given
in the Koran, by Rab, the Educator, one of the names of Allah.
Hence, Islam is the knowledge and practice of education
throughout its history. What modern educators must do is to
unearth the information on human nature from the Koran and
from the books by Islamic Ulema – because the verses in the
Koran are to be interpreted on the basis of their works and also,
perhaps, on the basis of modern natural and social sciences – and
embark upon a reconstruction of Islamic educational theory and
practice. This is what the author claims to do in his 300-page
book.

A comprehensive profile of *İslam*, one of the monthly journals
of a Nakşibendi network (see Chapter 6) is given by Ayşe Güneş-
Ayata (see Chapter 11). This journal has developed a holistic
conception of Islam, by encompassing both the Sunni orthodoxy
of the centre and the Sufi–mystical inclinations of the masses at
the periphery. This manifests itself in the field of Islamic education
through equal emphasis on both the glories of medrese education
in the past and ongoing education within the Sufi orders. The
school-educated Ulema and the more inspirational shaikhs seem to
be equally central to their project of educating the masses into a
holistically-conceived Islam. Meeting the challenge of modern
sciences and technology from the point of view of Islam requires
education in both fields. Hence, in the pages of *İslam* and the
allied journal *İlim ve Sanat* (Science and Art), it is possible to read
articles by teachers from the faculties of theology in various

universities. As might be expected, the increase in numbers of Imam–Hatip schools and faculties of theology has been welcomed, defended, and also demanded, by İslam.

In the other Islamic journal, *Ribat*, whose character is described by Sencer Ayata (see Chapter 10), the attitude towards Imam–Hatip schools has not been made very explicit. However, in its call for the militant and radical mobilization of individuals and groups for jihad against non-Islamic elements within self and society, *Ribat* has been opposed to the creation of a special occupational category of religious functionaries, the *din adamı*. According to *Ribat*, the division of believers into religious functionaries and followers is a Western notion and should be totally rejected. Every believer is an educator and someone to be educated. With the immediacy of the internal as well as the external jihad, *Ribat* seems to leave tackling the challenge of modern sciences to others who have the time and energy for it.

From this brief and partial survey of Islamic books and journals in contemporary Turkey it is possible to say that little advance in resolving the problem of reconciling Islam, modernism and the nation-state has been made since the time of Ziya Gökalp. Some of the possible combinations and permutations between these three world views have only been partially explored in Turkey.

CONCLUSION

The materials surveyed in this chapter do not yet permit clear, explicit and definitive formulations. I have presented a number of tentative arguments and suggestions in earlier sections, together with the 'data'. There is one observation, however, that can be explicitly emphasized here.

During the Young Turk Medrese Reform of the 1910s, Islam had been on the defensive and seemed ready for reconciliation, as exemplified by Ziya Gökalp's venture at synthesizing Islam, modernism and nationalism. During the Kemalist revolutionary era of the Unification of Education in the 1920s and 1930s, Islam institutionally became almost extinct, though its presence continued in terms of networks and symbolic codes. The reopening of the Imam–Hatip schools in the 1950s and their expansion during the 1960s signalled its re-emergence at official institutional level.

During the 1980s there have been 376 Imam–Hatip schools, 9 Faculties of Theology, approximately 50 monthly journals and daily newspapers with a total circulation of a million, numerous Koran courses, legal and illegal, and increasing numbers of vakıfs. These are clear indications of the official as well as non-official institutional proliferation of Islam.

So it seems that Islam has been one of the beneficiaries of modernization in Turkey. It is not clear, however, whether Islam and modernization are reconciled with each other or merely co-exist in a compartmentalized way. If the latter, is it due to the consolidation of modern–secular–democratic pluralism or to the internal fragmentation of Islam into official Islam, the orthodox Sufi orders, the mystical Sufi orders, the neo-orders as offshoots of the old ones, and independent supra-order groups? It may also be that the present proliferation of Islam is transitional and that future transformations might consist of a further Islamization of the institutions of state and society, or a further consolidation of modern democratic pluralism. These are some of the questions to be answered by further research.

NOTES

1. The research on which this chapter is based has been supported by two grants from the Ford Foundation. The first was obtained in 1978 in the context of a project carried out by F. Rahman, Z. Binder, H. Atay, myself and others. The second grant has been to support a project carried out by F. Acar, A. Ayata, S. Ayata, G. Şaylan and myself. The writing of the chapter itself was one of the products of a Middle East Award-supported academic visitorship at the School of Oriental and African Studies, London and a five month sabbatical from the Middle East Technical University, Ankara.

2. A. M. Kazamias, *Education and the Quest for Modernity in Turkey*, London, Allen and Unwin, 1966, p. 189; N. Dinçer, *1913'ten Bugüne İmam-Hatip Okulları Meselesi*, İstanbul, Yağmur Yayınevi, 1974, pp. 51–64.

3. Dinçer, *1913'ten Bugüne*, pp. 66–7; F. Yavuz, *Din Eğitimi ve Toplumumuz*, Ankara, Sevinç Matbaası, 1969, pp. 63–4; State Institute of Statistics (SIS), *Statistical Yearbooks 1952–1987*, Prime Ministry, Ankara, State Institute of Statistics Publications.

4. SIS, *Statistical Yearbooks*.

5. *Third Five Year Developmental Plan*, Ankara, State Planning Organization Publications, 1973, p. 755.
6. B. Akşit, 'Imam–Hatip and other secondary schools in the context of political and cultural modernization of Turkey', *Journal of Human Sciences*, 5 (1), 1986, pp. 25–41.
7. Ibid., p. 30.
8. Idem, 'Social Change and Cleavage in a Middle-Sized Turkish City', unpublished PhD thesis, University of Chicago, 1975; idem, *Köy, Kasaba ve Kentlerde Toplumsal Değişme*, Ankara, Turhan Kitapevi, 1985. Such 'ecological correlations' do not tell us anything about the behaviour of individuals or households in the provinces. This level of analysis takes into account the characteristics of provinces or other ecological units, not of individuals. Hence the fact that a province exhibits a high Justice Party vote as well as a high rate of Imam–Hatip schooling does not mean that Justice Party voters send their children to Imam–Hatip schools. They might or they might not, but we cannot make inferences about the behaviour of individuals on the basis of ecological correlations.
9. R. B. Scott, 'Qur'an Courses in Turkey', *The Muslim World*, 61 (4), 1971, pp. 239–55.
10. Ibid. During the workshop discussions, Professor Mardin argued that the area east of Sivas has a very different cultural history: various centres in eastern and southeastern Turkey have been honeycombed with medreses that are not included in the official statistics. Said Nursi's biography indicates very clearly the existence and high degree of development of medreses and other centres of learning in Eastern Turkey; Ş. Mardin, 'Bediüzzaman Said Nursi (1873–1960): the shaping of a vocation', pp. 65–79, in J. Davis, ed., *Religious Organization and Religious Experience*, London, Academic Press, 1982.
11. During the workshop discussions, Professor Turan made the suggestion that Imam–Hatip schools might be channels of upward mobility for the marginals in semi-modernized provinces, constituting a more conservative élite integrated with the system. See also Scott, 'Qur'an courses'.
12. B. Gökçe, S. Tüzün, G. Etkin, Y. Akpınar Sökmensüer, D. Atalay and K. Gürtan, *Orta Öğretim Gençliğinin Beklenti ve Sorunları*, Ankara, Milli Eğitim Gençlik ve Spor Bakanlığı Yayınları, 1984.
13. Ibid., p. 123, annex table 8.
14. N. Berkes, *The Development of Secularism in Turkey*, Montreal, McGill University Press, 1964, p. 142.
15. Gökçe et al., *Orta Öğretim . . .*, pp. 136–7, annex tables 26 and 27.
16. Akşit, 'Imam Hatip'.
17. Ibid., pp. 33–4.
18. E. Wolf, *Europe and the People without History*, Berkeley, University of California Press, 1982.
19. A. Y. Al-Hasan and D. Hill, *Islamic Technology*, Paris, Cambridge University Press and Unesco, 1986, p. 282.

20. Wolf, *Europe*; M. Nakosteen, *History of Islamic Origins of Western Education: 800–1350*, Boulder, University of Colorado Press, 1964.
21. C. Baltacı, *XV. ve XVI. Asırlarda Osmanlı Medreseleri*, İstanbul, İrfan Matbaası, 1976; H. Atay, *Osmanlılarda Yüksek Din Eğitimi*, İstanbul, Dergah Yayınları, 1983; F. Rahman, *Islam*, New York, Doubleday, 1968; Nakosteen, *History of Islamic Origins*; S. H. Nasr, *Science and Civilization in Islam*, Cambridge, Mass., Harvard University Press, 1968; Al-Hasan and Hill, *Islamic Technology*.
22. In 1983, Şerif Mardin presented a paper entitled 'Mysticism and Science' at the Middle East Technical University, Ankara, and argued that at the time of Copernicus there were intense relationships between mysticism and science in the West, whereas in the Ottoman Empire and Turkey, Ulema scholasticism and positivist social sciences were separated from mystical sources of inspiration and became formalized and subject to protocol.
23. P. B. Berger, B. Berger, and H. Kellner, *The Homeless Mind: Modernization and Consciousness*, New York, Vintage Books, 1973; E. Gellner, *Muslim Society*, Cambridge, Cambridge University Press, 1981.
24. Berkes, *Development of Secularism*; Carter V. Findley, *Bureaucratic Reform in the Ottoman Empire: the Sublime Porte 1789–1922*, Princeton, Princeton University Press, 1980.
25. Ç. Keyder, *State and Class in Turkey: A Study in Capitalist Development*, London, Verso, 1987.
26. Berkes, *Development of Secularism*; Osman N. Ergin, *Türkiye Maarif Tarihi*, Istanbul, Osmanbey Matbaası, 1977.
27. Berkes, *Development of Secularism*; Kazamias, *Education and the Quest*; Engin, 1977; Atay, *Osmanlılarda*; D. Kandiyoti, 'Women and the Turkish state: political actors or symbolic pawns', in N. Yuval-Davis and A. Anthios, eds, *Woman–Nation–State*, London, Macmillan, 1988.
28. Ergin, 1977; İ. Tekeli, *Toplumsal Dönüşüm ve Eğitim Tarihi üzerine Konuşmalar*, Ankara, Mimarlar Odası Yayınları, 1980; B. Braude and B. Lewis, *Christians and Jews in the Ottoman Empire: The Functioning of a Plural Society*, London, Holmes and Meier, 1982.
29. B. Akşit, 'Türkiye'de Sosyolojik Araştırmalar: Bölmelenmişlikten Farklılaşma ve Çeşitlenmeye', in S. Atauz, ed., *Türkiye'de Sosyal Bilimlerin Gelişmesi*, Ankara, Türk Sosyal Bilimler Derneği Yayınları, 1986, pp. 195–232.
30. Berkes, *The Development of Secularism*, pp. 400–23; Ergin, 1977, pp. 1657–67.
31. Berkes, *The Development of Secularism*, pp. 400–10.
32. Z. Gökalp, *Turkish Nationalism and Western Civilization* (trans. and ed. with an Introduction by N. Berkes), London, Allen and Unwin, 1959; Berkes, *The Development of Secularism*; T. Parla, *The Social and Political Thought of Ziya Gökalp 1876–1974*, Leiden, Brill, 1985.
33. Gökalp, *Turkish Nationalism*, pp. 202–47.

34. Berkes, *The Development of Secularism*, pp. 400–23; Ergin, 1977, pp. 1657–67.
35. Ergin, 1977; Atay, *Osmanlılarda*. For the study of medrese reform in the years after the Young Turk Revolution, Ergin and Atay have brought many documents together and presented their own analyses. My own analyses and interpretations have mostly relied on the documents and information in their books, which have been very valuable sources for me.
36. Atay, *Osmanlılarda*, pp. 214–31.
37. Mardin, 'Bediüzzaman Saidi Nursi'.
38. Atay, *Osmanlılarda*, p. 235.
39. Ibid., pp. 233–43.
40. Ibid., pp. 237–43.
41. Ibid., pp. 244–51.
42. Ergin, 1977, p. 1276; Tekeli, *Toplumsal Dönüşüm*, pp. 84–9; Atay, *Osmanlılarda*, pp. 251–8. There are some doubts about the fate of the Faculty of Islamic Sciences in İstanbul Darülfünun. Tekeli (*Toplumsal Dönüşüm*, p. 87) seems to agree with Mehmet Ali Ayni that Islamic sciences moved out of the university with the opening of higher-level medrese in 1915, whereas Atay (*Osmanlılarda*, p. 255) agrees with Hilmi Ziya Ülken that they were purged out of the university in 1919, when İstanbul Darülfünun was reorganized. The first opinion might be true in actuality, whereas the second seems to be true in legal terms.
43. Atay, *Osmanlılarda*, pp. 260–321.
44. Ibid., pp. 322–34.
45. Ergin, 1977, pp. 1735–42; Dinçer, *1913'ten Bugüne*, pp. 20–32.
46. This is my own summary of developments in education during the 1920s and 1930s. For other accounts see Ergin, 1977; Berkes, *The Development of Secularism*; Dinçer, *1913'ten Bugüne*; Tekeli, *Toplumsal Dönüşüm*; Atay, *Osmanlılarda*.
47. This intensity of Turkish secular nationalism, together with its exclusiveness, emphasis on reason, and oppositionalism is explained by Richard and Nancy Tapper (Chapter 3 this volume) in terms of fundamentalist nationalism.
48. I shall discuss in a later work other issues, such as Islamic sciences (*ilim*) and modern sciences (*fen*), faith and reason, innovation and continuity, mystic inspiration and reason, as discussed in some contemporary books and Islamic journals. In the present chapter, illustrative examples will be given to complement the discussion of discourses in the previous two sections.
49. Gellner, *Muslim Society*; C. Geertz, *Islam Observed: Religious Development in Morocco and Indonesia*, New Haven, Yale University Press, 1968.
50. In the research project being carried out by F. Acar, A. Ayata, S. Ayata, G. Şaylan and myself, I plan to study conceptions of education, ulema, schools, convents (tekke), mosques (cami), forces of social change and continuity, Islamic sciences, modern sciences,

reason, faith, and so on in various Islamic journals in Turkey. Here only two journals are briefly reviewed.

51. A. Gürtaş, *Atatürk ve Din Eğitimi*, Ankara, Diyanet İşleri Bakanlığı Yayınları, 1982.

52. Around the time this book was published, the 'religious course' in secondary schools was made compulsory by the 12th September Administration, and the relevant sentence in the 1982 Constitution was formulated in such a way that a course on 'religion and morality culture' was to be included in the curriculum of secondary schools.

53. Epistemologically, science cannot give final and definitive answers on any issue, so there will never be a time when modern sciences and the Koran will be in contradiction. Another point to be noted is that Gürtaş seems to assume that scientific theories are 'provable', whereas modern philosophies of science start from the Popperian requirement of 'falsifiability'.

54. O. Keskioğlu, *İslamda Eğitim ve Öğretim*, Ankara, Diyanet İşleri Bakanlığı Yayınları, 1987.

55. H. Atay, N. Armaner, B. Bilgin, R. Ayas and A. Uğur, *Atatürk'ün 100. Doğum Yılında Türkiye'de 1. Din Eğitimi Semineri*, Ankara, İlahiyat Vakfı Yayınları, 1981.

56. Ibid., pp. 336–53.

57. H. Ayhan, *Eğitime Giriş ve İslamiyetin Eğitime Getirdiği Değerler*, İstanbul, Damla Yayınevi, 1982.

58. B. Bayraklı, *İslamda Eğitim, Batı Eğitim Sistemleri ile Mukayeseli*, İstanbul, Anda Dağıtım, 1983.

8

MUSLIM IDENTITY IN CHILDREN'S PICTURE-BOOKS[1]

Ayşe Saktanber

INTRODUCTION

In recent years Islam has begun to occupy an important place in political debate in Turkey. Few observers can deny that the Islamic ideologies widely articulated in Turkey today constitute themselves as an alternative to Western-oriented secular modernization.[2] The increased visibility of Islam has prompted many social scientists to study various facets of this growing ideological current. Approaches have ranged from labelling the 'new' Islam a 'resurgence' to seeing it as an obscurantist reaction to republican ideology.

Turkish social scientists have provided various explanations to account for the transformation of Islam into an active ideology. Socio-economic changes experienced between 1950 and 1980 have, according to some views, provided the conditions for such a development. It was during this period that the masses were integrated into the political and economic process and that mass education began to affect the perceptions and aspirations of a wide section of the Turkish population.[3]

The most important consequence of the spread of education was the creation of a new type of élite raised traditionally but educated in the new secular universal educational institutions.[4] According to some observers, the members of this new élite brought their cultural baggage into the political and socio-cultural

171

environment in which they were moving. Thus, it is argued, it was this élite that later became the producers and supporters of the new Islamic ideologies. Apart from their role in the formation of political cadres espousing right-wing religious ideals, this new type of élite was also quite successful in creating new channels through which these ideas could be communicated. It was these people who were and are instrumental in the formation of new generations of Islamic intellectuals and lay sympathizers.[5]

The increase in Islamic publications in recent years is a sufficient indication of the new literacy of Islam. This new literacy in effect produces its own realm of knowledge and information and expresses its own politico-religious claims at the intellectual level by using modern social vehicles.

Some social scientists, notably Mardin, claim that Islam now constitutes a 'second culture' which is in interactive relation with Islamic sources in contrast to the culture of the secular intelligentsia who draw their inspiration from the West.[6] Various Islamic movements in the modern Middle East are often evaluated. as a reaction of indigenous forces to the failure of modernizing political orders to improve the concrete conditions of life for the people.[7]

Although this argument can be applied to the Turkish case, in order to explain the specificity of the Islamic movements it has to address itself to the content of the actual demands put forward by the people themselves. The demands that these movements make of the specific social order in which they exist can be read from their ideological discourses.

If it is possible to argue that Islam has become a powerful ideology in Turkey, it is necessary to identify the elements that constitute this ideology. One way of doing this is to seek to explain how Islamic ideologies transform individuals and construct them as Muslim subjects.[8] This construction not only defines the Muslim subject as an 'ideal type' but also delineates Muslim identity within the specific social context. The construction of the historically and culturally specific Muslim subjectivity cannot be simply the function of religious institutions, but has to proceed through different channels, including the political, cultural and educational institutions of society.

In this chapter, I focus on children's literature as a way of constituting Muslim subjectivity. This area of social enquiry has received very scant attention, a strange omission given the importance attached by sociologists to the process of socialization, whether in the school, in the family, or through the media. Children's books are among the basic socializing agents which transmit social values, norms and behaviour, and Islamic values constitute no exception to this. These books provide children with the cultural definition of gender-specific appropriate behaviour, and with acceptable reasons for obeying various forms of authority. Through books, children learn how other children in different circumstances behave, think, speak and play.[9]

Children's books can be considered as part of the popular literature available to Turkish readers. As such they can be transformed into codes used for the symbolic construction of identity. In the past, popular literature, especially in the form of illustrated stories, has played an important role in defining opposed political identities. Two fictional pre-Ottoman Turkish warrior-heroes, Karaoğlan and Tarkan, symbolized left and right political identities respectively, and during the 1970s Bülent Ecevit, leader of the social-democrat Republican People's Party, became known as Karaoğlan by large sections of the population of all ages.[10] These forms of popular 'literature' are also appropriated by Islamic journals and magazines, and I argue that children's books should be considered in the same context: to the extent that they also use drawings and other visual images, they too belong to this semi-pictorial mode of communication. Illustrations not only make the books attractive for children, but they also play an important role in communicating the narrative content. Thus, the main emphasis in this chapter will be on illustrated stories.

CHILDREN'S PICTURE-BOOKS

Children's picture-books in Turkey are based on and espouse different ideologies. This diversity, which creates an element of choice among those who are exposed to it, can be interpreted as an outcome of the prevailing cultural diversity in Turkey.

In studying these books, one can identify three major categories:

traditional tales, modern children's books, and religious stories.[11] I shall not be discussing the first, which includes fairy-tales of foreign origins and tales of the Turkish folk hero Keloğlan. These tales do not speak directly to the here and now, but exhibit concepts of time and space pertaining to a different, perhaps mythical, plane of existence where past, present and future are connected. The way such stories are made to address issues related to everyday 'normal life' necessitates a different analysis from one appropriate to stories whose 'present' can be seen to correspond with that of the 'readers'.

Children's stories in the second category are modern in that their real referential contexts are contemporary Westernized ways of life. Of course they also give place to imaginative aspects of the world of children, but this is not the world of fairies and witches and queens and kings, nor is it guided by superhuman, supernatural or divine rulers. On the contrary, the realities of this world are organized according to rational and secular social values. Here a world is constituted which is thought to be specific to children. In this world, children are over-protected from the harsh aspects of life. They face neither cruelty nor inconsistency in social relations. Many of these books, written by Turkish authors, are imitations of foreign originals, in terms of style, content and illustrations. However, there are particular types of Turkish books which emphasize the role of Turkish republican ideology in the socialization of the child. Rather than encouraging children to take part in diverse social activities, they orient children towards institutions thought to be the bastions of the Turkish social order: family and school.

Religious stories for children are of different types. Although there are certain differences between them with regard to narrative form and contents, they are similar in that they are all written to convey the basic principles and moralities of Islam.

First, some are written to transmit the important historical events in the spread of Islam. They are said to be stories from the Koran, but they also focus on events after the revelation was completed. They are quasi-mythical narratives in which the Jihad of Muhammad and his disciples is recounted as well as the wars and conflicts between Muslims after his death. These stories relate the courage, self-sacrifice and wisdom of pioneering Muslims, and their adventures while trying to preserve Islam.

Here the important point is that the stories are told in an authoritative tone which tries to convey a stamp of authenticity. In other words, the events are related as they 'actually' took place. Similarly there are other quasi-mythical stories which recount the lives of prophets such as Adam and Abraham, and their campaigns and miraculous adventures on the path of true faith.

A second type of children's religious picture-books are those which are directly aimed at teaching Islamic rules and obligations and also practices of worship. Some of them are produced as a series and collected under the heading *My Religion*, with specific topics such as *Towards Religion, The Child who Searches for God, Our Prophet with Children, I am Performing Ritual Ablution, I am Performing Ritual Prayer, I am Praying*, and so on. The series ends with a book on death and how to face it as a Muslim. These books have been recommended for primary school children since 1983–4 by both the Ministry of National Education and the Directorate of Religious Affairs.[12]

In these books, religion and the basic practices and observations of religious worship are taught to childen by their parents and especially by their fathers in the home environment. Another point specific to these books is that some of them are illustrated by photographs, thus resembling the photonovel, a highly popular literary form in Turkey, in which photographs carry the narrative. These books thus bring Islam into the very home of the child, emphasizing the place of Islam in everyday life.

There are also books that deal with the duties of a Turkish Muslim child. These try to teach what their authors see as Turkish Islamic morality, which comprises, first, moral qualities such as compassion, generosity and thrift, modesty and truthfulness. These qualities also have behavioural correlates: thus a Turkish Muslim child should show respect for his mother and father, shown primarily by faithfully heeding what they say. The kind of tragedy that can befall an unruly child is depicted graphically: he might be abducted, fall into a well, cut himself with a knife, and so on. A good child is one who is kind and even-tempered, knows how to address people and desists from making fun of others. The underlying feature is restraint in word and deed: for example it is said that God gave man one mouth and two ears, so that he should talk once and listen twice. What distinguishes these books from others teaching good conduct, and makes them religious, is their constant invocation of God's name. Consequently they enjoin children to do the same, to think of God at all times and show awareness of his omni-presence.

There is, finally, a third kind of children's religious picture-book, which also has a specific author but where the narrative is conducted in the form of either fables or realistic stories. In both cases the fictional character determines the nature of the narrative. The distinguishing feature of these books is that they are neither represented as historical truth nor delineated as overtly religious books of manners. This is not even explicit in their titles, but they communicate their understanding of Islamic rules and obligations as well as values and moralities by articulating them during the course of events. In these picture-books, unity and order in life depend on the power of God, and the moral inclusiveness of the guiding principles of life is the consequence of his will. Gender socialization, the organization of the family, the formation of authority relations, and the acquisition of cultural skills and values within the school and home environments are primarily arranged in terms of religious maxims. Instead of talking about prophets and religious obligations separately, these books recreate the world as a whole according to an Islamic world view. Some of them are published by the Directorate of Religious Affairs, and some by the same publishing house that produces the religious teaching picture-books mentioned above as recommended for primary school children.

WOMEN'S SILENCE, MEN'S AUTHORITY

I shall first discuss gender differentiation among characters in religious picture-books. I focus on those books which are not overtly religious but have a strongly religious content. In these stories, gender differences are rigid and marked. Men take a more active part and are seen as engaged in a wide variety of roles and occupations. Men's role as family bread-winners is particularly emphasized. They are also the dominant figures who provide the family's communication with the outside world.

Young boys are depicted as students, apprentices, shepherds; adult men are usually teachers, imams, local landlords, tinsmiths, blacksmiths, drivers, tailors, clothsellers, coffeehouse owners, and, less frequently, civil servants, doctors, rich businessmen, and sometimes thieves, gamblers and beggars. Thus a wide variety of male identifications is covered in these stories.[13]

By contrast, females are either non-existent or described in vague terms; when they do appear they are usually passive and dependent mothers. Girls are almost completely absent. In the series *My Religion*, however, religious obligations and practices of worship are taught primarily to girls; but this teaching is of a special kind. Girls are made to understand the justice and truth of Islam by someone in authority (usually the father) rather than reaching an understanding of Islam as a result of the everyday struggle for a decent life. Since girls are not supposed to face life outside the home, it is necessary for them to be given such instruction by someone who does. Therefore it is their fathers rather than their mothers who are influential in this teaching process. Thus, in teaching the basic principles of religion the role of fathers and the father–daughter relationship are intensely emphasized. Sometimes elder brothers also take part in the process, together with their fathers. If we remember that the books in the series *My Religion* are usually made up of photographs, the absence of adult women can be ascribed to Islamic notions of modesty.

In religious stories, women in most cases stay motionless and silent, rarely making any gestures other than modest smiles and very brief occasional comments. When they appear in the series *My Religion* they sit somewhere in silence and read the Koran. When women do figure in religious stories they are often depicted as mothers worried about their sons, spending time praying for them. The only thing that a mother can give to her family apart from her services is her affection and blessing. But the reward for this self-sacrifice is a sacred place given to them by their family. Since they are respected but also dependent, they must be taken care of by their sons. The duty of respect towards mothers is regarded as self-evident. As shown in traditional folktales like *Keloğlan*, respect for the mother is an aspect of traditional Turkish culture. Keloğlan's mother is a figure whose approval and happiness are constantly sought but whose advice is rarely heeded. Dependence on the mother's goodwill is also a feature of religious stories. For instance, the importance of mothers is emphasized by the fact that no one can go on pilgrimage without obtaining their mother's permission (if she is alive); this is one of the rare fields in which mothers can exercise some authority over their sons. Predominantly, however, mothers are not disciplinarians in the family, but rather they are seen as the most important source of love and affection.

In the series *My Religion*, fathers are also shown to be very affectionate while teaching Islam to their children. With their daughters, men's facial expressions and bodily gestures are quite soft and they usually look at their daughters' faces with warm and affectionate eyes. One gets the impression that girls are such fragile creatures that their vulnerability arouses extreme caution.

Relations between spouses are also not elaborated upon. Parents are rarely shown together, they do not talk to each other, and women are not seen in encounters with other men. There is a total absence of anything that could remind the reader of sexuality. The most frequent contact that a woman has with a male is in the mother–son relationship; and mothers are inevitable figures in the lives of their sons. Moreover the significance of the mother–son relationship is indicated by the expectation that sons should make sacrifices for their mothers.

In these stories, the way women dress is always in accordance with orthodox Muslim codes, with headscarves and very simple, long-sleeved dresses. Only in the *My Religion* series do girls not cover their heads in the family environment, except when they read the Koran or go to the cemetery. However, a second type of woman is often introduced as the polar opposite of the pious Islamic mother, immediately recognizable by their different dress and behaviour. These are 'modern' women, non-believers, morally corrupt, who display all the evils of sacrilege. Perhaps because of this they are not associated with the peculiarly feminine role of motherhood. Unlike the soft, warm, devoted and dedicated Islamic women, they are selfish and ignorant. In the pictures, all their wrong-doings are defined and illustrated in great detail. The story *Masa* (The Table) is illuminating in this respect.[14]

In this story, a table witnesses a dinner party. The women and men sit around the table, eating the meal greedily, drinking alcohol and laughing loudly. Meanwhile they discuss the reasons for the scarcity of food in the world. After dinner, 'these women with polished finger-nails and cigarettes between their lips' begin to play cards, gossiping at the same time. They have feigned, artificial faces with heavy make-up, and they are bedecked with earrings, necklaces and bracelets. The husbands, who are not really any better, are kept in the background while the women's behaviour is emphasized.

Here, as in other such books, modernity and Islam are seen as divergent and incompatible world views. Modernity itself can only mean deviance from Islamic morals and values. Moreover, the story tries to underline the hypocrisy inherent in the modern intellectual who seems concerned about poverty while greedily consuming huge amounts of food. In the story, this does not escape the notice of 'the table', which seems thoroughly ashamed of all this moral corruption.

So these stories equate the good woman with the pious woman. This equation also holds for men, who are usually depicted as fathers, teachers and imams, while within the family the father is the absolute authority figure, a position occupied by teachers and imams outside the home. In fact, imams are not often mentioned and it is the teacher who usually takes the role of moral adviser. Teachers are not shown teaching their students how to read and write, or anything particular about nature and science, but rather as imposing the virtue of patriotism, and giving advice on moral issues and on being a true believer in Islam. They also teach the boys what is improper, wicked and sinful. Unlike the teachers, fathers are sometimes shown in a very angry mood, shouting at their children with scowling faces, while every member of the family obeys them.

As a concluding point, I may say that although boys are represented in more exciting and adventurous roles, and as engaged in a variety of pursuits, they do not ask for more autonomy. Compared with girls, they are more independent, active, achieving, brave and intelligent, but they are just as obedient to the authority of their male elders.

Yet not all men are good. Deviants who play cards or sit idly in coffeehouses are depicted as examples to be avoided; so are greedy and stingy men, who usually have dark and dirty faces. Respectable men are pious fathers and teachers, and conscientious sons who dedicate themselves to doing good things for the love of God. Respectable men, finally, are tender and merciful in their approach to all God's creatures.

THE ORDER OF THE WORLD: MODERNITY VERSUS ISLAM

The Islamic world view as communicated to children depicts two contrasting worlds, each of which corresponds to distinct ethical values, personality types and authority relations. The first of these, the religious world, is the one that is deliberately emphasized and explicitly advocated in these stories; it takes as its point of departure a spiritual as against what we might call a temporal world view.

In this respect, the religious stories try to communicate the idea that behind the seemingly natural or social course of events one should see an ultimate cause, that is, the work of God and his divine order and justice. This basic truth is manifest in the teachings of the Koran, and a pious Muslim who can grasp this essential point can effectively impute reason, meaning and light to an otherwise blind, meaningless and shallow world. It is only submission to the will of God and Islam that can make life intelligible, orderly and eternally beneficial for the mortal human being.

Those who properly adopt this view are true, honest, benevolent, generous and thrifty people. An important point is that these qualities are also emphasized in secular (Turkish) stories, but in them it is as a Turk that such qualities have to be cultivated. Religious stories, by contrast, show these qualities as emanating from God. People and children especially should strive to be generous, thrifty, and so on, in order to be closer to God, regardless of the sacrifice this may involve.

They may suffer because of self-sacrifice, but only in the short run, for their true belief eventually brings them prestige and prosperity. They are represented as ideal human beings who are admired by the various characters in the stories. Often the reader is implicitly instructed to follow the example of these true believers in Islam.

The second world view is thoroughly materialistic and hedonistic in nature and is adopted by those people who are unable to see the fundamental fact that the material world is temporary. They are deceived by the superficial, illusory and non-essential joys of life. The selfish, egoistic, ruthless, greedy and self-deceiving hypocrites are always punished by God for their worldly, hedonistic actions and avarice. Their punishment shows that neither material wealth nor illegitimate power can provide security and affluence in life if not backed by religious belief and conviction. These points are well illustrated in the story *Zelzele* (Earthquake),[15] which contrasts the two world views, presenting a more holistic picture of the Islamic one.

The hero is a young boy, a Junior High School student. At the age of puberty he is at a turning-point in choosing for himself a world view and a way of life; the alternatives are the materialist–hedonist and the Islamic ones. The story begins with a series of dramatic events. An earthquake shatters a small town. In the widespread panic, two men are trying to help save others, especially children. Another man, who is drunk, somehow rescues himself from the ruins of a bar; he tries to loot a jewellery shop, ignoring a little girl's cries for help. His greed for money makes him so blind that he fails to notice the collapse of a building, which proves fatal for him. His death is a tragic one, since his head is completely crushed beneath huge stone blocks. In fact, this was a cinema in which pornographic films had been shown.

The young boy manages to escape from this disaster and climbs a small hill. While thinking that his school days are over and feeling sorry for himself, to his surprise he sees that both the school. building and the mosque have remained intact, totally unaffected by the earthquake, which has completely destroyed all the other buildings in the town. Then the muezzin's voice comes from the minaret, inviting people to the mosque by praising the greatness of God: Allahu-Akbar.

All this was a dream, however, and he wakes up to discover his mother sitting just behind his bed. He tells her his dream; she wants him to stay in bed to get some sleep, but he decides to go to the mosque for the morning prayer. This time his mother gets excited and says, 'hurry, catch your father up!' The boy gets up, saying the bismillah first, and then does his ablutions to go to the mosque. On his way he sees the dark windows of the houses, with no light coming through. He thinks: 'Alas! People who live in these dark houses are so ignorant that they don't know that prayer is more valuable than sleep.'

In the mosque he realizes that the imam in his dream was the same as the imam in the mosque. He notices another man standing just behind the imam, whom he also recognizes from his dream. He learns from his father that this is the newly-appointed teacher in his school. The boy recalls the intact school and mosque and the religious men from his dream, and so thanks God for it.

The identity of the dream teacher and imam with those in real life indicates that the dream was a divine intervention, a gift bestowed upon him to show him the true way. In this way, fairies and supernatural beings in folk tales are replaced by God to help the hero choose the correct path.

ISLAMIC MORALITY

Choosing the right way, however, is only a starting point and does not immediately bring rewards. One should internalize the prescribed moral norms of Islam and act accordingly in order to be rewarded. In these books, examples of moral prescriptions are telling the truth, keeping promises, helping others and the poor, building mosques, schools and fountains for them, taking care of mothers, being kind and honest, working hard, being merciful to animals (and all kinds of creatures), respecting the blessing of God, parents and elders, fighting injustice and performing religious obligations. The fundamental moral prohibitions are deceiving others, lying, stealing, betraying a trust, inflicting physical harm on others (especially small animals), hurting others' feelings, despising others, idleness and breaking rules.

A person who does not behave according to these moral prescriptions will be disappointed regardless of age, status and wealth. He will lose prestige and self-esteem as well as material wealth, and live in misery for the rest of his life. He may even end up as a beggar. But if he repents, he may be accepted and can have another chance to be saved. If he continues to be a good person he will be rewarded by regaining his wealth and prestige. Rewards mainly take the form of acceptance as a good person, first in the eyes of God, then in the community, and then in his own eyes. Thus, a young boy will be praised by his parents and teachers, and an adult man will prosper in business life.

Although rewards are similar in kind (well-being and prestige), punishments vary in their intensity. If one intends to deceive others, one ends up being deceived oneself. Boys who kill pigeons have pangs of conscience, and so on. Sometimes this applies to natural objects as well, though symbolically. A piece of rock which despises other objects, boasting too much of its power, is shattered to pieces and becomes dust, thus being reduced to a smaller size than everything that it once had scorned. There is a one-to-one correspondence between punishment and misconduct. Punishments are neither secular nor institutional, however, but stem from the divine order of things and from the divine justice of God: neither judges, policemen nor teachers play a significant part in meting out this justice.

In some ways, the father's authority can be as significant as God's, but even if a father punishes his son physically, this punishment is not as severe as punishment by God, which can entirely determine his future. Reward by the father is shown in his approval and affection. The teacher's authority is not discussed in terms of punishment and reward: he is authoritative rather than authoritarian; the authoritarian type being very similar to the assertive parent.

Submission to the authority of the state is not a major issue. Although the school environment as represented in these stories is secular, republican ideology is largely absent, and in this sense religious stories play no part in reproducing the dominant secular ideologies of the Turkish state. Loyalty to the Turkish flag, however, is regarded as a virtue, and it is often stressed that even a child should be ready to sacrifice himself for his flag. Patriotism is mentioned in the context of the liberation from occupational forces at the end of the First World War, and references to the Turkish War of Independence are common. None the less, patriotism and loyalty to the flag are not associated with love of Atatürk and the Republic. Official state ideology does not play an influential part in the formation of authority relations. This clearly contrasts with the approach in school-centred modern stories. Cin Ali, the hero of a series of such stories, is asked what he wants to become when he grows up: he promptly replies 'Atatürk!'

A good example of the kind of choice a child has to make is often shown with regard to his friends. In modern stories, friendship is talked about in terms of intimacy, common interests, companionship, support, affection and fun. By contrast, religious stories turn friendship into a choice between competition and jealousy on the one hand and loyalty and faithfulness on the other. The child is urged to make the right choice and find good friends. Being influenced by the bad habits of friends, and being misled by a friend into morally proscribed behaviour, are shown to be the undesirable aspects of friendship. For instance, a person may want to have all the things which his friends have, and such emulation may lead him to corruption or theft. A bad friend can easily lead to drug addiction, alcohol abuse, and so on.

THE ISLAMIC ENVIRONMENT

In religious picture books, home, the school and the mosque are the three major elements of the physical and social environment. There is little naturalism. The countryside, always depicted in modern stories as a precious territory to be discovered, loved and protected, does not figure prominently in religious stories. Children's interaction with nature is emphasized only to advise them to be kind to animals and warn them not to hurt pigeons and sparrows. Besides these, they are not encouraged to observe nature. They have no animal friends; on the contrary, playing with dogs, for example, is seen as a sign of naughtiness.

The home environment is not defined in detail; everyday life at home, including family pastimes, is not taken into account. Children's relationship with their environment is restricted to a few activities such as going to school, working part-time as apprentices, doing homework, worshipping God, and sometimes, though as a bad habit, hunting animals. In real life, children play in the roads, but this is not shown in the religious stories; nor are children depicted as playing at home or in the garden. Indeed playing, alone or with friends, is not emphasized, and is only secondary to other activities. Entertainment, such as going to the cinema, the theatre, the circus, or on a picnic, having birthday parties, meeting with friends at home or outside, playing interesting games, listening to music, watching television or reading, have no place in the world of children.

Children's adaptation to the social environment is not orientated to the development of individual skills and talents. Similarly, neither general knowledge nor knowledge of specific subjects constitutes a significant part of the formal or hidden school curriculum as shown in these books. Education in school emphasizes ethical notions of honesty, patriotism and loyalty to the flag. Students wear black uniforms and white collars as is compulsory in Turkish schools. They appear neat and clean, but this is not the result of school teaching, by contrast with secular stories, where teachers are depicted as active in creating and maintaining order and cleanliness in the pupils' personal habits. In religious stories the teacher is always a man, with the moustache typical of Turkish religious people,[16] but he dresses in a modern and formal way with a suit and a necktie.

As opposed to modern stories, these religious books are not concerned with keeping children protected from the strong and extreme emotions of real life. On the contrary, as argued above, children are faced with the problems of deciding what sins or good deeds are, and of being conscious of the divine order. These stories can thus be summarized as moralistic depictions of a world full of sin, where the child should learn to save him/herself by being loyal to God and his religion.

CONCLUSION

The world view that emerges in these story books is extremely empiricist and this-worldly. The main point made in the stories is that an individual's actions are judged in this world. There is no sense in which the consequences of divine justice are postponed to the hereafter.

The child (usually a boy) is presented with generally accepted social values – goodness, intelligence, conscientiousness, obedience and dutifulness – which are nevertheless depicted as intimately connected with an Islamic way of life. Although Islam occupies a central position in the stories, one can also see efforts at defining relations between religion and society. And yet the forms of sociability advocated for children are very limited in scope. What is striking is the absence of an image of a 'happy childhood' with its implications of free time reserved for visiting parks with playmates and a relaxed and pleasurable home life. Nor is there any concern to encourage the development in the child of an inquisitive, independent, creative mind, able to acquire the skills needed to function in society. Instead, what is stressed is the importance of a 'true' essential self, capable of dedication to God and Islam. All other aspects of life are deemed to be ephemeral details. The central guiding concern of the authors of these books is to impart to the child the central concepts and categories of Islam, according to which he will learn to place all aspects of life in their correct focus. These categories define, above all, the essential qualities and hence the actions expected of men and women. Thus women, on the basis of their procreative capacities, under the guardianship of fathers and husbands, are assigned to the home, to seclusion and invisibility, where their single function will be to service others. Men, by contrast, as earthly representatives of the divine, entrusted with spreading His message and executing His will, are burdened with the organization of social life. Those whose earthly passions prevent them from comprehending the Divine Order are turned over to suffer the consequences of His wrath.

The way to control the self (*nefs*) and limit its greed is indicated in the stories by the limitation of the social environment to a few loci of interaction such as home, school and mosque. This limitation of sociability is complemented by a reduction in the number of possessions. A few austere, functional pieces of furniture and articles of clothing suffice for leading the correct life. It is suggested that only in this way can the individual hope to deal with the complexities of life and, with the guidance of God, to attain true faith as well as material and spiritual well-being.

This message is directed first and foremost to boys, since the social existence from which lessons are to be drawn belongs exclusively to men. Women are not even direct observers of this life of moral struggle. Social life for women is the execution of God's command, of which they become cognizant only through the mediation of fathers, husbands and sons.

NOTES

1. I wish to thank my friend Dr Nükhet Sirman who first read this chapter and made valuable criticisms which were extremely helpful, and also Dr Sencer Ayata, who first drew my attention to religious stories and guided me with his scholarship.
2. This point is clearly made in Michael Meeker's chapter in this volume.
3. Mardin, for instance, argues that the widening revival of Islam in

Turkey should be explained partly in terms of the economic achievements of the 1950–80 period and partly as a result of the consolidation of the universal education system of the Republic. According to this view, with a certain level of economic growth it became possible for a large section of the population to make use of educational facilities. Şerif Mardin, 'Culture and religion towards the year 2000', in *Turkey in the Year 2000*, Turkish Political Science Association, Ankara, Servinç Matbaası 1989, pp. 163–86.

4. The literature on this subject shows that this phenomenon is not specific to Turkey. Besides the above-mentioned study by Mardin, see also Michael Fischer, 'Islam and the revolt of the petit bourgeoisie', *Daedalus*, 111 (4), 1982, pp. 101–25.

5. For the impact of these new political cadres on the recent political life of Turkey, see for instance Ali Yaşar Sarıbay, 'Türkiye'de siyasal modernleşme ve Islam', *Toplum ve Bilim*, 29–30, spring–summer 1985, pp. 45–64; and also İlkay Sunar and Binnaz Toprak, 'Islam in politics: the case of Turkey', *Government and Opposition*, 18 (4), 1983, pp. 421–41.

6. Mardin, 'Culture and religion', pp. 2–3.

7. Bassam Tibi makes this point for almost all Middle Eastern societies: 'The renewed role of Islam in political and social development of the Middle East', *Middle East Journal*, 37 (1), winter 1983, pp. 3–13.

8. The theoretical concept of subject construction in ideology is one of the most important parts of the Althusserian thesis on ideology; see Louis Althusser, *Ideoloji ve İdeolojik Devlet Aygıtları*, prepared for publication by Murat Belge, Istanbul, Birikim Yayınları, 1978. Here I assume that 'the Muslim' is the subject of Islamic ideologies, where individuals are first interpellated as Muslims, i.e. Muslim subjects, before their subject construction is completed through different channels of ideological apparatuses.

9. For detailed discussions of these points, see L. J. Weitzman et al., 'Sex role socialization in picture books for preschool children', *American Journal of Sociology*, 77 (6), 1972, pp. 1125–50; S. Béraud, 'Sex role images in French children's books', *Journal of Marriage and the Family*, February 1975, pp. 194–207; R. Kulbe and J. La Voie, 'Sex role stereotyping in preschool children's picture books', *Social Psychological Quarterly*, 44 (4), 1981, pp. 369–74.

10. The impact of heroism and hero-worship in Turkish political culture is so important a topic that it should be investigated in all its aspects. Mardin's study of the cultural heritage influencing the thought of Young Ottoman modernizers of the late nineteenth century shows how military valour is an important component of the 'Little Tradition', that is, the folk tradition that forms the culture of the masses: Şerif Mardin, 'Super westernization in urban life in the Ottoman Empire in the last quarter of the nineteenth century', in Peter Benedict, Erol Tümertekin and Fatma Mansur, eds, *Turkey: Geographic and Social Perspectives*, Leiden, Brill, 1974, pp. 403–46. Accounts of various heroes' feats of courage are found both in oral

tradition and in almost all kinds of Turkish literature, including primary- and secondary-school Turkish and History textbooks. Mardin also gives a good idea of how strongly hero-worship affected the behaviour of Turkish youth at one period: 'Youth and violence in Turkey', *Archives Européennes de Sociologie*, 19, 1978, pp. 229–54.

11. Leftist organizations seem to be content with modern children's books, and do not create their own forms, catering in their publications only for children over the age of ten.

12. All the books in the series are by the same author, M. Yaşar Kandemir, and were published between 1983 and 1984: *Dinim Serisi*, Istanbul, Damla Yayınevi.

13. It is interesting to note that the first set of adult male identities can be seen to constitute the world of *esnaf*, that is, artisans, craftsmen and small traders, or in Mardin's words 'men of the bazaar'. Mardin in effect argues that it is these very people of the 'Little Tradition' who felt threatened by the erosion of their communitarian way of life: 'Super westernization', p. 431.

14. A. Efe, *Masa*, Ankara, Kandil Yayınları, n.d.

15. H. Demir, *Zelzele*, Ankara, Kandil Yayınları, n.d.

16. In the recent political history of Turkey, physical appearance has continued to be a way of showing political leanings. For men, different moustache styles were an important way of demonstrating political identification, and they were and are classified according to their appearance. See, e.g. Ayşe Çağlar, 'Greywolves as metaphor', in Andrew Finkel and Nükhet Sirman, eds, *Turkish State, Turkish Society*, London, Routledge, 1990; see also Emelie A. Olson, 'Muslim identity and secularization', *Anthropological Quarterly*, 58 (4), 1985, pp. 161–71.

9

THE NEW MUSLIM INTELLECTUALS IN THE REPUBLIC OF TURKEY

Michael E. Meeker

INTRODUCTION

During the last decade, a new kind of columnist and essayist, the 'Muslim intellectual' (*müslüman aydın*) or 'Islamist intellectual' (*islamcı aydın*) has attracted a considerable audience among Turkish believers. The term 'Islamist intellectual' is preferred by observers, while 'Muslim intellectual' is preferred by these writers themselves. For the latter, the important point is that they write as believers, not that they write from an Islamic perspective. They therefore see themselves as Muslim rather than Islamist intellectuals. I have used the term Muslim intellectual in line with an anthropological preference for categories of self-reference. However, it should also be noted that some of the writers designated as Muslim intellectuals accept this label only reluctantly, since they see it as tinged with a Westernist outlook.[1]

The Muslim intellectual is a critic of republican political and cultural institutions who calls for re-Islamization of the way of life of believers in Turkey. While he is more or less indebted to a century of Islamist criticism of Westernization, the new Muslim intellectual is very much the product of the post-1950 secular Turkish Republic. This background differentiates him from earlier Islamist thinkers in Turkey. The kind of language he uses, the literary works he cites or analyses, the stance he takes toward Westernism and secularism, together with less tangible features of his discourse, are unprecedented, even though much of his thinking falls more or less squarely within what might be called a tradition of Islamist resistance and opposition.

In general, the new Muslim intellectual in Turkey is always a writer who has published columns in newspapers, short articles in journals, or books consisting of collections of short essays. His prose is contemporary Turkish. His writings are critical and reflective. He addresses an audience whose social and educational background is similar to his own. He often appeals to personal experiences which his readers are likely to have shared, and he often attempts to reach conclusions which serve as an orientation for personal thought and action. He may pronounce on political events past or present or insist on the principle of political activism, but he does not generally speak for specific tactics, groupings, or parties. He sets himself apart from earlier Islamist thinkers by rejecting the question of how an accommodation is to be reached between Islam and the West. He rejects specifically the problem to which earlier writers devoted so much attention: how Western science and technology are to be integrated within an Islamic society. He argues instead that science and technology, as practised in the West, contradict and are therefore incompatible with Islam. More importantly, the Muslim intellectual is sensitive to any attempt to justify Islamic principles from the standpoint of a Western perspective. This, he argues, was the basic mistake of Islamist thinkers of the late nineteenth and early twentieth centuries. Out of a feeling of lowliness before the power of the West, he contends, they lost touch with the distinctiveness of an Islamic outlook as they attempted to develop Islamic versions of Western concepts and institutions.

From the blurbs on the jackets of their books, the following social portrait of the Muslim intellectual emerges. He is somewhere between thirty and fifty years old and lives in Istanbul or Ankara.[2] He was born to a family of provincial townsmen or officials and attended provincial primary and middle schools. Later, after coming to Ankara or Istanbul, he completed one or more programmes of secular higher education in Turkish universities. Following this, he became a permanent resident of Ankara or Istanbul. He knows one or more European or Middle Eastern language other than Turkish. He has had a serious, long-standing, interest in Western literature, philosophy, or social history, and there are more references in his work to Western writers and Western scholarship than to Islamic authorities or sources, although the latter are not infrequently mentioned and are sometimes discussed in detail. One suspects that this portrait also applies to the reading audience of the Muslim intellectual, save that the ages of readers extend downwards beyond thirty years, and their residences are not restricted to the metropolitan centres of Turkey.

Any further generalization about the writings or backgrounds of the various individuals known as Muslim intellectuals is more difficult:[3] some occasionally address questions with a direct bearing on doctrinal belief and practice and make frequent references to Koran and Hadith, but others rarely do so; some usually write as columnists in newspapers or publish short articles in journals, others also publish book-length studies; some have attended religious schools or institutes, others have not; some have spent one or more years in Europe or America, others have not. Like most writers in Turkey these days, they must make their living in a variety of ways other than by writing alone: one has had appointments at a fairly high level of the government. Another teaches in a private school; another is active in editing and publishing; another holds an academic appointment; another works for a private company.

The very term 'Muslim intellectual' indicates how these writers have adopted a new style and stance that has no exact precedent in the Republic. In recent decades, the term 'intellectual' (*aydın*) has implied a secular writer. The intellectual was perhaps a humanist, a rationalist, a liberal, a Marxist, a nationalist, but he was certainly not an Islamist. For Turkish secularists, then, it must seem a contradiction in terms that an individual who sees himself as debunking humanism, rationalism, liberalism, Marxism, and nationalism should be called 'intellectual'. But in fact, the term 'Muslim intellectual' is appropriate, for he writes in a conceptual and semantic field that has considerable overlap with his secular counterparts. The cultural problems he addresses, the historical incidents he cites, the stereotypes of Turkish society to which he refers, fall within the boundaries of the political and cultural discourse of the urban, educated Turkish élite of the 1960s and 1970s.

This fact explains in part why Muslim intellectuals have tended to become spokesmen for the Islamic opposition in public fora and in the mass media. They appear on panels discussing political and cultural issues ranging from art, literature and drama to politics, economy and communications, and they are interviewed or quoted by reporters of secular newspapers and weeklies. When such a reporter wants to know 'What are the Muslims thinking?' he naturally consults the Muslim intellectual who is able to represent the Muslim viewpoint, not only in language that the secularist can understand but in a way that speaks directly, even if more or less antagonistically, to him. (I would not like to leave the impression, however, that educated readers of a secularist persuasion in Turkey are generally familiar with the thinking of those individuals who have come to be known as Muslim intellectuals. Name and face recognition is one thing; actually reading their columns, articles and books is quite another. My impression is that exceedingly few readers of a secularist persuasion either know what the Muslim intellectuals are writing or understand their different orientations.)

Neither the neighbourhood imam or hoca, who may be in closer contact with the ordinary believer, nor the believing religious scholar, who may have a more perfect mastery of Islamic tradition, can play such a role, but the Muslim intellectual is more or less comfortably in his element in the public fora and mass media of Istanbul. In effect, the Muslim intellectual is a believer who is now, perhaps more than ever before in the history of the Republic, responding to the same problems and experiences as the secular intellectual.

While the Muslim intellectual is quite conscious of an overlap, he is also careful to make a distinction between himself and secular intellectuals who are in a sense his principal antagonists. He sees secular intellectuals as symptomatic of the ills of Western society, in that they base their reflections on appeals to science and reason alone, without any reference to revelation. The Latinate term 'intellectual', he points out, implies purely abstract mental capacities, as opposed to sentiments and convictions. But purely abstract mental capacities are likely to fall into vicious error if they are left unframed by religious conviction. They therefore cannot attain the truth. The Muslim intellectual accepts science and reason but only so long as their practice is guided by fear of God (*takva*) and the recognition of God's oneness (*tevhid*). This means he unequivocally rejects humanism and secularism, the cultural ambience which results from appeals to reason and science as sources of absolute truth. Accordingly, the Muslim intellectual rarely if ever refers to himself by the Turkish cognate *entelektüel*, but instead by the term *aydın*, another modern neologism whose connotation of 'enlightened' is more ambiguously linked with the West.[4]

Beyond this, the Muslim intellectual also has a sense of how his thinking has been directly influenced by contemporary conditions. He sees himself as living in a Westernized, humanistic, and secularized society. This means that he is not in the same position as the late-nineteenth-century Islamist thinker whose experience was framed by a more or less Islamic society. Thus the concerns and interests of the Muslim intellectual naturally overlap with those of his antagonists, secular intellectuals, in a way that was less typical of earlier Islamists. As a consequence, the Muslim intellectual is often in an uncomfortable position and required to perform a difficult balancing act. While he must engage secularist intellectuals on their own ground to develop a strong case for the Muslim point of view, he risks losing contact with the ordinary Muslim as he traffics in the concepts and problems of his secular counterparts. Often the ordinary Muslim, who is inclined to seal himself off from any alien social environment, sees the Muslim intellectual as similar to, rather than different from, his secular antagonist. Among more conservative believers in Turkey, the Muslim intellectual may well be denounced as 'modernist', 'radical', 'leftist', 'Khumaini-ist', or even 'Shi'ite'.

THE APPROACH

Before I review the writings of three Muslim intellectuals, however, I must say something about my approach to their work. Since the authors I discuss have all written a thousand pages or more of essays, it will not be possible to give exhaustive accounts of their thinking. I shall try instead to locate their writing within the framework of contemporary Turkish social and cultural life. To do this, I shall argue that Muslim intellectuals are responding to the 'constructedness' of social relations and personal identity in contemporary Turkish experience.

To explain what I mean by this will require a brief digression into a sociological distinction, that between society as *Gemeinschaft* and society as *Gesellschaft*. Society as *Gemeinschaft* designates a community which consists of face-to-face relationships with known persons, many of whom are related by blood or marriage. The members of the community accept a common moral convention which is more or less unquestioned, and their experience of social relations involves many occasions on which the individual is able to identify strongly with social others. Society as *Gesellschaft* designates, in contrast, organizations, associations and arrangements which are based on formal institutions, legal statuses, or passing fashion. It includes not only government, bureaucracy, army and school, but also corporations, clubs and partnerships. Society as *Gesellschaft* is based on devised contracts, legal fictions and popular fancies. It is not experienced as morally given but as subject to revision, revocation, or transition. So society as *Gemeinschaft* is experienced as enduring and constraining while society as *Gesellschaft*, which has a more or less temporary and provisional dimension, is experienced as 'constructed'. The latter is made, and can be unmade or remade.

This sociological distinction was first developed to describe social changes in nineteenth-century Europe, but it has also been used to describe similar changes that have been taking place in contemporary Third World societies. For example, social change in post-1950 Turkey, as in nineteenth-century Europe, has generally brought with it a shift in emphasis from society as *Gemeinschaft* to society as *Gesellschaft*. Not so very long ago, the identity of most individuals in Turkey was largely determined by the social positions and social constructions of their parents and the community and region in which they were born and grew up. The individual had a family and a place of origin which more or less told you everything about him. After 1950, this kind of personal identity began to be eroded by many factors. Some of the most important of these were the move of many people from provincial to metropolitan areas, the steady growth of large urban conglomerations, and the increasing numbers of people educated beyond primary and middle schools. In particular, young people who moved from provincial to metropolitan areas and acquired some higher education increasingly found themselves in a constructed social environment that had less definite normative foundations than they were accustomed to. In contrast to their experience of a given personal identity in a moral community, they were faced with choosing who to be, with whom to associate, what to think, even with choosing how to dress, what to eat, where to go and what to see, all matters that were more or less socially given in Anatolian villages and towns. Consequently, these young people were pressured to work out for themselves a new form of personal identity, one that required the ideologization of experience. As they left behind their provincial identity, which was not chosen but determined as a *fait accompli*, mental maps of social reality became all the more important to them. And because they were moving from a given to a constructed social environment, these mental maps tended to take the form of ideologies, often only tenuously related to social realities past and present. While the ideologization of identity and relationships was the means for them to regain a sense of grounded experience, this process did not simply replace their traditional social moorings. Often their experience of society as *Gesellschaft* brought with it an intimation of a void, a sense that identities and relationships were artificial and abstract and hence meaningless and inconsequential.

While this feature of contemporary Turkish experience has its direct counterparts in Europe and America, the recent Turkish case has at least three special features. First, an unusual degree of social mobility in Turkey in recent decades has led to a fairly impressive erosion of the personal ties and roots of individuals at many levels of Turkish society. This has not been a matter of rural–urban migration alone, but of a broad top-to-bottom transformation of Turkish society which has changed the very character of villages, towns and cities as social conglomerations in a relatively short period. Secondly, Turkish social traditions, somewhat more than European and much more than American social traditions, could be said to be designed to minimize the sense of 'constructedness' of social relations and personal identity. In Turkey, the importance of group loyalty and group norm resolutely casts the fictional or contractual dimensions of social relations and personal identity into the shadows. The result is a stronger tradition of *Gemeinschaft* than of *Gesellschaft*. Thus, experience of the emptiness of a 'constructed' society has been a more emphatic feature of social change in Turkey.

The third factor, however, sets the Turkish case apart altogether from both Europe and America. In contemporary Turkey, *the culture of Gesellschaft is secular and Western* while *the culture of Gemeinschaft is Islamic and Eastern.* This observation is only basically accurate rather than absolutely true; nevertheless, it pinpoints a distinctive factor in the Turkish social equation. As large numbers of individuals have moved from the environment of *Gemeinschaft* to that of *Gesellschaft* in Turkey, they not only face the loss of social moorings and the need to ideologize their identity and relationships, they are also faced with a cultural divide.

The sociological distinction just outlined has a close kinship with the analysis of Muslim intellectuals themselves. They also make the case that the Western and secular *Gesellschaft* in contemporary Turkey is artificial and abstract in comparison with the Islamic *Gemeinschaft*. Furthermore, in my interviews with them, they have acknowledged, two explicitly and one implicitly, that their own careers involved the problem of identity associated with a shift from Islamic *Gemeinschaft* to Western *Gesellschaft*. At the same time, they are very much at odds with the theory of modernization implicit in this distinction. Social scientists have usually seen the shift from *Gemeinschaft* to *Gesellschaft* as a process of social evolution, and have attempted to understand this process in Third World countries by comparisons with nineteenth-century Europe or America. In contrast, the Muslim intellectuals – and here I find the case they make a very forceful one – see Islamic civilization as basically different from Western civilization. In the former they see the contractual and fictional side of society (*Gesellschaft*) to be more perfectly rooted in moral conventions and moral solidarities (*Gemeinschaft*).

For the Muslim intellectuals, Islam is a social discourse which represents an *alternative* to the Western and secular *Gesellschaft* in contemporary Turkey, one which would be free of the emptiness and injustice that they attribute to modern society. The notion of an alternative social discourse is perhaps a unique feature of the Muslim intellectuals as writers in contemporary Turkey. They resemble in this respect the Westernists and secularists of the late Ottoman and early republican period, who were intent on the introduction not simply of new ideas but of new paradigms of thinking and behaving. To confirm this novelty on the part of the Muslim intellectuals, compare their writings with those of two recent republican ideologists who see Islam as an important factor in Turkish identity: Alparslan Türkeş and Nurettin Topçu.[5] In the work of the latter two, one finds an arid discussion of Turkish identity in terms of general concepts such as 'culture', 'nation', 'religion', 'tradition', rather than a search for a distinctive outlook and attitude through discursive or graphic practice.

I shall now turn to a brief review of three of the most prolific of the Muslim intellectuals and attempt to make an assessment of their different writing projects, all of which aim at the mobilization of Islamic discourse as an effective address of contemporary Turkish experience.

ALİ BULAÇ

Biography

Ali Bulaç was born in 1951 in the southeastern town of Mardin, where he attended primary and middle school. Later he moved to Istanbul, where he graduated from the Istanbul Higher Islamic Institute (1975) and from the Sociology section of Istanbul University's Department of Literature (1980). Of the three writers, he is the only one with a religious education. He studied for seven years in a medrese, probably before he left Mardin for Istanbul. He knows Arabic and is familiar with the classical Islamic sources.

From the middle 1970s Bulaç has been active as a writer and editor in connection with different journals, newspapers and publishing houses. He has published articles in various magazines, including *Hareket, Düşünce, Girişim, İlim ve Sanat*, and others, and has written columns in various newspapers, including *Yeni Devir, Milli Gazete*, and *Zaman*. He is also the author of a number of books, which discuss various aspects of contemporary Islam from a historical or sociological point of view.

His first book, *Concepts and Orders of Our Times*, which came out in the later 1970s,[6] can be seen as a kind of manifesto of the

Muslim intellectuals. Having sold over 40,000 copies, it must be one of the most, if not in the most successful of their publications – sales of between 10,000 and 15,000 would normally be considered a thumping success for any book, secular or religious. He has since published two other books which address contemporary issues and others which discuss aspects of the Koran and Hadith.[7] The two different types of books reflect his interest in developing an Islamic intellectual position while also addressing matters of religious belief and practice that are often the more immediate concern of ordinary Muslims.

Analysis

The appeal to Turkish youth. Ali Bulaç's writings are a good place to begin. His work illustrates how the Muslim intellectual is responding directly to the ideologization of identity among Turkish youth during the 1960s and 1970s. Bulaç tells us that he conceived his first and most successful book, *Concepts and Orders of Our Times*, during the early years of his higher education, that is, sometime in the first part of the 1970s, when he was a little over twenty years old. This was a very difficult time for any serious young man concerned with what was taking place in Turkish society. Bulaç addresses himself to the problems that he and others were facing. On the back cover of the most recent edition he writes:

> The book is written for the young generations who feel the need for understanding the cultural and social environment in which they live, especially for those students who are in the course of their lycée and higher studies, and for researching and investigating intellectuals. Its aim is to provide them with true, realistic and healthy information regarding the socio-economic orders which make up the modern world, and concepts which underlie them and give them life, and in doing so to offer criticism and open up alternative avenues of research.

In the preface, the author tells us that the book

was taught to the senior class of three different *lycées*

attended by children of three different social segments, and
their opinions regarding the book were sought out. Taking
into account the viewpoints, criticisms and proposals of
almost 300 students, the book was rewritten and at each
printing reviewed once again.[8]

In the book, Bulaç analyses what many Turkish youths held to be
the only available political alternatives: capitalism, scientific
socialism and fascism, each of which is seen as representing both a
regime and an ideology. To understand these political alternatives,
Bulaç argues, it is necessary to understand the problem of class
conflict in Western society.

Class conflict is a social ill. In the West, it has its origin in the
corrupt form of Christian spiritual authority; however, the cruelty
and injustice associated with class were enormously intensified by
the development of capitalism. In his later writings, Bulaç
presents the argument that capitalism itself has its origins in the
Protestant reaction to the illegitimate spiritual authority of the
Church. Revising the Weberian thesis here and there, he maintains
that the Protestants spiritualized the attainment of wealth so that
they might escape the authority of a corrupt priesthood. In turning
to the accumulation of power and wealth as a cure to a spiritual
ill, the Protestants multiplied rather than resolved the problems of
a sick civilization. This argument has a distinct appeal for
believers who are caught up in debate over modernist political
ideologies, since it traces the latter to features of Christianity
which have been the target of Muslim criticism since the time of
Muhammad and his Companions.

One of the by-products of the capitalist intensification of class
cruelty was the launching of colonial ventures, the result of which
was to propagate capitalism, as well as the social maladies it
engenders, to all the world. As a consequence, class has become a
focal problem of the modern age, one that is a concern of all
peoples. Scientific socialism, as regime and ideology, emerged in
the course of a search for a solution to the crisis of class conflict.
Having failed as such, scientific socialism inevitably led to social
problems even worse than those spawned by capitalism. Fascism,
like scientific socialism, was also an attempt to find a solution to
the crisis of class conflict. As regime and ideology it emerged in
underdeveloped, capitalist societies as a reaction to the threat of

scientific socialism. Because such societies were politically vulnerable and economically backward, fascism was even more
pathological than either capitalism or scientific socialism.

Thus capitalism, a highly expansive and exploitative system,
gives rise to a vicious circle of political reactions and counter-
reactions which do not alleviate but instead exacerbate the social
ills from which they arise. The result is the worldwide demoralization of society: individuals have become dissolute, family life has
disintegrated and women have been reduced to wage-labour. This
moral degeneration is accompanied by a pathological form of
foreign relations. Countries are ruthlessly pitted against one
another ideologically, politically and economically.

In the final sections of this book, Bulaç argues that Islam
provides a means for coping with these contemporary conditions.
He begins by refuting the secular stereotypes of Islam as a
mediæval religion that has been bypassed by modern life. Islam is
not traditional, conservative or reactionary. It is a religion for all
times and places which stands outside of history. Islam is itself not
implicated in the vicious circles of Western political regimes and
ideologies; it is the basis of a moral social order in which property
rights are recognized but the rich become the willing guardians of
the poor. The regeneration of the social order by a return to Islam
will have the further benefit of resolving international tensions
since these have their causes in internal conflicts within all the
world's societies.

To draw upon the resources of Islam to deal with contemporary
problems, believers will have to do more than passively embrace
Islamic beliefs and practices. They must also, Bulaç explains,
engage in a struggle which has an important mental dimension.
This is where the work of the Muslim intellectual is of
significance. Westernization has divided the community against
itself and led to a war of ideas. The result is a vast array of false
concepts which result in confusion among believers. Notions like
civilization, democracy, art, secularism, socialism, morality,
spirituality, holiness, conservatism, rightism, feudalism, feminism,
nationalism, communalism, class, science, modernity, progress,
nation, liberty, freedom, culture, tradition, backwardness, development and so on have all come from the West and are alien to an
Islamic outlook. The Muslim intellectual will subject these
concepts to systematic examination from an Islamic perspective.

When this is done, believers will be able to arrive at a proper understanding of contemporary life and to work out Islamic remedies to contemporary problems. According to Bulaç, this project was not accomplished by earlier Islamist thinkers who confronted the Western challenge. They were too often ready to incorporate Western principles and institutions into their thinking, giving them an Islamic veneer as they did so. In this way, they themselves contributed to the mental confusion which was part of Westernization, rather than enabling Muslims to resist the intrusion of foreign notions and attitudes.

In *Concepts and Orders of Our Time*, it could be said, Islam becomes one more mental map in an urban society and mass culture, one more alternative that stands alongside free market, class struggle, or national essence ideologies. However, in drawing Islam itself into the net of constructed experience, Bulaç intends to demonstrate that Islam leads the believer away from modernisms back to the truth and justice of an authentic community. The Muslim intellectual is, then, a new kind of believer who arises in response to the special challenges of contemporary life. His task is not to rework Islam so that it takes the form of yet one more modernist construction, but to show how its beliefs and practices remain a sufficient foundation for community in contemporary life.

Secular intellectual, Muslim intellectual and Muslim scholar. In his second book, *Intellectual Issues in the Islamic World*, Bulaç shifts from the analysis of ideologies and regimes to a more reflexive stance. How does the contemporary believer understand his situation and communicate it to others? How is his thinking divided from Western science and philosophy? How is it joined with Islamic belief and practice? Though the answers to these questions are prefigured in his first book, they are articulately developed and provocatively illustrated in the second.

Bulaç begins by comparing Judaism, Christianity and Islam in order to show how the principles of the oneness of God (*tevhid*) and fear of God (*takva*) endow the Muslim with a perspective quite different from that of the Jew or Christian. This allows Bulaç to draw a clear line between Muslim thought and that of its historical antagonists. In the second section of his study, he sketches how an intellectual crisis in the Islamic world followed upon the rise of the Western imperial powers. His account of the virtual collapse of Muslim thought in Turkey after the founding of the Republic is of special interest. During this period, he notes, Islam was sustained only on the level of ritual belief and practice, largely as a consequence of the efforts of provincial women who refused to countenance that their children should be raised as unbelievers. In the following section, Bulaç explains how the Muslim intellectual is participating in the revival of Muslim thought in contemporary Turkey. Here he compares the secular intellectual (*entelektüel*), the Muslim intellectual (*aydın*) and the Muslim scholar (*alım*). Both the secular and the Muslim intellectual analyse history and society out of a concern with contemporary social ills; however the two are otherwise very different. The secular intellectual is inspired by the Western image of a Prometheus who challenges divine authority, makes man the measure of everything and rises above the common people as a superman. In contrast, the Muslim intellectual is guided by a belief in the oneness of God and fear of God as he considers contemporary problems. This is where the Muslim intellectual and the Muslim scholar resemble one another. The first seeks to apply lessons of history at the front lines of contemporary experience; the second keeps secure the foundations of Muslim belief and practice through the study of the Islamic sources. Bulaç concludes his book with a case-study that exemplifies the kind of problems with which the Muslim intellectual is concerned. He discusses a family of 'progressive' and 'enlightened' concepts, such as modernism, atheism, civilization and humanism, in order to show how they are implicated in imperialism, itself a product of the ills of Western society. Because of the worldwide effects of Westernization, the mental confusion inspired by these concepts is not an affliction restricted to the Muslims, but one suffered by all the world's believing peoples, including Buddhists, Hindus and Confucians. He concludes that believers will be able to cope with contemporary problems because Islamic principles provide them with a clear insight into the true nature of contemporary life.

Intellectual Issues in the Islamic World illustrates how in the present age the work of the Muslim intellectual complements the work of the Muslim scholar. While the Muslim intellectual looks primarily to contemporary life, the Muslim scholar looks primarily to the Koran, Hadith and Sharia. Working together, they will be able to harness contemporary life to right-thinking and right-acting. The special role and task of the Muslim intellectual, a thinker and writer who was not heretofore part of the Islamic community, is thereby conceived in terms of the project which inspired *Concepts and Orders of Our Time*. The Muslim intellectual is responding to the peculiar challenge of contemporary experience, a time when believers have been misled by all manner of modernist concepts and principles. The Muslim intellectual will serve to re-connect contemporary life with Islamic belief and practice, making possible a rebirth of the Islamic community.

Bulaç's third book, *Social Change in the Islamic World*, reveals his ability to tackle very different kinds of materials, proves his intuition for appropriate polemical strategy, and offers a further poignant illustration of the character of his project. In this study, Bulaç analyses cultural, political and economic changes in the later Ottoman Empire, a period which has recently become crucial in Turkish assessment of contemporary social and cultural life. In a prelude, he reminds his readers of the intellectual potential of Islamic civilization by evoking the ascendancy of Islam over Europe during the Middle Ages. He then engages in a lengthy analysis of the travails of the latter-day Ottoman Empire, aimed at demonstrating the inadequacy of Westernist solutions for an Islamic society. In his conclusion he expresses the hope that secular intellectuals will be moved by the historical truth of the Islamist analysis he offers, and looks to the time when all intellectuals might come together to understand Islamic, Ottoman and Turkish history. Once again, Bulaç is confident that the Muslim intellectual will be able to sweep away the confusions of modernist ideologies. Just as the latter should be able to aid believers to understand contemporary experience by means of Islamic beliefs and values, so too he should be able to unravel historical and social problems which meet the most exacting standards of secular intellectuals.

From modernist ideologies to canonical belief and practice. Bulaç's argument is an attractive one for Turkish youths caught up in, but troubled by, the constructedness of modern Turkish life. Foremost among these are educated, middle-class young people in cities who are the children of conservative families with provincial backgrounds. Bulaç is telling these individuals that an aspect of their background which sets them apart from the majority of their peers offers an appropriate, if not an ascendant, response to contemporary life. In this respect, the appeal of Bulaç's studies is similar to the appeal of the writings of other Muslim intellectuals. What sets him apart is the specific way in which he sees Islam as having a place in contemporary life. In each of his three major studies, he argues that the social injustices and cultural conflicts of the modern age have their origins in the West, where they are the inevitable consequence of a corrupt form of spiritual authority. If believers re-examine contemporary life from an Islamic perspective, they will be able to dispel the confusion that has accompanied Westernization and to understand how Islamic beliefs and values provide a firm foundation for a society free from the manifold ills of modernity.

Judging from his writing alone, there seems to be a difficulty inherent in this stance. Even as he anticipates a restoration of Islamic community, Bulaç writes as an inhabitant of twentieth-century urban society and mass culture. His subject matter is modernist ideologies and regimes, how they are all of a piece even though they are none the less in conflict with one another. To make the point that Islamic beliefs and values are the basis for putting right what has gone wrong in the modern age, he is obliged to draw Islam itself into the polemical terrain of these modernist ideologies. Accordingly, his books are similar in various ways to those written by secular intellectuals. They have the character of historical monographs. Their covers feature provocative modernist representations. Their texts are equipped with footnotes, cited references, statistical summaries and bibliographical lists.

Has Bulaç underestimated the problem of modernity? Is a constructed personal identity as much the attribute of the believer as of the non-believer in the present day? If this is the case, is it not necessary for the believer to place more importance on how he will express himself than on how to escape from the condition of modernity itself? While I could not say how Bulaç might respond to these questions were they directly put to him, a passage in his second study suggests that he has not yet thought through the issues they raise. In a discussion of tradition, culture and intellectuals, Bulaç observes that a revival of artistic and literary activities is especially important for Third World peoples because of the way their colonial experiences have served to weaken their powers of imagination. However, when he considers whether believers should not begin to engage in graphic and literary experimentation, he insists that such endeavours should be postponed until concepts appropriate to contemporary life have been worked out by Muslim intellectuals. He defends this view by claiming that graphic and literary experimentation may lead believers away from reality into artificiality and abstraction, the main dangers of modern experience. Having stated a key problem – how is the contemporary Muslim to express himself? – Bulaç turns away from it. He resumes his argument that the Muslim intellectual will aid believers to work their way out of modernity back to Islamic belief and practice. But if the Muslim intellectual must rely on discursive and graphic practices firmly rooted in the modern age, how is he ever to attain the Islamic community which makes these practices unnecessary?

RASİM ÖZDENÖREN

Biography

Rasim Özdenören was born in 1940 in the southeastern town of Maraş. He attended primary and middle school in Maraş, Malatya and Tunceli. During the 1960s he graduated from Istanbul University's Law Faculty and Journalism Institute. In 1967 he joined the State Planning Organization, and in 1970 he was sent to the United States where he completed a Master's Degree in Development Economics. From 1975 he served for three years as an advisor and inspector in the Ministry of Culture. Leaving state service, he worked for two years as a writer for the newspaper *Yeni Devir*. In 1980 he returned to the civil service once again, and he is now an assistant general secretary in the State Planning Organization.

Özdenören has had a long-standing interest in literature, literary criticism and philosophy. He has been publishing articles on these topics since the early 1960s, usually in literary journals with an Islamist connection. As a writer, however, he is best known in

Turkey for his fiction. He has published a novel and five volumes of short stories.[9] Two of his stories have been adapted for television and screened by TRT, and one of the adaptations won an international prize. Here, however, our interest is in his essays on Western culture and contemporary Islam. Özdenören has recently been focusing his attention on this topic, publishing seven volumes of essays in less than three years. Some of these have been well-received, selling between 15,000 and 20,000 copies.[10] He has also published a translation of Orwell's *Animal Farm*, written plays (at least one of which was adapted for television) and been closely associated with the literary journal *Mavera*.

Analysis

Cultural differences: West versus Islam. In his later essays Özdenören has been successful in analysing distinctive features of Western culture and explaining how they are at odds with Islamic principles. He brings to this project the skills of a good story-teller and an entertaining essayist. This enables him to discuss literary, philosophical and other cultural issues in a way that can be easily grasped. With equal facility he can draw a parable from T. S. Eliot's analysis of Hamlet, Bertrand Russell's attitudes towards piety, the relationship of automobiles to pedestrians in Istanbul and America, or draw contrasts in the designs of pitchers and bowls in the West and in Turkey. But there is also something more to his accomplishment than writing skill. For many years he has taken the question of cultural identity very seriously, not only in his writing but in his personal life. It must also be kept in mind that his most recent books were written at a time when he was able to take advantage of the trail-blazing efforts of other Muslim intellectuals, such as Özel and Bulaç.

Some years ago, Özdenören published a collection of about sixty essays which had first appeared between 1962 and 1983. These essays, which are listed with the date of their original publication, exhibit an interesting evolution over this period. In his earliest pieces he is preoccupied with a feature of Western literature that he alleges to be absent from contemporary Turkish literature: this is an explicit concern with a spiritual dimension. Özdenören finds this dimension even in the work of Western authors who profess no religious convictions, but it is lacking, he maintains, in the fiction of modern Turkish authors. Fairly early, in the 1960s, he links this spiritual preoccupation of Western authors with their clear sense of cultural identity, a sense which he claims is missing from the work of the Turkish modernists. Later, after his trip to the United States in the early 1970s, he is able to articulate his perceptions of cultural difference with all the expertise of an academic sociologist or anthropologist. He begins to write persuasive essays about the character of Western culture in general, about differences in the cultural traditions of different Western countries and about the confusion of cultures in contemporary Turkey. When reading his work, I convinced myself that he must have had courses in the social sciences at some point during his education; but he tells me this is not the case. He describes instead a period of personal uncertainty in which he was struggling to understand his own confusion about his Islamic and his Turkish identity. This led him to examine critically seemingly insignificant incidents, such as newspaper headlines, street behaviour, family custom, and so on. This approach is very well exemplified by his recent book, *At Which End is the Egg to be Broken?*, in which he presents a model of Western culture and then, in a series of analyses of a wider range of Turkish and Western writers, illustrates how the problems of Western culture surface in their thinking.

In the essays written in the later 1970s, Özdenören begins to address more specifically the way in which Western culture differs from Islam. In this respect he views Islam not as a compendium of dogmatic beliefs and practices, but as a religion which inspires in the believer an active attitude and outlook.[11] Later, in the early 1980s, he begins to stereotype Western culture as the antithesis of Islamic tradition, and his analyses of Western authors and works become more disapproving than approving. While he never ceases to write pieces illustrating how Muslims can learn from Western fiction and analysis, he is more inclined to uncover contradiction, exhaustion and dead-ends in Western literature and philosophy. The theme of suicide in Western literature, for example, has been one of his special interests.

The striking feature of Özdenören's most recent work is his notion of reconstructing Islamic tradition in Turkey. Part of his efforts is clearly aimed at restoring the believer's pride and dignity in the face of the urban stereotype of him as backward, ignorant and irrational. References to a Muslim 'feeling of lowliness', which occur in the writings of most Muslim intellectuals, are especially prominent in his work – the concept of a Muslim or Turkish 'inferiority complex' (*aşağılık duygusu*) is a time-honoured one dating back to the beginnings of Westernization during the nineteenth century. According to Özdenören, the project of renewing an Islamic outlook and attitude in social life cannot be accomplished by simple dogmatic assertions of Islamic belief and practice. When the Ottomans first turned to the West they did so uncritically, with the result that there was a confusion of Western culture and Islamic tradition. This confusion has to be sorted out and understood. Contemporary Turks have to know very clearly what is Western and what is Islamic if they are to rebuild Islamic society in Turkey.

The opposing of Western and Islamic culture. Özdenören's differentiation of Western culture and Islamic tradition is based on the absence and presence of religious conviction. For the Muslim, 'fear of God' (*takva*) has a decisive effect on his thought and behaviour. At the same time, the distinctiveness of Western culture is derived from the absence of this essential Muslim attribute. In this respect, modern secular culture in the West is but the final outcome of an imperfect understanding of the relationship of God and Man, one which dates back to the corruption of scripture by Saint Paul.

Özdenören explicates numerous contrasts between Western culture and Islamic tradition by reference to 'fear of God'. For example, science, rationality and philosophy all have an important place in Islamic tradition; however, religious conviction serves as a frame within which they are developed. In the West, the absence of the frame, or its faulty formulation, means that science, rationality and philosophy all have pathological dimensions. They must always be shaped by a set of givens and are not methods which themselves lead to the truth. In Islam, revelation is given by God, but in the West man himself is the source of all values. In the West man is made the measure of all things: the result is madness and savagery. Rationality leads to absurdity. Philosophy strays into all kinds of formal intellectualisms and baseless fictions which have no intimate relationship with human experience. Science is worshipped as a source of knowledge. It is taught as dogma and ultimately leads to human destruction.

Humanism is also a direct consequence of the absence of a 'fear of God'. The West is obsessed with the virtues of heroism, the extraordinary accomplishments of the Great Man. But humanistic virtue, which involves an extreme individualism, is wild and out of control. The result is the adulation of all kinds of cruel and barbaric behaviour and accomplishments. Ungoverned by fear of God, the development of human powers has led to imperialism, colonialism and slavery on a worldwide scale. Moreover, the internal contradictions of Western culture are a clear indication of its pathological development. There is an intimation of the absurdity of life and an obsession with suicide. An extreme cultural relativism in the West lies behind its progressive demoralization and decline.

According to Özdenören, the contrast between Western culture and Islamic tradition can be seen on the gross level of differences between the histories of Western and Islamic societies. Western society is a scene of inter-class and inter-ethnic conflicts of the worst kind, an extreme ethnocentrism which views other peoples as primitive and savage, the ruthless exploitation of weak peoples in distant lands, the destruction of the environment and the development through science of monstrous weapons and techniques that threaten the destruction of humankind. In a number of essays on Western writers, Özdenören is able to show how intimation of the absurdity of life, the obsession with self-destruction, and blindness to religious sentiments and sensibility are characteristic of modern Western literature and philosophy.

While Özdenören provides many lively illustrations of how Western culture is at odds with Islamic tradition, this very project limits the extent to which he is able to develop a reflective and critical perspective on contemporary Turkey. The portrayal of Western culture as composed of fantasies and inventions, the attribution of all that is good to Islam and all that is bad to the West, the idealization of Islamic history and the vilification of Western history, are more or less prominent features of the writings of all Muslim intellectuals. However, Özdenören's ultimate dependence on such stereotypes is especially significant. He is a writer who understands very well the complexity of cultural and historical differences, and yet he finds himself –

especially in his recent work – in the grip of black and white stereotypes. Along with this, he is moving more and more to a conception of Islam in terms of Asrı Saadet, the time of Muhammad and his Companions when an ideal Islamic society was realized. Thus there are signs that he is adopting a position in which a stereotype of the West signifies all that is bad in human experience, while an ideal of an Islamic Golden Age signifies all that is good. In so far as this is the case, he is not directly addressing the issue of how an Islamic outlook and attitude are to be brought to bear on contemporary Turkish experience.

İSMET ÖZEL

Biography

İsmet Özel was born in 1944 in the central Anatolian province of Kayseri, the sixth child of a police official. He attended primary and middle school in Kastamonu, Çankırı and Ankara, and he finished lycée in Çankırı. He studied for a period at the Political Science Faculty of Ankara University, and later graduated from the French Language and Literature Faculty of Hacettepe University. He speaks and reads both French and English, and is familiar with a wide variety of Western authors. Özel is identified with the 1960s generation of Turkish poets, a group that came to be recognized as unusually innovative and accomplished, and he is now considered to be one of Turkey's outstanding poets. He began to publish his poetry in a variety of journals when he was not yet twenty years old, and from the later 1960s he was recognized as a prominent poet of a leftist persuasion. Later he began to turn to Islam. This shift is assumed by public opinion to have taken the form of a conversion from Marxism, but Özel himself, who is reluctant to discuss this period in his life, minimizes the extent to which he changed his thinking. He hints that Islam had always been of some importance to him personally, even if it has become increasingly significant, and says that he has always remained concerned with the dignity and honour of the people and with finding practical solutions to their problems. In the 1970s, he says, he had begun to conclude that there was no solution, when his turn to Islam was accompanied by a renewal of hope.

During the period from 1977 to 1979 and from 1981 to 1982, Özel wrote columns in the newspaper *Yeni Devir*, in which he explored and defended the possibility of a return to Islamic sources as a basis for coming to grips with contemporary problems. His first book of essays, *Three Problems: Technique, Civilization, Alienation*, is seen by some as a new departure in Islamist thought, and it very likely had an important influence on other writers such as Bulaç and Özdenören. In this book, Özel sets aside the issue of how Western science and technology can be integrated with Islamic belief and practice. This is one important way he and other Muslim intellectuals differ from Islamist writers of the late Ottoman and early republican periods. He insists instead that the central problem for contemporary Muslims is the reconstitution of an Islamic way of life, an objective that begins with the individual reconstituting his personal thought and practice. When an Islamic way of life is achieved, he argues, Muslims will have no difficulty in developing theoretical and practical sciences that fulfil their needs.

In recent years, half a dozen books consisting of collections of his daily newspaper columns have appeared, and he has also continued to write and publish poetry.[12] While his books are not as widely read as those of some other Muslim intellectuals – they sell between 10,000 and 15,000 copies – some authorities consider Özel to be the most original Islamist thinker of the republican period and anticipate that his views will have a lasting influence. Furthermore, he is the one Muslim intellectual who is taken seriously by believers and secularists alike. It is even likely that a sizeable number of his readers are of a secular, if not a leftist, orientation.

Analysis

The reaction to modernist ideology. Özel's turn, or return, to Islam can be understood as closely linked to his sense that the ideological alternatives of the 1960s and 1970s had come to a dead-end. In this respect, he looks to Islam for something that was missing from these ideologies, and attempts to articulate his discoveries in these essays. He does this, not by reviewing Islamic principles of belief and practice, but rather by what might be termed an Islamic discursive practice. Ironically, this makes him a more difficult writer for ordinary believers to understand than other Muslim intellectuals like Bulaç or Özdenören, but at the same time a writer whose import is more easily appreciated by secular intellectuals.

Before discussing this aspect of his work, however, some qualifications are necessary. Özel writes with a consciousness of his place in the community of believers. He has a respect for the opinions of Muslims, and he asserts the justice of their cause at all times and places without qualification. He refers with approval, either directly or indirectly, to the hard-line stereotypes which appear in the work of all the Muslim intellectuals, and he writes, like most of them, with the conviction that he stands at a crossroads of history. Like other Muslim intellectuals, one finds in his writing the same peculiar combination: a warm personal modesty before others and events that follows from the principle of recognition of God's oneness (*tevhid*), and a sense of pride and dignity, occasionally verging upon stiltedness and pomposity, that follows from a sense of being close to what is essential and unchanging in human experience. It has been suggested to me that Özel writes in the tradition of the Ottoman diplomat who felt no need to bow or defer before the West. Perhaps the stance of the Ottoman diplomat was also influenced by the two factors of a Muslim identity that I have mentioned.

On the other hand, there are features of his writing that are not to be found in the work of other Muslim intellectuals. Reading his essays, one has the impression of being able to follow the writer thinking things through on his own, fully aware that others who share his religious convictions will see the matter differently or take exception to his conclusions. Thus, his religious convictions do not free him from taking responsibility into his hands as someone who must think and act for himself; rather they enjoin it. This gives Özel's stance a fresh quality. If we were to search for his equivalent in the West, we might say that his writing is reminiscent of the early Protestants in that there is an emphasis on the conscientiousness of a believer with serious, sometimes overwhelming, moral responsibility. And indeed, he has on at least one occasion drawn a parallel between himself, as a Muslim intellectual, and Christian evangelicals. Özel makes this point in the course of a denunciation of Binnaz Toprak's characterization of himself as bearing a likeness to Christian adventists who anticipate a return to the golden age.[13]

In the final analysis, however, Özel must be seen through the lens of Turkish, if not Islamic, intellectual and religious history, a point which all Muslim intellectuals are keen to make. He is a distinguished poet who discovered in the Islamic tradition a response to contemporary experience rather than the dead principles of a mediæval dogma. Özel's move from Marxism to Islam explains in part, I think, why he was able to set aside, as a matter of secondary importance, the question of the relation of technology and science to Islamic belief and practice. The question for late-nineteenth-century Muslims was how a social tradition could be reconciled with the necessity to respond to Western modernism. A century later a Marxist poet, living in a secular urban milieu and faced with the culs-de-sac of modernist ideologies, could rediscover the active power of a tradition that existed for the most part only as passive social practices and cultural transmissions. In this respect, Özel's essays explain the appearance of the Muslim intellectual in the 1980s more satisfactorily than do the writings of Bulaç or Özdenören. When the secularist reads the latter two authors, he might sometimes wonder why intellectuals with a taste for reflection and criticism would be attracted to religious dogma. Since Özel's essays are more successful in demonstrating that what we perceive to be dogma makes possible a distinctive intellectual outlook and attitude, he enables us to understand better what inspires, but is not always realized by, the writings of other Muslim intellectuals.

The scene of Özel's writing. The aim of Özel's first book, *Three Problems: Technique, Civilization and Alienation*, is to construct a Muslim way of thinking.[14] This is achieved by critiques of the three aspects of the contemporary Western world view denoted in the book title.

Alienation is an integral part of the definition of man in the West. It is a dimension of Western humanism, the attempt to make man the focus of social and cultural life rather than to found it on divine revelation. Alienation is a problem for all peoples, but it is an unusually exaggerated phenomenon in the contemporary West.

Civilization, which is equated with culture, can be understood as the institutional elaborations which are part of complex social structures and power hierarchies. It is not peculiar to the West, but has also been a feature of the history of Muslims. In the West, however, the concept of Islamic society has been confused with Ottoman, Abbasid and Umayyad civilization. This is a mistake. Islam is not itself a civilization although it has the potential to engender one which is free of class differentiation and power hierarchy.

Technique or technology is an inevitable dimension of the material framework of our lives; in the contemporary world, however, technology is out of control. This is a consequence of the failure to accept any moral limits on technological developments and exploitation. These limits are only to be found in Islam, but they are denied in principle by Western humanism.

These arguments of *Three Problems* are the forerunners of Bulaç's *Intellectual Problems in the Islamic World* and Özdenören's *Words which Confuse our Thinking*. At the same time, Özel's work exhibits features which place it in a class apart from Bulaç and Özdenören. In his essays, the scene of writing is the writer speaking to the reader. While the reader to whom the essay is addressed remains anonymous, a sense of intimacy arises from the writer's reflection on his own experiences as he attempts to reach conclusions consistent with Islamic principles. The fact that his conclusions are not necessarily consistent with popular Muslim opinion lends the essay an atmosphere of frankness and sincerity, and on some occasions confession. The result is a distinctive discursive practice that is reminiscent of the dialectical thinking of the French intellectual but conveys none the less the peculiar Muslim atmosphere of moral concern and personal restraint.

Didacticism versus discursive practice. Many of Özel's essays seem at first to be motivated by a didactic purpose. This in itself would imply that they are a more traditional form of Islamic prose, akin to the sermon if you like. Speaking frankly to the reader, the writer raises questions about various unfounded hopes that are current among believers. He refuses to look to the state, whether the present Atatürkist state or a future state based on Islamic principles, for a solution to the problems of believers. He refuses to nourish the expectation of radical or utopian solutions, and he explicitly rejects force and terror. These are all elements of the power game of the modern ideologist. Islam is not about triumph and victory over others; it springs from personal convictions on the part of individuals. These convictions will have important political consequences because they are true. He insists on political actions and organization, but not for the purpose of revolutionary hopes, and not for the purpose of establishing regimes. He also recommends against any illusions about the future. Muslims are invariably on the side of what is right and just, but they cannot expect that the future of Turkey lies in their hands. This is a matter that will be decided, in the short run at least, by the power game. He also declines to idealize the Ottoman past and is reluctant to engage in tendentious comparisons of Western and Islamic civilizations. The problems of imperialism, exploitation, colonialism and class are not a monopoly of the West, but inevitable features of all civilizations. That is why one must not confuse Islam with civilization as Western Orientalists are wont to do. He expresses the same distrust of Turkish parliamentary democracy that one finds in the writings of other Muslim intellectuals, but he reminds his Muslim readers that they have fared better under a multi-party than a one-party regime. He discounts the popular belief that a wave of conversions is sweeping certain groups or classes in Europe or America, and he warns Turkish Muslims to look upon advice offered by Western converts with scepticism, since the latter rarely understand conditions in Turkey. He even discounts the frequent claim that the overwhelming majority of people are devout Muslims. He places the numbers of genuine believers at 6 per cent of the population, but he adds that this small proportion is a crucial one.

But should we see Özel as a thinker who is attempting to raise the level of the political maturity of Muslims by demolishing false hopes? Perhaps at one level this is the case, but the issue of authors and audiences is not one-dimensional. I would suggest that Özel, in raising questions about so many of the myths current among believers, is also diverting their attention away from dogmatic consensus and towards an active outlook and attitude. The poetry of *tevhid*, if I might be allowed to put it that way, is made possible by religious convictions even though this poetry is not itself dogma. As Özel himself remarks, his essays are sometimes presented, not in order to arrive at firm conclusions, but for the style and manner of thinking that they exhibit as well as for the occasion which they make possible between writer and reader.

Three Problems is organized as a book-length study, but it largely consists of essays which had earlier appeared as daily newspaper columns. Since then, Özel has not felt the need to organize his columns in the form of a book-length study. He has allowed them instead to appear as collected essays, unorganized by topic. In effect, then, Özel is not really the author of books. His prose has been almost always limited to the format of a 500-word newspaper column. He has recently remarked that he will no longer continue to write as an essayist, but the import of this intention is not clear.

That he has been recognized as an original Islamic thinker on the basis of such a restricted form is remarkable, but it is also possibly not accidental. His prose may take the form of brief essays because of its underlying kinship with poetry. This conclusion is consistent with points Özel has made himself about the characterization of Islamic social discourse. It involves, not a matter of a rationalizing organization and scientific demonstration, but a kind of harmony, a harmony that Turkish Muslims are privileged not so much to perpetuate as to rediscover. A kind of prose close to poetry would seem an appropriate form in which this rediscovery could be worked out.

CONCLUSION

The question of why Muslim intellectuals made their appearance in the later 1970s, and succeeded in attracting a large audience in the 1980s, is partly explained by restrictions on Islamic authors which only began to be eased in the 1970s and by the policies of 're-Islamization' which were favoured by the military authorities during the 1980s. I would suggest, however, that the Muslim intellectuals also make their appearance in the wake of a period of ideological exhaustion precisely because Islam is perceived as an alternative to the conflicting constructions of modernity. But when they speak of Islam, they do not have in mind the traditional beliefs and practices of the Turkish *Gemeinschaft*; rather, they envision an Islam that was never perfectly realized in Turkey, one that is based on divine revelation and orthodox practice, not on past customary practices in the Ottoman or any other Islamic Empire.

In this respect, the Muslim intellectuals are not unwilling urban residents yearning to return to the security of the rural town or village where there was no need to think through who one was and what one was to do. They are very much creatures of the contemporary Turkish city, like their secular counterparts. The difference is not that they do not traffic in ideology, and hence inevitably in social constructs, but rather that they have committed themselves to an Islamic outlook which aims uncompromisingly at the moral grounding of personal identity and social relations.

To understand what they are trying to achieve and the appeal of their writings, we have to recognize that the Islamic alternative of which they write is a very real one. The Islamic tradition, among many other things, embodies a powerful criticism of the mainsprings of Western civilization. In the Islamic tradition, the relationship of *Gesellschaft* to *Gemeinschaft* is conceived and instituted quite differently from how it is conceived in the Western tradition. In fact, the *Gesellschaft* of the Republic itself is on close inspection not entirely secular and Western, but has always had, and will always have, aspects that are rooted in Turkey's Islamic traditions. So the Muslim intellectuals are not writing about a blurry ideal which appears only in sacred texts rather than in the real world. They are bringing into focus an important side of Turkish political and social culture.

At the same time, this does not mean that just anyone at just any time is going to be successful in bringing Islamic tradition to bear on contemporary experience. What the Muslim intellectuals *want* to say and do is not the same as what they are *able* to say and do, given their individual capacities and circumstances.

NOTES

1. See note 4 below.
2. There are many Islamist women writers in Turkey today. I have not scanned the journals and newspapers to determine if any of them

takes the stance of the men who are identified in this chapter as Muslim intellectuals. None were brought to my attention by male writers or readers. Similarities and differences of stance between Islamist women and men writers might be a very revealing indication of the experience of believers in contemporary Turkey.

3. Here are the names that have come to my attention: Ali Bulaç, Rasim Özdenören and İsmet Özel (the three writers considered in this chapter), İlhan Kutluer, Ersin Gürdoğan, Abdurahman Dilipak and Hüseyin Hatemi. Most of these writers are mentioned by Binnaz Toprak in an article which places them in the context of the role of religion in Turkish party politics: 'Islamic intellectuals of the 1980s in Turkey', *Current Turkish Thought*, 62, Istanbul, Redhouse Yayınevi, 1987. This item is not a periodical. The Redhouse Press irregularly publishes little booklets on aspects of Turkish life. This is one of them.

4. For some Muslim intellectuals, *aydın* is just as unacceptable a term of self-reference as *entelektüel*. The modern Turkish term *aydın* is the successor to the later Ottoman term *münevver*. The latter, an Arabic cognate, signifies 'enlightened' and points at one and the same time to the traditional Islamic concept of divine enlightenment as well as to the humanistic values of the Western Enlightenment. As such, the term *münevver* is an instance of the way late Ottoman thinkers represented Western concepts in the guise of Islamic concepts. Such practices are attacked by Muslim intellectuals as having facilitated the breakdown of Islamic ideals and values during the nineteenth century.

5. Alparslan Türkeş, *Milliyetçiliğimizin Esasları*, Istanbul, Dergah Yayınları, 1975. Nurettin Topçu, *Temel Görüşler*, Istanbul, Dergah Yayınları, 1978.

6. *Çağdaş Kavramlar ve Düzenler*, Istanbul, Pınar Matbaacılık, ca. 1978, rev. 1987.

7. *İslam Dünyasında Düşünce Sorunları*, Istanbul, İnsan Yayınları, 1985; *İslam Dünyasında Toplumsal Değişme*, Istanbul, Nehir Yayıları, 1987. *Kur'an-ı Kerim'in Türkçe Anlamı*, Istanbul, Pınar Yayınları, 1983. *Kur'an ve Sünnet Üzerinde*, Istanbul, Beyan Yayınları, 1985.

8. *Çağdaş Kavramlar ve Düzenler*, p. 10.

9. The novel is *Gül Yetiştiren Adam*, Istanbul, Akabe Yayınları, 1979. *Hastalar ve Işıklar*, Istanbul, publisher unknown, 1967, *Çözülme*, Istanbul, Akabe Yayınları, 1973, *Çok Sesli Bir Ölüm*, Ankara, publisher unknown, 1974, and *Çarpılmışlar*, Ankara, publisher unknown, 1977, *Denize Açılan Kapılar*, publisher unknown, 1983.

10. The volumes of essays, most of which appeared in either *Yeni Devir* or the literary journal *Mavera*, are *İki Dünya*, 1977, *Müslümanca Düşünme Üzerinde Denemeler*, Istanbul, İnsan Yayınları, 1985, *Yaşadığımız Günler*, Istanbul, İnsan Yayınları, 1985, *Ruhun Malzemeleri*, Istanbul, Risale, 1986, *Yeniden İnanmak*, Istanbul, Nehir Yayınları, 1986, *Yumurtayı Hangi Ucundan Kırmalı*, Istanbul,

Akabe Yayınları, 1987, *Kafa Karıştıran Kelimeler*, Istanbul, İnsan Yayınları, 1987, *Çapraz İlişkiler*, Istanbul, Risale, 1987, and *Müslümanca Yaşamak*, Istanbul, Akabe Yayınları, 1988 .

11. See the recent books *Words Which Confuse Our Thinking* (*Kafa Karıştıran Kelimeler*, Istanbul, İnsan Yayınları, 1987, see above n. 10) and *Essays on Muslim Thought* (*Müslümanca Düşünme Üzerinde Denemeler*, Istanbul, İnsan Yayınları, 1985, see above n. 10).

12. Özel's poetry has been published in the following volumes: *Geceleyin Bir Koşu* (1966), *Evet, İsyan* (1969), *Cinayetler Kitabı* (1975), *Celladıma Gülümserken* (1984), publishers unknown, but see *Erbain: Kırk Yılın Şiirleri*, Istanbul, İklim Yayınları, 1987, for collected poetry. *Üç Mesele: Teknik, Medeniyet, Yabancılaşma*, Istanbul, Dergâh Yayınlari, 1978, *Şiir Okuma Kitabı* (1980), *Zor Zamanda Konuşmak*, Istanbul, Risale, 1984, *Taşları Yemek Yasak*, Istanbul, Risale, 1985, *Bakanlar ve Görenler*, Istanbul, Risale, 1985, *Faydasız Yazılar*, Istanbul, Risale, 1986, *İrtica Elden Gidiyor!*, Istanbul, İklim Yayınlari, 1986, *Surat Asmak Hakkımız*, Istanbul, Risale, 1987, *Tehdit Değil, Teklif*, Istanbul, İklim Yayınlari 1987. More recently, he has published an extended autobiographical essay, *Waldo Sen Neden Burada Değilsin?*, Istanbul, Risale, 1988.

13. 'Amaç doğruya yaklaşmaksa', *Gösteri*, October 1986, p. 31. Toprak's characterization appears in 'İki Müslüman Aydın: Ali Bulaç ve İsmet Özel', *Toplum ve Bilim*, 29–30, 1986. Toprak's reply to Özel is 'İsmet Özel'e cevap', *Gösteri*, November 1986, pp. 34–5. This is a fairly rare example of an interchange between a 'Muslim' and a 'secular' intellectual in the 'highbrow' secularist press. It is conducted with a fair degree of strong feelings.

14. In the preface to the first edition of *Uç Mesele: Teknik, Medeniyet, Yabancılaşma*, he notes that he originally thought of giving the book the title, 'Introduction to the Muslim Way of Thinking' (Müslümanca Düşünmeye Başlangıç).

Part III

ISLAMIC LITERATURE IN CONTEMPORARY TURKEY

10

TRADITIONAL SUFI ORDERS ON THE PERIPHERY:
Kadiri and Nakşibendi Islam in Konya and Trabzon

Sencer Ayata

INTRODUCTION

Three salient features of the revitalization of Islam in Turkey in the 1980s were the increase in the number of publications, especially the monthly journals, the emergence of religious networks associated with local power centres and a shift of emphasis within the Islamic movement itself in favour of traditional Sufi brotherhoods, for example the Nakşibendi.

At one point in 1987 I identified some fifty different Islamist journals on the counters of bookstores and newsagents in Ankara. The vast majority of these, especially those affiliated to the traditional Sufi orders, began publication in the early 1980s. Also striking is the fact that some of these journals are not published in Turkey's three major cities. Although monthly journals have for long been an important element of Turkish political and intellectual culture, I doubt whether any leading journal has ever been published in peripheral towns.

On the other hand, the significant role played by peripheral towns in the revitalization of Islam is a theme that has received due emphasis in the literature. One way of looking at this relationship is from the perspective of political participation; Islam, it is argued, becomes an ever more potent political force as the popular dimension of politics increases.[1] The role of the periphery is also conceptualized in ideological and organizational terms: the provincial town is seen as a highly suitable social environment for the conversion of traditional religious views into fundamentalist beliefs. The fact that the Muslim Brotherhood developed its militant base and political support in peripheral towns is shown as a case in point.[2] In relation to Turkey, Mardin makes the following comment: 'under various guises of Islamic revitalization we have encountered a thrust which comes from the provinces and the small towns which are the operational nodes of this thrust ... The periphery has set out to conquer the center.'[3]

The traditional Sufi brotherhoods are commonly identified as centres of opposition to the orthodox religion of the state and the Ulema in the Ottoman Empire. Although latterly the tarikat networks were used by Sultan Abdülhamit as communicative channels to reach the masses, to counter the political influence of opponents,[4] they were legally abolished in the early days of the Republic. A sociological account of their underground history has not yet been attempted, but we know that the enthusiasm of some tarikats has survived throughout republican history and shown a tendency to rejuvenation in the past two decades. In the 1980s, monthly journals published by the traditional tarikat circles and their various subdivisions gradually came to outnumber the Nurcu journals as well as those initiated by the independent Islamic groups. The Nakşibendi dominate both the grassroots and the national leadership of the religious Welfare Party, as they did in the case of its predecessor the National Salvation Party. More significantly, the same tarikat is powerfully represented both in parliament and in cabinet, with numerous MPs and supposedly five ministers. In the same period, the relationship between the traditional orders and various economic institutions and private enterprises has consolidated. The flow of capital from the Gulf States was used to found new banks to finance primarily investments undertaken by people in Nakşibendi circles. Another interesting example is a chain store with branches in almost every Turkish town of size. This company finds its customers among Muslim women who want to follow the latest fashions in religiously approved dress.

In this study I examine two monthly journals published by subdivisions of two leading traditional orders and in two provincial cities particularly known for the vigour of their religious activities. The Nakşibendi journal *Ribat* comes from Konya, the symbol in Turkey for religious conservatism, and the Kadiri journal *İcmal* from Trabzon in the Black Sea region, the small towns of which are commonly identified as strongholds of Islamic fundamentalism.[5]

I examine only what is in the text, to dwell on the perspective itself, to explicate the way in which religion provides an understanding of a general order of existence. The major focus will be the interpretation of the systems of significance in terms of which subjective frameworks are ordered. Of course, as Geertz maintains, uncovering an image of world-construction can also give us clues as to the programme for human conduct that is either implicitly or explicitly suggested.[6] A discussion of the possible ways in which the teachings of the Sufi orders can influence social action is attempted at the end of each section.

Underlying the Sufi vision of the cosmos is a sharp distinction between worldly and other-worldly realms, accompanied by a moral evaluation of the former as essentially negative. Denigration of the physical world and repression of material desires and interests, in short rejection of this world, constitute the central problematic in the two journals, around which other issues revolve. Strong disapproval is expressed of a wide range of Western schools of thought, presented in the two journals under the generic term 'materialism' and what is described as a materialist culture, usually identified with the self-indulgent individual who acts according to whim, that is, without taking religious standards into consideration. From this perspective, I compare the Nakşibendi and Kadiri journals in terms of how they approach, handle and elaborate this problem. One of my main conclusions is that the Nakşibendi journal lays greater emphasis on withdrawal from the material joys of life, while arguing for supremacy of and commitment to politics and political action, whereas the Kadiri approach advocates rejection of the world for the sake of attaining a higher level of moral integrity and inner spiritual perfection.

THE RADICAL ISLAM OF A NAKŞIBENDI ORDER

The journal *Ribat* has a nationwide circulation of 20,000. It began publication in late 1981; at the time of writing, six volumes had appeared, each containing twelve issues. Each 32-page issue contains some 15 articles by different authors,[7] though consecutive issues often give the reader the impression that the articles are actually written by only two or three people. The Nakşibendi leaning becomes obvious in the discussions and by the fact that the writers refer almost exclusively to Nakşibendi authorities to seek support for their arguments. However, the basic views developed in the journal, and many of its minor discourses, are different from those put forward by other strands of Nakşibendi thought in Turkey. For instance, *Ribat* adopts a line of thinking that foresees wholesale rejection of the West, including science and technology; others, while fiercely rejecting Western political and cultural infiltration, are silent about economic relations with the Western world; and still others do not even oppose Turkey joining the EEC.[8] Similarly, some leading sub-orders give active support to the ruling Motherland Party, whereas others join the opposition in siding with the religious Welfare Party. As Rahman indicates: 'in many cases a sub-order only keeps a titular affiliation with the parent order and launches itself on an entirely independent career where it may keep certain rites of the original order but adds new emphasis and sometimes introduces an entirely new orientation'.[9] Thus it would be highly misleading to take *Ribat*'s interpretation of Islam as typical of other Nakşibendi interpretations of Islam in Turkey.

Basic Assumptions about Human Nature

On the pages of *Ribat* there are repeated references to the idea that human beings are made of two components, matter and spirit. God created the universe in such a way that these two entities stay in balance. In the case of human beings, however, this balance has the propensity to get distorted. The matter component is a combination of earth and water – mud – whereas human spirit contains divine spirit. Given this, men can move in two directions, very much opposed: downwards, beneath all living creatures, to a most degrading and inferior status, and upwards to the top, to a status above that of the angels.

The degradation of man emanates from three sources. First, at the psycho-physiological level, man is a combination of flesh and animal spirit. This first level of matter is interpreted by *Ribat* as *nefs*, which relates to men's inordinate appetites. The animal spirit is always inclined to make men betray the original purpose of God's creation, which for *Ribat* is single and one-dimensional: to obey the ordinances of the Creator. The second form of matter, posing a threat to man's relations with God, is the material world itself. Important in this context are goods, property, titles and women. The material world is conceived as the prison of the spirit of God that exists in man. The third force is of a different, external order and is constituted at a more general cosmological level. This is Satan, who implements his vicious plans through the carnal mind, which in its own shrewd way attempts to challenge the truth of revelation.

Now we can move to discussion of the concrete manifestations of these evil forces in the present-day world, to see how *Ribat* actually portrays social life, social institutions and social structure. The interaction of the *nefs* and the material world has brought about what is called 'the Islam of the Ancestors' (*Atalar dini*). This is seen as some sort of half-way religion and its constituent members are half-hearted Muslims. This inherited Islam is dualist in essence: an absurd mixture of Islamic and non-Islamic traits. In terms of its values, inherited Islam is characterized as individualistic, utilitarian, rationalistic (in the sense of investing too much trust in human beings' small and feeble minds), liberal, hedonistic and above all thoroughly materialistic. Such deviation from Islam inevitably leads to a deep spiritual crisis, marked by such tendencies as egoism, anarchy, aimlessness, alienation and a loss of a sense of responsibility. In terms of personalities and everyday practices, the Islam of the Ancestors brings forth various major types, whose common feature is their half-heartedness.

One type, the *secularist-minded Muslims*, employ the standard of reason to evaluate what is right and wrong in Islam, taking only what they see as rational and contemporary. Distinct from them, and much more important, is *common man's religiosity*, or folk Islam. In this, the performance of rituals is taken seriously, though not always practised uniformly. However, common men's Islam is highly superficial and formal and full of contradictions, and it is based on a weak foundation, the self-indulgent individual. It is worldly and materialistic: providing for subsistence needs has become the first priority in people's lives. Saving money to accumulate wealth, working hard to transfer property to future generations, eating too much food, buying furniture for the home, preparing trousseaux for daughters, gazing at shop windows, going to the movies, listening to music, watching television and resting are some examples of sinful acts taken in this direction. Common man's religion also contains non-Islamic cultural traits such as family-centredness, too much love of children, love of animals and of nature, an indiscriminately friendly attitude, optimism, keeping good intentions about others, being good-humoured, and especially having a sense of humour, cracking jokes to make people laugh, caring too much for family honour, the attitude of tolerance, leaving others on their own, preaching fraternity and peace in relations with one's workmates, fellow-townsmen or fellow-countrymen.

Various contributors to the journal do admit that common people pray and fast regularly: the vast majority would at least go to Friday prayers, while many go on pilgrimage at a later stage in life. Those who prefer comfort and lust to Islam ask for God's forgiveness and repent later in life. On the other hand, many of the religious practices of the common people are superstitions or false beliefs: using the Koran to decorate walls, opening shops with prayers by the imams, reciting *mevlûds*, cooking special foods on various religious days, visiting saints' tombs and making sacrifices, veiling women improperly, practising usury in trade, offering guests luxury foods and beverages on Ramazan feasts. Common men's religion has created ambitious, acquisitive, assertive, haughty, ostentatious, self-indulgent and materialistically oriented individuals, who cannot save themselves from an ever-deepening spiritual crisis.

A third type of Religion of the Ancestors is that of *Muslims in outward appearance*, who control their passions and perform pious deeds, but only to take religion as a solitary affair. To avert trouble for themselves and their families, they compromise with or yield to the state or political authorities.

Taken altogether, the half-hearted Muslims of the Religion of the Ancestors are not to be regarded as Muslims, nor in fact as human beings. Since they are directed primarily by their desires and material interests, they constitute an internally weak and highly vulnerable mass that can easily be defeated, captivated and enslaved by the enemies of Islam: more specifically, by the material world and Satan.

The various categories considered under the generic term Religion of the Ancestors are not invented by *Ribat*'s authors. The Sufi notion of the stages of spiritual perfection can be recalled: those who do not perform at least the minimum of exoteric religious obligations (the Sharia) are commonly regarded as animals, who take not the essence but only the form of humanity. Passing through other stages, the adept gradually attains the perception of religious truth.[10] What is required is a higher endeavour towards complete submission to Islam, not merely the adoption of exoteric codes of behaviour pertaining almost exclusively to worship. In other words, aspects of religiosity such as devotion, performance of rituals, achieving subjective experience of transcendental entities, knowledge and information about religion and belief, that is, acknowledging the truth of religion, are not sufficient conditions to make one a true Muslim. What is being hinted at is a distinction between extrinsic and intrinsic religiosity: the former, seen as dependent and infantile, is essentially utilitarian and self-serving and confers safety, status, comfort and talismanic favours upon the believer, whereas the latter emphasizes commitment based on high moral purpose.[11]

The concrete shape that the material world has taken is Western culture, the two main variations of which are capitalism and communism. The Western system, the trap for half-hearted Muslims, is neither new nor original; it is only the contemporary form of ignorance; but ignorance has always prevailed and will always prevail. The Western system however appeals to Muslims by means of new idols and through new forms of associationalism (*şirk*). Property, science, technology, power, mind, various objects of pleasure and material comfort are some examples of such contemporary idols. Another specific feature of the Western system is that with it associationalism began to take an increasingly concealed form: women, children, the football team, cars, music, civic principles, political views, are all modern idols that men indirectly associate with God. Materialist Western civilization defeats the Muslims by attacking the very centre but at the same time the weakest part of their defence: the inner core, not sufficiently equipped with the defensive armour of Islamic faith.

And finally, Satan: the eternal enemy, plotting to dissociate men from God. If the material world stands for the modern economy, I think symbolically Satan here pertains to the political level: the level at which conscious plans are made and instituted through various agents with the deliberate aim of undermining the power of the Muslim world. This level has two components, one internal and the other external. The former is the 'unjust and oppressive' rule: by definition any system of government which deviates from the Sharia is, and indeed almost all systems of government in the present-day world are, unjust and oppressive, that is, the exact opposite of the Islamic state.

To analyse the nature of political, ideological and economic power in non-Islamic societies, *Ribat* adapts the symbolic frame developed by Ali Shariati.[12] Three major pillars uphold oppressive rule: Pharaoh, the despot, the tyrant, or in general the political authority and the machinery of the state; Croesus, the very rich man, the tycoon, who stands for the commanding heights of the capitalist economy; and Balaam, a man of knowledge who tries to mislead the faithful – here the reference is to education and ideology in general, and the so-called 'men of religion' of the Directorate of Religious Affairs in particular. Externally, the two major Satanic powers are the USA and the USSR, and behind them Zionism. Together, the internal and the external Satanic powers try to deceive the believers by creating false desires, expectations, aims, ideals, hopes and emotions.

This then completes our survey of the three major enemies of Islam: *nefs* – the vulnerable Religion of the Ancestors; the material world – Western civilization; and the Satanic powers – the state, the rich, the scientist, men of religion and finally the world superpowers. At this point I want to use some verses by Rumi as an illustrative metaphor: 'we human beings are like hungry and greedy birds; spread all over are hundreds and thousands of grains; the route to each grain however is full of traps and dangers'. For *Ribat*, the most treacherous and serious of the three great dangers is the greed of the bird – the nature of the human being itself, the *nefs*. Why? I think that *nefs* represents the subject, the inner core, the essence, the inside: in short, Islamic society itself. If in the past the believers had remained firm and intact, neither the Western politico-military apparatus nor the power and inducements of the capitalist economy (grains) would have proved so successful in defeating the Islamic world. In fact *Ribat* makes it clear that the dangers and traps awaiting the greedy bird, that is, the plans and operations of Satan, are not very difficult to trace and counteract.

Satan's front or the front of the infidels thus identified, we can move to a discussion of *Ribat*'s response. What is to be done about the united front of greed, grain and trap?

Withdrawal

To answer this question we need to elaborate on a philosophical assumption at the very foundation of Sufism, that has to do with the conceptualization of the relationship between this world and the next. The Sufi line of thinking may be summarized as follows: this world is only a low order and its relationship with the higher one is conceived of as contingent; this life is a necessary passage during which the soul undergoes various tests; more precisely, the world is transitional, it is an uneasy guest-house, a place of suffering for the true believer, who is sent to the world to suffer.[13] Tests, trials and suffering may involve starvation, disaster, torture and distress, and often the true believer faces such trouble under highly unfavourable conditions. Therefore the believer must have strength and knowledge of what he is doing. Both in fact are provided for him by Islam, which prepares the believer for the examination and shows him the road to success, not in this world of course, since salvation comes only in the next. Islam can thus be seen as a worldly religion only in a very specific sense: in guiding the passenger on the short trip to his ultimate destination, the Day of Judgement and the next world.

According to *Ribat*, Islam is a complete and perfect system. It is always up-to-date and is the everlasting guide of man, with a unique capacity to instruct him on every single detailed issue. Islam's first message to the believer is that suffering in this world begins with a process of withdrawal from everything connected with faithlessness, associationalism and idolatry, to seek final refuge and protection under the principle of the unity of God (*tevhid*). This in fact is essentially a battle against one's own self, a strengthening of the essence, of the inside. Therefore it is called the Great Struggle (*Cihad-ı Ekber*): this is a matter of the suppression of evil desires, and involves leaving behind all the comforts and joys of life. Conquering the carnal mind and submitting it to Islam also receive special attention. Mind and reason as human capacities can always go astray to mislead the believer: therefore, it is essential to render the mind under the full command of the superior truth of revelation.

A related idea is that of 'short duration'. One whose world is filled with the thought of death reaches the highest level in renouncing this world. He no longer plans or accumulates for the future. This in turn is based on an attitude that considers only the world to come, while seeing this world as if there were no tomorrow, that is, as a world of short duration.[14] By adopting this attitude in its extreme, *Ribat* argues for withdrawal even from the very basic aspects of daily life. The true believer should also show other-worldliness by distancing himself from property, goods and indeed any other objects of consumption. To attain this, he should realize that the world, the totality of material objects, belongs to God himself and is His blessing. Men are allowed only to use these objects and can neither save nor spend as they wish. The reader is asked to keep in mind that the flesh is buried naked; just as one leaves one's clothing behind on entering the bathroom.

The most difficult aspect of withdrawal concerns emotional ties, which are strongest in primary relations. For instance, the household head should remember that his responsibility is first to God and only then to his family. He should force (for there is use of force in Islam) those under his authority to live and practise Islam thoroughly: wife, children, sons who disobey should be rejected and sent out of the house at once. The believer should recognize that those who live Islam in society are extremely few. This requires that neighbours and relatives be approached with caution; when such people drop by for a visit, the believer should not hesitate to shut the door and send them away. In establishing relations, the principle is 'believers first'. Similarly, young men are instructed to be ready to abandon half-hearted parents when this is required by the Islamic cause.

Rejection of the dominant values, norms and customs of the people is yet another essential step to be taken in moving away from an essentially non-Islamic social order. Traditions have two major characteristics: first, they are deeply affected by Western civilization, and secondly, the common attitude of the majority is one of subordination and even deference towards Westerners. Conformity with the values and beliefs of the people will bring adoption of Western culture and ethics. A Muslim should refer to Islamic standards alone: he needs neither the opinions of others nor their rules of conduct.

Since there is no Islamic state, there is a wide discrepancy between the rules and regulations laid down by the political authority (the oppressive state) and God's order and commands. One important consequence is that being a good citizen of the state and being God's servant on earth become two incompatible objectives. The believer who remains faithful to God must also avoid relations with all existing political institutions. In this perspective democracy and political parties are modern forms of associationalism, which the true believer should abandon immediately. Moreover, withdrawal from politics should also include resignation from government jobs, for this again means taking part in repression of faithful Muslims.

The conflict between society and polity on the one hand and the Islamic way of life on the other is formulated in a vivid and striking way. If the believer chooses not to conform to society's customs and traditions, this brings shame and disgrace upon him. But breaking laws and disobeying the authorities is an offence: he becomes guilty. Here in fact is the tragic paradox: following God's order and commands and being loyal only to God (religion) brings the believer disgrace and guilt, whereas escaping from disgrace and guilt will make him sinful. Thus he knows that in present-day society it is impossible to be a good companion, a good citizen and a true believer simultaneously. Not to commit sin, the believer ought to renounce both the traditions of society and the laws of the state.

Equally important for the believer is the need to protect himself against the negative influences of non-Islamic ideas, whether religious or non-religious in character. The Muslim should know that there are in fact only two kinds of thought systems: those of human origin and those of divine origin. Liberalism, humanism, communism, positivism, democracy, etc., are all human systems which start from materialistic viewpoints and assumptions. The believer should also immunize himself against Balaam. At present, the most dangerous form is the so-called 'man of religion': the mouthpiece of the Pharaoh, the oppressor, who, with the deliberate aim of confusing the minds of the faithful, attempts to show as Islamic truth what is actually blasphemy, idolatry and associationalism. The reference is clearly to the personnel of the Directorate of Religious Affairs. *Ribat* also recommends its readers to stay away from various misleading interpretations of Islam. These are, first, the attempt to justify the truth of revelation by showing the scientific nature of the Koran (here the reference is mainly to some Nur sects): shall we say that God is wrong if a half-baked experimental scientific discovery seems to contradict the Koran? Secondly, there are the Muslim intellectuals who deny the truth and relevance of the Sunna and the traditions of the saints: if the Prophet was an example, and God sent him to interpret the verses, how can the Sunna be denied? Thirdly, the so-called Turkish–Islam synthesis is simply absurd: Islam itself is the only thesis, it needs no synthesis.

Finally, withdrawal can also assume a concrete geographical form: that is, the actual migration of believers to a place where they can live Islam fully. I will return to this in a moment.

Total withdrawal from the non-Islamic world, though difficult and painful, involves a process of purification of the believer's soul and total devotion to God. *Ribat*'s understanding of self-denial and self-mortification is sometimes taken to the extreme of living as one of the dead, with no desires or material needs. The Great Struggle, the decisive repression of inordinate appetites, desires and temptations, the struggle in one's own heart to yield to divine ordinances, is won by means of pious asceticism (*zühd*). This requires that the *zahid* (ascetic) despise the world, seeing it as only a temporary abode and giving it no value. Purging one's heart of the effects of this world brings immunity against all Satanic influences. This strength of the inner core is further consolidated by worship, which by imposing the observance of a detailed code of behaviour leaves no time for worldly preoccupations.

Retaliation

True faith can be attained as the outcome of withdrawal from, and the Great Struggle against, Satanic forces. Hence faith, withdrawal, asceticism and worship mutually reinforce each other to make the believer all the more powerful for the second stage of the Struggle. Now it needs only one more step to be taken for Islam (the guide) to take the true believer to his salvation in the next world.

The goal of withdrawal and asceticism is not an isolated religious life. On the contrary, it is retaliation, to return to the attack, to launch a second Struggle. The aim is to conquer all the areas from which the true believer has withdrawn, one by one. The target is the totality of the non-Islamic society. In the first stage the believer rejects all possibilities of compromise with the non-Islamic order, and in the second he moves to put an end to it: to wage the Lesser Struggle (*Cihad-ı Asger*) against the infidel.

The religiosity of the individual believer, individualized or privatized religion that legitimizes only the relationship between man and God, is detrimental to Islam. In other words, the believer can have no existence apart from the community which is the basis of solidarity and action. This requires that Islam should be transmitted to other people by word and letter. It is through the community that the younger generations are to be educated. The method of communication is from inside to outside, through concentric circles: one's own self, the family, relatives, fellow-villagers and townsmen, the whole world. However, the believer should be well aware of the fact that people are essentially conservative and it is very difficult to change their traditional customs and beliefs. Moreover, people know that change entails suffering, and that is what people fear.

Struggle against the infidels is the work of 'Hizbullah', the party of God. Some contribute to Hizbullah by putting people on the right path, others join with their wealth and property, and finally there is physical participation. I have already mentioned that for *Ribat* the aim of religion and of asceticism is not to achieve happiness on earth for humanity, not even for believers. Even the supposedly happiest life on earth is no more than an experience of dreadful slavery. On the other hand, there is no escape from death. Sweet, warm, beautiful and affectionate death, with all its compassion and kindness, is waiting to welcome and caress the believer with its tender touch. This is the aim of life: not just to die once, but to experience this most marvellous of all experiences a thousand times, to return a thousand times to die again, though not in a lowly or ordinary fashion but as a martyr. Once the true believer has divorced himself completely from all worldly concerns he will easily achieve this. Moreover, *Ribat* further upgrades the morale of true believers, relating how on many occasions it has been witnessed that the corpses of the martyrs do not decay and their blood always remains fresh.

The party of God then is based on the self-sacrifice of true believers at all levels. Hizbullah is further defined as a community for itself: it is conscious of its mission as a divine agent of change, and acts on behalf of a major historical epoch. The relation between the leader of the movement and the community of believers is one of total responsibility and obedience. Hizbullah is united in faith and action, and in aims and methods. The rival party is Hizbüşşeytan (the party of Satan). When this party is defeated, suffering comes to an end, and the Islamic state is established. But before that come the Greater and Lesser Struggles, which also include geographical withdrawal to retaliate. This Medina of the contemporary world (the place where the Muslim community should gather to retaliate as did the Prophet Muhammad with his companions from Mecca to Medina) is Afghanistan, and the struggle of the Afghan Mujahidin.

Islamic Radicalism

A few comments are needed, finally, on the sources of the radical tendency adopted by the journal *Ribat*. The following four dimensions seem particularly noteworthy.

First, some of the basic themes adopted by *Ribat* from Sayyid Qutb's teachings are the conception of Islam as a barrier to human indulgence, whims and desires, and the perpetuation of wants, and the idea of counterposing religion to the Western conception of the individual so as to provide the latter with a goal greater than himself. With his principle of constancy (*thabat*), Qutb was emphasizing that Islam has a core which immunizes believers against the threat of appropriation by Western values which create a state of aimlessness among Muslim people. This, as well as the more fundamental categorical distinction between man-made social systems and Islam as the only system of divine origin, is also echoed on *Ribat*'s pages: hence, when sovereignty is in human hands, the source of power also becomes human, making some people masters of others. Following Qutb, *Ribat*'s authors argue that liberation from bondage to other men and to human desires can be brought only by Islam. The legitimate use of physical force in achieving this aim is advocated by Qutb and this idea finds ready acceptance in *Ribat*.

There are important parallels between the strategy of withdrawal as put forward by *Ribat* and Qutb's formulation of a revolutionary strategy for Islam in the contemporary era: the formation of an independent and separate community of believers (*jama'a*) to act as a vanguard committee of Muslims; the notion of hijra, that is conscious separation from the prevailing order to effect a detachment from the oppressive system. The distinction between the two major combating forces as the Party of God and the Party of Satan is directly adopted from Qutb's framework. Finally, the strategy of withdrawal as a period of separation from society, for the sake of consciousness-raising, nurture and growth, is also developed from Qutb's ideas and arguments.[15]

Secondly, the journal draws heavily upon the vast stock of Nakşibendi ideas and practices. In the first place, the Great Struggle, or that essential stage during which the individual severs all his ties from existing society, to be exposed fully to radical Islamic consciousness and to give total commitment to the movement, is made possible by means of the Sufi doctrine and practice of pious asceticism. Effective withdrawal from all kinds of non-religious preoccupations is consolidated by emphasis on orthodox as well as Sufi rituals and practices, a unique feature of the Nakşibendi order. Finally, the tarikat network, which generates hierarchical relations of domination and subordination, obedience and loyalty, is an important institutional and organizational asset inherited from the past which is easily geared to the functioning of a radical militant movement. To sum up, the contribution of the Nakşibendi tradition to *Ribat*'s radical Islamic discourse is an effective combination of three fundamental notions: spiritual renewal, a detailed code of social conduct, and human companionship. This combination indicates the transformative potential of the Nakşibendi order which in terms of its dominant discourse is not fundamentally radical as such. As Eisenstadt argues, 'religions may foster new types of activities, which go beyond the original religious ethic: transformation of the original responses which may lead to the transformation of social reality'.[16]

Thirdly, in *Ribat*'s interpretation of Islam, cosmological explanations occupy only a marginal place. The ideals of total obedience and complete self-sacrifice are justified on moral and eschatological grounds: a peculiar combination of the two is used so as to legitimize other-worldliness and 'martyrdom'. Here, the direction taken by world-rejection is essentially economic. The individual stripping himself of material interests becomes an invaluable asset to be mobilized for political ends. In the words of Khomeyni, 'asceticism is not a turning away from the world but a refusal to be seduced by the concerns of materialism and hedonism'.[17] The other side of the coin, as Shepard indicates, is using other-worldly concern for the sake of this-worldly action.[18]

Ribat's dichotomous interpretation of human nature recognizes no place for intermediate statuses and situations. *Ribat* addresses mainly young students, many of whom, as we understand from the text, must be very poor. With reduced or blocked social mobility, these youngsters must be content with low-status jobs and positions, or at best they might expect a moderate degree of material comfort and social security. However, even achieving such mediocre positions may require a good deal of hard work and material suffering, as well as resort to various undesirable means – corruption, flattery, cheating, fraud, immoral consumerism. Moreover, the position to be attained may not seem at all desirable or even acceptable: an ordinary life with no intrinsic value or charm of its own. It brings with it no distinction, whereas lives that do may seem quite impossible to attain.

Hence, the reader is asked to consider two possibilities: either to mix with mud, and become mud, to look only miserable, to become the filth or the wretched of society; or alternatively to elevate himself, to distinguish himself from the ordinary, to become a hero. Although Sufism is very different from modern humanitarianism, it gives an extraordinarily high status to humanity, presenting man as perfect and as a divine product reflecting the qualities of God.[19] This notion is recurrently elaborated on *Ribat*'s pages to communicate to the reader a sense of dignity, self-worth and high self-esteem. In Islam, it is emphasized, distinction and elevation derive not from money, titles or rank, but from the degree of one's devotion to the Islamic cause. To a social environment marked by insecurity, corruption, chaos and various odds, *Ribat* tries to bring stoicism, discipline and determination. Commitment to such qualities, however, should be carried to the point of self-mortification if and where it becomes necessary. Hence, *Ribat*'s fundamental message to the reader can be summarized as follows: if you cannot afford a meaningful and decent living, why not risk an honourable death?

İCMAL: THE SPIRITUAL WORLD OF THE SAINT[20]

Many present-day Sufi orders are either influenced by or directly descend from the Kadiri order. The organizational character and mode of appeal of this order are marked by looseness and adaptability: these enabled the continuous emergence of semi-autonomous sub-orders out of the main branch, a fissiparous tendency which helped the order spread all over the world. It is also known as one of the most peaceful of the Sufi orders, distinguished by piety, charity and humanitarianism, the ethos inculcated by al-Gilani, the founder.[21]

The contract

The day of man's creation is marked by the instance that the human spirit recognizes and accepts God as the sole and ultimate possessor. Following this, the material world, including men's physical bodies, was created. The Sufi tradition takes this contract as its basic point of departure to explain the nature of the relationship between God and men and human nature itself. In order of creation, however, the human spirit did exist before the universe and human flesh came into being. At this stage the spirit was completely pure, that is, not yet mixed with matter. In its worldly existence by contrast the spirit is imprisoned: the walls of a mud cell, the body, are inserted between the spirit and its possessor. A dark curtain separates the two from each other. The curtain, defined as everything except God, includes the world, the flesh and the realities of life. The aim of creation is to return to God with a soul as pure as the original spirit, and to show real subordination to God as prescribed by the Koran, the Sunna, the traditions of the great Imams and finally the Sufi way. The two polar opposite states of purification and pollution cannot however be known or predicted, since man can move in both directions. Thus human nature is conceived as dynamic, and hence the fate of each individual is problematical.

Humanity is the quintessence of the universe: the material world, including all living things, is created by God only to serve the various needs of human beings. It is of its own kind and therefore not subject to the laws that other creatures are. Thus, whereas the various objects in nature stand in a state of perfect balance, incessant contradictions and a continuous state of disequilibrium pertain to human nature. The in-built tension is between man's inordinate desires (the *nefs* again) and the divine spirit. *İcmal*'s Sufism recognizes free will as well as predetermination. God endowed human beings with a power to reason, and the human mind is taken under the protection of revelation. Man must know that he is not his own creator, and his reason and effort are not sufficient to overcome the deep-rooted problems embedded in his nature. Hence, reason and free will are of use only to the extent that they lead man to submit to God. Since man is naturally good, he is always inclined to act in this direction, but evil influences that misdirect him are also powerful.

The dark curtain

The world, which attracts the self-indulgent individual, stands on the three major pillars of women, children and property. The *nefs*, acting as Satan's agent, moves man away from divinity. The *nefs* has three evil qualities: bestial – lust, pleasure, joy, illicit sex, gluttony and greed; predatory – wildness, outrage, anger, grudge, oppression and aggression; and Satanic – cheating, fraud, haughtiness, pride, envy, lying, disloyalty, treachery and hypocrisy. *Nefs* in this sense then is a combination of uncontrolled desires and the carnal mind. It enslaves man by passions, worldly interests and corruption.

However, if properly controlled, the instinctive drives act as the prime mover of life, and without them all activity would cease. World rejection is not as powerful a message in *İcmal* as in *Ribat*. On the contrary, establishing the right balance between this world and the next, between matter and spirit, is posited as the highest value to be attained. As Kinberg indicates, since total rejection of the material world is not possible even for the most extreme ascetic, his commitment is inevitably one of compromise and not desertion. In simple terms, this amounts to living without giving much importance to the physical world: ideally, thinking very little of it, the *zahid* takes only a sufficiency of the world.[22] What is essential here is abstinence from the superfluous. *İcmal*'s emphasis is less on physical asceticism and more on maintaining a high standard of religious morality.

Secondly, *İcmal*'s criticism of the *nefs* and the world is less universalistic and abstract and more particularistic, concrete and historical. What the journal identifies as modern forms of blasphemy, idolatry and associationalism are elaborated as historically specific categories.

Critique of the Western system

İcmal treats Western civilization as a historical product in the sense that its genesis and development mark the disappearance of various institutions and structures and their replacement by new ones. The two major institutions considered in this context are feudalism and Christianity. Each a despot in his own right, feudal landlords exploited and tortured people under arbitrary rule, whereas Western Christianity was a distorted religion very different from the original form. Christian religious courts were instruments of repression and torture. Finally, the religious institutions actually took part in the economic exploitation of people, so that members of the Church led extravagant lives amidst widespread misery and poverty of the people.

At this stage, Islamic civilization was in its heyday. Europe eventually turned to the East to emulate its success and reap its fruits: scientific method, Islamic principles of justice, liberty and equality were all borrowed, one after the other. Then feudalism and Christianity were destroyed in four major stages. The Renaissance attacked religion, to replace it with the ideology of material progress, while the Reform movement skimmed off the last remnants of divinity from Christianity. The French Revolution consolidated the power and position of all modern irreligious institutions. Finally, the Industrial Revolution gave rise to the two dreadful ideologies of Comtean positivism and Darwinian evolutionism.

However, Western people were to fall prey to a new form of tyranny. The reason was that the West borrowed from the East only the form and not the essence of civilization, which was nothing other than Islam. Eventually the vacuum was filled by materialism. This term is used generically so as to cover a wide variety of Western philosophical schools. The vantage point of materialism is to take sensual experience as the ultimate basis of knowledge and to recognize no reality other than the material. The universe is composed of matter in its various physical and chemical states. Matter is supposed to exist as objective reality that can be seen and studied as independent from spiritual essence. Pre-empted of any notion of divinity, however, what is dissociated as objective reality reveals itself as a state of chaos that operates in the absence of an Initial Cause, or a well-defined aim. Materialism focuses on particles of matter and their isolated relationships with each other, but the aim of genuine science ought to be the explication of the masterly work of God who unites the infinite number of particles in an intricate, perfect and orderly fashion.

Comtean positivism rests on a denial of the role and importance of religion in favour of a narrow-minded conceptualization of science, while its Durkheimiam version elevates society and social change to the level of God, making these the most important contemporary idols. According to Durkheim, society has a collective conscience – a spirit – which, acting as God, distinguishes between right and wrong. Since humanity comes before society, however, this formulation rules out not only divine but also human will.

According to *İcmal*, Darwin's theory of evolution is a deliberate attempt to reduce man to the status of an animal. Freudian psychology serves exactly the same purpose, for there is hardly any difference between an animal and an aggressive sex maniac motivated solely by his instincts. Finally, there is Marxism, which reduces human life to economic motives. Man is conceived as a digestive system, taking in food, consuming part of it and defecating the rest. Hence human worth is esteemed according to the criterion of contribution to production, that is, to the digestive system. As materialistic premises were gradually adopted by Europeans, animal instincts began to dominate human qualities. The emergent social system was fundamentally oriented to the satisfaction of man's untamed appetites.

Capitalism as a social and economic system is based on the deification of money, property and prosperity. The logic of competition is that one should keep the most for oneself in order not to be dominated by others. The absence of moral rules to restrain the animal ego in man is an outstanding feature of capitalism. This keeps stimulating the drive to accumulate and consume. Under capitalism, wisdom refers to possession of more property. Capitalism works according to the principle of satisfaction of the unlimited desires of greedy individuals. Therefore the major idol that this system introduces on the historical stage is the individual ego.

At the cultural level, capitalism consolidates the hegemony of the *nefs*, which dominates and enslaves man. The capitalist system tries to make men forget death and the other world by bringing heaven down to earth through increased material prosperity. This, however, is suicidal, since accumulation of material wealth signifies the increased alienation of man from himself. Man is actually searching for himself, not for any external object of discovery. Under capitalism he is increasingly oriented to the market to look for what he has lost. The resultant anarchy, the fetishism of sexuality and reason, political oppression, the reduction of sublime values to utilitarian standards and the virtual absence of moral principles in everyday conduct have nothing to do with the extension of human rights and freedom as is often argued.

At this point, *İcmal* argues a relationship between a particular civilization and a personality type: the corrupt capitalist system and mentally sick Western man. The increase in property and material prosperity made Western man ever more greedy and insatiable. Having no higher aims or ideals, he is totally bewildered and lost. Moreover, the ethic of competition which pervades all aspects of life imposes enormous strain on the individual: confusion, anxiety, panic, exhaustion and stress. Under all these negative influences, the psycho-space of Western man has turned into a battlefield. A deep spiritual crisis, firmly grounded at the very roots of this civilization, is leading to its collapse. Western civilization is producing ever-increasing numbers of mentally sick people and as a result the whole society has become a huge mental hospital. This system is now being exported by the West to Islamic countries under the guise of world system and world culture.

Although economic exploitation is an integral part of it, Western imperialism is primarily a cultural phenomenon. Cultural invasion proceeds in two main directions: in the first place, as the spread of a hedonistic culture which saps the internal strength of Eastern societies; secondly, the Western ideological propaganda machine created a severe identity crisis among Muslims, for example by presenting Islam as an obstructionist force inimical to the growth and spread of modern science and technology. Similarly, changes were introduced in the educational system to eliminate the Islamic men of wisdom and profound knowledge, while a new intelligentsia was implanted to defend Western interests and spread Western views and values.

The Islamic response

Whereas *Ribat* limits the boundaries of the *nefs* with inordinate appetites, *İcmal* recognizes other stages. The difference is one of emphasis, for the whole idea of the classification of stages involved in the repression of the *nefs* is part of traditional Sufi teaching. The first stage in this hierarchical ordering is a *nefs* dominated totally by animal instincts. At the second stage, the person can distinguish what is right and what is wrong for Islam; yet, he is unstable and unpredictable, moving between the two extremes of repentance and non-conformity. In the third stage, observance of religious obligations is almost perfect, and the heart begins to wonder at the secrets of the other world. Moving up to the further stages involves lifting the dark curtain and attaining true faith, the gnostic *haqiqa* and *ma'rifa*. In this endeavour, however, personal effort remains insufficient, since these can be achieved only under special spiritual guidance.

The emphasis on control of desires is, according to *İcmal*, what distinguishes Islam from systems of thought which assume that human needs are unlimited. Once this assumption is made, all human activity becomes oriented to the satisfaction of needs and leads to a social system marked by the anarchy of endless wants. In stark contrast, Islam makes a first-order distinction between wants and needs, asserting that only the former are unlimited. Even if we suppose that needs are unlimited, we have to recognize that they cannot be satisfied in this world, which is itself finite. According to Islam, man is created to do what is expected of him, and religion provides the individual human being with a comprehensive list of actual human needs. Hence, whereas endless human desires are suffocating capitalism, Islam is teaching man how to get his life under control and to discipline himself. In this sense, religion is self-control and it is this that animals do not have.

This in turn is achieved through moral education. In the recent past, however, proper educational facilities were denied to Muslims. The current education system places the ideals of the state, society, and economic development above divine virtues and ideals:

> Islam as a religion was little affected by the 350 years of Christian missionary endeavour. As a polity, it was little affected by the 150 years of colonial conquest and imperial rule. But there was one sphere – education – in which colonial rule did have a profound effect on Muslim society: because the foreign powers ... sought to give as little education as possible, the wrong sort of education when it had to be given and also to bring about a schism in the soul of the Muslim community ... The local educational system was either destroyed, ignored, or allowed to collapse through 'benign neglect' by the colonial regimes. For militant Islam today the real field of battle is the school room ... matters of teacher training, curricula and school textbooks are actually of far greater and more long lasting importance than heroism in ancient battles.[23]

As Parsons says, it is essential to understand ultimate frustrations to have a full grasp of the basic religious messages.[24] I shall dwell further on this point.

According to *İcmal*, education involves teaching a divine programme to give pure Islamic consciousness to Muslims. On the one hand, this will help Muslims to overcome the negative effects of the forces of idolatry on thought and action. On the other hand, Islamic education will bring peace of mind and emancipation from anxiety. Although the mind is an essential component of the educational process, it must be developed by Islam, strengthened by religious faith and enlightened by revelation. The key instrument of this educational process is a special agent who has mastery over the psycho-gnostic states that guide the human soul on its journey towards complete purification.

The Perfect Man

As a semi-divine character, the Perfect Man exists as an entity at the level of God, though he appears as one among people. This theosophic conception attributes immediate divine illumination to the Perfect Man: he enters into God's spiritual kingdom; speaks His secrets and mysteries; discovers hidden and invisible things; tells the future and life after death. He is created as God's Caliph on earth; he is the superior and the chosen one; God is manifest in his heart; his work is God's work; and his *nefs* is directly controlled by God. The two worlds are united in the Perfect Man: he is the spirit of the world and the world is his flesh. Nothing in this world or in heaven can remain unknown or concealed to him.

The spiritual genealogy of the Perfect Man is traced through al-Gilani to 'Ali and from him to the Prophet Muhammad. One of *İcmal*'s major contentions is that intercession with God can be possible through sainthood. The Perfect Man is the only legitimate heir of the Prophet, and submitting to his authority is the same as surrendering to the Prophet and to God.

The Perfect Man has the power to work miracles. Since he can acknowledge the spiritual essence of God, his decisions are final and his discoveries and observations are absolutely correct and pure. With his special insight, foresight and discernment, and with his 'vision of the heart', he can uncover the hidden realities of both worlds. His soul has reached that highest stage of perfection, annihilation in God.

According to *İcmal*, a true grasp of eternal realities requires religion to be 'concretized'. Attributing a special superhuman status to Muhammad as a model of salvation is part of Turkish Islamic tradition.[25] In its Sufi interpretation, the Prophet becomes the concrete form and living essence of the word of God, the Koran. His education is undertaken directly by God and therefore his deeds, the Sunna, are true divine ordinances. The abstract language of the Koran is transformed in his person into spoken word and action. In his concrete person, thought becomes praxis. His life is the externalization and concretization of Koranic realities. When the Koran is thoroughly examined, there emerges the portrait of an ideal person, who represents the highest values of Islamic society. As the argument goes, society is a single person with a single heart where God presides; the heart of society is the Perfect Man, and he gives sanctity to the Islamic community. On the other hand, intercession, guidance and mediation are all legitimate institutions in Islam. God created the chain of material and spiritual events to conceal his own essence. The statement that every happening or event has a cause does not contradict religious faith in so far as we distinguish between the immediate and the First Cause. Hence rain is due both to clouds and to God. The same principle holds in the spiritual sphere. The way to Islam is always from God, but the intercession of a mediator is necessary. The most prominent learned men of Islam had to go under the protection of such special envoys of God, for those who do not are indirectly accepting the guidance of Satan.

Education, self-discipline and spiritual perfection require neither books nor laboratories, since the appeal is only to the heart. The knowledge of the Perfect Man is not based on discursive reason, but is a higher understanding of divine mystery and love. His method of treatment is unique in that he adopts a genuinely totalistic approach, taking into account material as well as spiritual factors. He helps the patient to discover the inner secrets of his specific physical and psychological constitution. As Fazlur Rahman comments: 'to teach and treat people each according to his capacity and individual needs is a cardinal principle with Sufi Shayks ... [for] these have remarkable insight into practical psychology'.[26] Thus, the Perfect Man cures stress and psychosomatic disorders, saving Islamic society from becoming a huge mental hospital like Western society.

An Overview

İcmal's identification of its primary aim as one of education has important consequences in defining the limits of the target group and methods of dealing with Muslims, and in developing tactics and strategies for coping with non-Islamic groups and institutions. In the first place, for *İcmal* the call to Islam should be cast as widely a possible: this requires a cautious, patient and tolerant approach. The use of physical force in approaching Muslims is explicitly condemned. *İcmal*'s authors argue that it is both unrealistic and .unfair to expect non-Islamic beliefs and practices to change at once and for good. Those with the weakest faith should be treated as though seriously wounded in an accident, and as deserving of affection and care. The emphasis on peace, voluntarism and persuasion is closely linked with the traditional notion of the Perfect Man. In this view, the notion itself rejects the use of physical force: as the expression of ultimate power, his existence negates the possibility of any other source of power.[27]

The Perfect Man establishes a hierarchical spiritual order with himself at the top. Others are ranked, at least in theory, according to the degree of their moral perfection. The Perfect Man emerges as a traditional charismatic figure whose power and authority over his followers are absolute and unrivalled. Obedience to him requires the full suppression of individuality: as the traditional Sufi proverb 'goes, 'the seeker should be in the hands of his guide as a dead body in the hands of the washer'.

This complete self-annihilation before the authority of the saint has social, moral and political implications. Total submission means putting an end to the anarchy of desires and ruthless competition which governs everyday life. The individual learns how to be content with what he is and has, demanding only a sufficiency from others and from society at large. The ambitious, acquisitive, possessive individual is thus replaced by a satisfied, grateful, submissive religious devotee. The ascetic goals of contentment and trust (*tawakkul*) in God or simply self-control in the Sufi sense are thus attained. In practical social terms, this kind of self-control amounts to acceptance of any situation, learning to remain insensitive to misfortune. This involves both inculcating in the poor contentment with their lot and suggesting to the wealthy that they draw back at least partially from the drive for acquisition and consumption. As can be seen, the denigration of worldly affairs is also a way of arguing for the subordination of the whole worldly realm to the authority of the saint.

The moral element concerns the role of the Perfect Man as a supreme guide in resolving ethical disputes and curing psychological disorders. He gives advice to resolve moral dilemmas and acts as a point of spiritual refuge for those who want to escape from a competitive social environment which is rapidly eroding the warmth of hearth and home, the spontaneity of intimate relations, the sacredness of traditional values and all past identities. The psychological field, and the role of the Perfect Man as a therapist treating his patients' tensions and addictions by means of Sufi spiritual techniques, is the most recurrent theme taken up by *İcmal.*

Politically, the charismatic leadership of the Perfect Man is marked by absolute authority not subject, at least in principle, to rules and regulations. On the other hand, the form of political organization involved resembles a wide patronage network rather than a para-military revolutionary organization. When these two elements – absolute power and a patronage network – are considered together, we see how the saint judges opportunities, here compromising, there confronting various Islamic and non-Islamic forces, trying to enhance both his personal power and that of his order.

CONCLUSION

If the term 'self' is to be understood as 'an ability to conceive of the individual as standing outside society and nature, [as] an autonomous thinking agent acting on them',[28] this conception typifies the outlook of neither journal. Sufism seems to recognize three major states: the animal self which is a slave to material drives or passions; a deeper self which, if properly discovered and brought to the surface – only by means of religion – can win over the first; and various intermediate stages, which in the final resort come close to the first. The Sufi ideal is certainly the second: an individual totally encapsulated by the rules and ideals of the

Islamic community, and robot-like in observing the infinite multitude of Islamic regulations. Bellah provides a general account of this conception: 'a responsible self, a core self or a true self, deeper than the flux of everyday experience, facing a reality over against itself'.[29]

A differentiation between the experience of the self and the world which acts upon it, or simply between the self and the world, is the cardinal message of Sufi teaching. The second step is the degradation of the animal self and the empirical cosmos in favour of an ultimately superior 'community self'. This gives the individual the power to sever himself from ordinary life and to establish his mastery of it. The Sufi doctrine of world rejection, then, involves providing the devout Muslim with a sense of morality superior to the various norms and maxims of daily life. In attempting to establish religion on an intense inner life of conscience, Sufism aims at maintaining the affirmation of self-control over materialism and hedonism, and of the community over the individual ego, the *nefs*.

. Despite various minor differences, the Sufisms of *Ribat* and *Icmal* seem to have in common this ideal of strengthening the inner core; indeed a certain conception of privacy in the sense of personal integrity[30] but one that can only be achieved through total submission. Beyond this common message, differences begin to appear. The cluster of ideas and the dominant messages put forward at this second level are equally important, since these are indicative of different patterns through which revivalist movements of Sufi origins can develop. A general typology is not attempted here, but, on the basis of detailed evidence from the two journals, two patterns can be discerned that seem to be of great significance in understanding the phenomenon of revivalism.

The first pattern is characterized by a very strong emphasis on abstinence from material inducements, combined with a powerful eschatological stress that gives a high premium to death and martyrdom. Insistence on ritual and practice is associated with an ethos orienting the seeker to action rather than theological speculation or immediate spiritual gratification. The fundamental aim of world rejection is to distance the individual from various other aspects of social life so as to direct him to a single-minded political struggle.

The second pattern also strongly condemns immoral consumerism and greed, but it is marked by a tendency to compromise between religion and material concerns. Personal integrity and self-control attained as the outcome of moral education are conceived as necessary for developing a strong Muslim identity to counter Western ideological and cultural influences. This worldview-oriented religion focuses more on belief than on action. Moral integrity and emotional gratification come before immediate political action and struggle.

It emerges clearly out of this discussion that religious movements with very similar theological and intellectual backgrounds can produce very different outcomes. Adequate understanding of the phenomenon of Islamic revival requires the uncovering of these distinct patterns and styles of appeal.

NOTES

1. B. Lewis, 'The return of Islam', *Middle East Review*, Fall 1979, p. 29.
2. M. Kupferschmidt, 'Reformist and militant Islam in urban and rural Egypt', *Middle Eastern Studies*, 23 (4), 1987, pp. 403–19.
3. Ş. Mardin, 'Culture and religion towards the year 2000', in *Turkey in the Year 2000*, Turkish Political Science Association, Ankara, Sevinç Matbaası, 1989, pp. 163–86.
4. Ş. Mardin, 'Religion and politics in modern Turkey', in James P. Piscatori, ed., *Islam in the Political Process*, London, Cambridge University Press, 1983, p. 141.
5. *Ribat*, Aylık Islami Dergi, Konya, Sebat Ofset Mat., Vols. 1–6, 1982–8; *İcmal*, Aylık İlim Fikir Kültür Dergisi, Trabzon, Numune Basım, Vols 1–6, 1982–8.
6. C. Geertz, *Islam Observed*, New Haven and London, Yale University Press, 1968, pp. 95, 97.
7. I shall not refer to the authors by name when discussing *Ribat*'s religious views, for two reasons: first, there is little specialization among authors, so that they tend to step on each other's territory. The two major exceptions are Tahir Büyükkörükçü, a former MP from the National Salvation Party who writes short articles on Rumi, and Abdullah Hoca, who dwells on the relationship between the Prophet and his Companions. Neither, however, are discussed here. Secondly, *Ribat* does not seem to tolerate individual variations, so that, although different authors are mentioned, each issue or in fact each volume seems like a single book by a single author.

8. O. Açıkalın, 'Modernism/Westernism vs. Fundamentalism/Islamism: An Analysis of Two Islamic Periodicals in Turkey', unpublished M.Sc. thesis, Ankara, Middle East Technical University, 1987, pp. 3, 53.

9. F. Rahman, *Islam*, Chicago, University of Chicago Press, 2nd edn., 1979, p. 158. UK edn., London, Weidenfeld and Nicholson, 1966.

10. H. Dabbashi, 'The Sufi doctrine of the "Perfect Man" and a view of the hierarchical structure of Islamic culture', *The Islamic Quarterly*, 30 (2), 1986, p. 116.

11. R. Stark and C. Y. Glock, 'Dimensions of religious commitment', in R. Robertson, ed., *Sociology of Religion*, Harmondsworth, Penguin, 1969, p. 259.

12. M. Yadigari, 'Liberation theology and Islamic revivalism', *The Journal of Religious Thought*, 43 (2), 1986, pp. 46, 47.

13. See P. Worsley, 'Religion as a category', in Robertson, ed., *Sociology of Religion*, p. 221.

14. L. Kinberg, 'What is meant by Zuhd', *Studia Islamica*, 61, 1987, p. 35.

15. Y. Y. Haddad, 'Sayyid Qutb: ideologue of Islamic revival', in J. Esposito, ed., *Voices of Resurgent Islam*, New York, Oxford University Press, 1983, pp. 67–9; F. Ajami, 'In the Pharaoh's shadow: religion and authority in Egypt', in Piscatori, ed., *Islam in the Political Process*, pp. 12–36.

16. S. N. Eisenstadt, 'The protestant ethic thesis', in Robertson, ed., *Sociology of Religion*, p. 305.

17. M. Fischer, 'Islam and the revolt of the petit bourgeoisie', *Daedalus*, 111 (4), 1982, p. 119.

18. W. E. Shepard, 'Islam and ideology: towards a typology', *International Journal of Middle East Studies*, 19, 1987, p. 308.

19. A. Schimmel, *Tasavvufun Boyutları*, Istanbul, Adam Yayıncılık, 1982, pp. 167–9.

20. *İcmal* addresses the reader through an introductory article in which no specific names are given. Matters of general policy, evaluations of the present situation, and theological arguments to legitimize the role and authority of the Perfect Man generally appear on these pages. Social criticism and polemics with other approaches are usually taken up by Ali Gedik. Celal Mısır's writings are fundamentally eschatological. Presentation and critique of Western philosophies, ideologies and world views are attempted by Ali Yetimoğlu. Dr Abdullah Terzi focuses more on specific contemporary issues, such as homosexuality, AIDS, cybernetics, modern psychology, radio-activity.

21. Rahman, *Islam*, p. 159.

22. Kinberg, 'Zuhd'.

23. G. H. Jansen, *Militant Islam*, London, Pan Books, 1979, pp. 68, 107.

24. T. Parsons, 'Religion and the problem of meaning', in Robertson, ed., *Sociology of Religion*.

25. N. Tapper and R. Tapper, 'The birth of the Prophet: ritual and gender in Turkish Islam', *Man* (N.S.), 22, 1987, p. 86.
26. Rahman, *Islam*, p. 157.
27. Dabbashi, 'The Perfect Man', p. 128.
28. P. Abrams, *Historical Sociology*, Bath, Open Books, 1982, p. 228.
29. R. N. Bellah, 'Religious evolution', in Robertson, ed., *Sociology of Religion*, p. 277.
30. B. Moore, *Privacy: Studies in Social and Cultural History*, New York, M. E. Sharpe Inc., 1984, p. 247.

11

PLURALISM VERSUS AUTHORITARIANISM:
Political Ideas in Two Islamic Publications

Ayşe Güneş-Ayata

INTRODUCTORY

A review of the social science literature on Islamic revival in Turkey since the Republic shows three periods when this subject attracted attention. First was the early 1950s, when the main emphasis was on whether the Democrat Party, because of its populist outlook, would retreat from the secularist reforms of Kemal Atatürk.[1] The second wave of interest came in the 1970s with the establishment of the National Salvation Party and its consolidation as a major political force.[2]

The third wave, which began in the 1980s,[3] is radically different from the first two, because the nature of the subject, Islamic revivalism, has changed drastically. First, this new movement in Islam is a result of popular reaction but its proponents intellectualize it much more fiercely than before, so much so that they have published up to 45 monthly periodicals. Secondly, they are organized but not necessarily in political parties. Thirdly, although this is one of the rare periods when Islamic groups have been very close to power (such as Nakşibendis in the Motherland Party government), direct attacks on the secular Turkish state, as well as demands for a totalistic Islamic state, have greatly increased. Fourthly, radical Islamic elements are introduced for the first time in Turkish republican history, especially under the influence of the Islamic Revolution in Iran. The nature of this new movement in Turkey requires a thorough investigation of its distinctiveness and its position *vis-à-vis* the state.

State and religion can complement and at the same time conflict with each other as they seek to attract, monopolize and expand resources.[4] Their historical rivalry in the strictly secular Turkish Republic has been accentuated with the growing Islamic revival.

Religious revival is currently an important political phenomenon not only in Islam but elsewhere.[5] All such movements represent a response, often reactionary, to indigenous political factors distinctive to specific countries. However, parallels can be drawn among these movements, especially between the Turkish case and others in the Middle East, and revivalism generally reflects greater awareness of the existing world-system. In many ways, from developments in communication technology to the social transformations involved in industrialization, modernization has assisted revivalism. It has also been argued that revivalism is a conscious or unconscious response to the painful social consequences of rapid modernization, notably anomie, rootlessness and cultural alienation.[6]

The general usage of the concept of Islamic revivalism tends to treat the movement as a whole. Although distinctions may be made on the basis of country, for example the Iranian version from the Saudi Arabian, variations are not emphasized, especially in countries where Islam is not the dominant state ideology. However, divisions and rivalries within the movement can mean that competing groups, instead of accepting the domination of one group, may prefer to continue the struggle under a secular state. In a secular country like Turkey, the state's legitimation *vis-à-vis* Islam as an opposing force is highly dependent on such divisions.

The present chapter draws attention to divisions among Islamic revivalist groups in Turkey. The analysis of differences is important, first for practical political purposes, because it can indicate which groups have the potential for success, secondly, because it may allow us to identify diversity in their points of departure as well as different Islamic and non-Islamic influences on them.

These groups tend to vary along three axes: fundamentalism, modernism and traditionalism/neo-traditionalism, a common ground of the three being anti-Westernism. For the purpose of analysis here I briefly indicate some of the features of these axes.[7]

Fundamentalism finds its main authority in written scripture rather than in traditional practices or rituals or in spiritual leaders. It may express its anti-Westernism in the language of Third World opposition to imperialism. It argues that Islam has a flexible nature, but there is a necessity for a new *ijtihad* (re-interpretation of Koranic principles) in order to rebuild Islam as a distinct and integrated system; thus it accepts the idea of progress and may even support conscious attempts to achieve it.

Modernism is the acceptance that Islam provides an adequate ideological base for public life. It is flexible, and this flexibility allows for positive dialogue with one or more Western ideologies. It tends to place a high value upon material technology, to use modern techniques of social organization and mobilization, and to accept modern values such as democracy, freedom, equality and social justice as well as modern institutions such as parties and parliaments, even to the extent that sometimes Western practices are derived from Islam, for example democracy from Shura (assembly).

Traditionalism or *neo-traditionalism* is an eschatological response to the Western challenge. It has a strong sense of resistance to Westernization, but a selective adaptation of modern technology is possible. Islam, as it is, has to be transformed into a social practice. In this, traditional means are considered adequate. Local customs and traditional authority figures such as local shaikhs are valued. Traditionalism is obstructionist towards secularist governments, and has a gradualist approach to change.

This chapter discusses two very widely circulated monthly periodicals published by Islamic groups, namely *Girişim* (Initiative) and *İslam*, in the light of their variation along the three axes I have outlined.

GIRIŞIM

Girişim is an independent monthly, published in Istanbul since October 1985, which claims a circulation of about 10,000. It is predominantly political in content, while in terms of appearance it is not very different from any such journal of the left. Each issue contains about 48 pages, of which around 20 are reserved for

news and comment, 20 for independent articles, and 10 for arts
and culture. The first section usually has a topical coherence,
where an event such as the Iran–Iraq war, or a problem such as
youth, or the career of an individual such as Said Nursi, is
investigated and discussed in detail by different authors. In the
second section there is a great variation of themes. The third
section contains reviews of plays and films, but is mainly reserved
for book reviews, occasionally long but usually short and
informative. It is, however, indicative that the publishers are
trying to appeal to a clientele that reads widely.

The periodical articulates a distinct form of Islamic revivalism.
Classic features of belief and practice commonly associated with
Islam are absent. Practices such as prayer, fasting, almsgiving,
pilgrimage are very rarely mentioned, and if they are it is in
relation to political events such as the incidents in Mecca in 1987.
Reading *Girişim* one cannot learn much about Islam or its daily
practice, nor does it aim to convert people to Islam, nor will a
Muslim find answers to his day-to-day intellectual or practical
problems.

What *Girişim* proposes is a 'political theory of calling (*davet*)'.
In this it is original, claiming descent from no tarikat or earlier
movement, and it aims to create a forum for independent
discussion of both tarikat and non-tarikat views. Although a
careful analysis reveals that the publishers really are taking steps
in this direction, they are faced with problems. Authorities from
the tarikats either do not take this attempt seriously or oppose it
strongly; therefore the only people they can attract to their inner
pages are Westernized liberals, or Muslims from a tarikat
background who are already critical of their own position. With
this explicit initiative, however, they are successful in generating
some discussion in the periodical. Nevertheless, in the second
volume they show less timidity in delineating their own position,
especially in reaction to severe criticism from both Nurcu and
tarikat sources. Editorials begin to dictate programmes and
political doctrines, and they are full of polemics against other
Islamic movements. But *Girişim* does not hesitate to publish
criticism received, especially in the form of letters to the editor.
This, of course, shows the sincerity of their tolerance of different
Islamic perspectives.

Girişim appeals to a specific intellectual group: young people –

the problems of youth and their specific place in the Islamic movement are subjects frequently discussed in its pages – with urban experience, either university students or young graduates, and probably living in social situations where Western culture is dominant. In these situations the editors are likely to enter into frequent discussions with similar intellectuals from Western culture. The periodical is trying to equip its readers with the tools necessary to 'fight the other side'. Its readers are Islamic revivalists, but from intellectually varied backgrounds and not necessarily students in the Faculty of Theology.

Reading the volumes, I could trace some of the reasons why my revivalist students at the Middle East Technical University were such keen followers of *Girişim*. The dominant discourse and values in Turkish universities are highly determined by Western concepts. The periodical takes these concepts seriously, discusses them, tries to integrate them into the Islamic framework if possible, and, if not, gives detailed explanations of why they are to be rejected. The majority of such explanations refer to more recent Islamic scholars such as Mawdudi or Shariati, who use more modern concepts, rather than to Imam Maliki or Al-Ghazali. This Western discourse appeals to the youth, as it provides them with a framework that is different but not inferior. There are often references to and discussions of the works of Hegel, Weber and Marx, and meticulous care is shown not to say anything derogatory about them. Ali Shariati, who seems to have influenced *Girişim*'s point of view deeply, was aware of the domination of Western discourse among the youth, so he also used Western sociological terms, although he realized the problems involved.[8] By contrast, Islamic concepts (such as *şirk*, associationalism, or *tağut*, idolatry) are very rarely used. *Girişim* and its arguments can thus be followed easily by any intellectual, and demand no specific knowledge of Islam.

Girişim recognizes two dominant themes in Western sociology. First, modern society is highly differentiated and complex, which generates conflict. This conflict is encouraged and manipulated by the Western bloc, but it will continue even in an Islamic society, although probably at a decreasing level.

The second theme is that of change. The world is changing, it has changed since Muhammad's time, and it will continue to change. So *Girişim* argues the need to reinterpret not only *fıkıh*

(Fiqh, the system of Islamic law) but many other parts of Islam. *Asrı Saadet*, the period during which Muhammad lived, is no longer the perfect model for emulation. Probably this is one of the reasons why there is no reference in *Girişim* to pre-twentieth-century Islamic scholars, who are not considered adequate and recent enough for understanding the present-day world in general and Turkey in particular. The essence of the religion cannot of course be changed, but new rules of *fıkıh* can be integrated in accordance with *nass*, what is written in the Koran.

Girişim is specifically a political journal, and other aspects of life such as social or economic problems are not emphasized. It is argued that political philosophy and policy in Islam are immature and underdeveloped, so the periodical is trying to fill a gap. As for the society of the future, not much is proposed except very basic principles, for example that sovereignty lies in Allah, and that *nass*, being the word of Allah, cannot be changed. *Fıkıh*, however, is to be accepted as dynamic: with social change new rules can be obtained by *kıyas* (analogy) with the help of the Ulema in the Shura. All these have to be compatible with the Koran. A system is proposed called *dindar demokrasi* (pious democracy), which is not elaborated in detail but resembles Mawdudi's principle of 'Theo-democracy', according to which sovereignty is in God but also in the Caliphate of men; Muslims are agents for the realization of God's will; this can only be possible with constant consultations in the assembly of the community.[9]

In the search for an ideal future Islamic state, *Girişim*'s line of argument is faced with a major problem. Once *Asrı Saadet* is rejected on the basis that society has changed and developed, then there remains no model to emulate or to propose. The Islamic Republic of Iran is seen as a precious infant of great promise, who must be looked after with the utmost care, but, as with any infant, including one's own, one cannot predict how it will grow up. Moreover, Iran has one more disadvantage, that the state is predominantly Shi'ite, which creates much resentment in popular Muslim culture in Turkey, therefore for an Islamic movement openly to preach a pro-Iranian stance is playing with fire.

Instead of discussing a model for a future society, *Girişim* prefers to devote attention to the politics of 'calling' (*davet*). This is not presented as a coherent, step-by-step theory and praxis, yet lately the framework has been crystallizing. This theory of calling, although it seems at present to be timid and unassertive, claims to be original. It is argued that the theory should overcome all differences of sect, opinion and practice in Islam; it should aim at integrating popular Islam with the Islamic movements in a basically anti-Western and rational ideology. The theory of calling necessitates a leader who is realistic and aware of contemporary social and philosophical problems and has a profound knowledge of Islam, who can entrust the believer with communicating, diffusing and inculcating these ideas, and can command respect and obedience.

This theory of calling turns around six recurrent themes: anti-Westernism, realism, the problem of geographic specificity, pluralism, leadership and the people, and the means of preaching the theory.

Anti-Westernism

This is an underlying theme, not only in this periodical but in all Islamic publications. Compared with other journals, such as *İslam*, however, articles in *Girişim* dealing specifically with anti-Westernism are few. They are not anti-Marxist, in fact they are silent about Marx, whereas the Soviet Union is criticized alongside the United States for its imperialist activities.

Westernism is viewed in many aspects. In the first volume, it is more of a cultural system, in the second volume its imperialistic nature is stressed. It is argued that the West wants to condition human beings to be part of the world production system. The Western economy creates a consumer society associated with competition and waste, leaving the individual in solitude and alienation from the system. The political dimension of the West is democracy, which they regard as unreliable and slippery because it does not recognize the idea of *tevhid* (the oneness of Allah) and proposes a system which denies Allah's sovereignty. In democracy there can be no freedom, only slavery to people, to a government chosen by people and to a state imposed by people.

On these grounds they criticize the Turkish democratic system, claiming it was imposed on the people by the Westernized élite, especially after the War of Independence, when people were worn out by the conditions of war. The present-day Western democratic system is used as an example of unreliability, where liberties are only for those inside the system and no tolerance is shown to Muslims who want to practise Islam as a whole in worship and ideology. However, as people come to notice the unreliability of the system, they will adhere to Islam and bring about the Islamic resurgence. So the ultimate and inevitable solution is Islam.

Realism

'The contemporary theory of calling has to be realistic, thus accordingly the preachers of Islamic calling have to know the detailed particularities and differences of their own countries.'[10] The realism proposed by *Girişim* marks an approach that clarifies this movement's relation to existing Turkish state and society. Turkey is a specific country where there is secularism, Westernization and capitalism, but with Islam as a popular religion. These conditions must be assessed specifically, leading *Girişim* to adopt a practical attitude, ready to make use of all available resources for the Islamic calling without being an integral part of any of the other movements. One should be cool and calculating towards political parties; for example, parties such as ANAP (the Motherland Party) can be used instrumentally to serve some Muslim demands, but Muslims should not be blindly attached to them. The role of Islamic tradition in popular culture should be realistically assessed, and popular religion should be used if it contributes to the mission.

However, this realism brings major problems that are not common in Islamic politics: the problem of contemporaneity, and the problem of geographic specificity, both of which were made core issues by Shariati in his theory.[11] The notion of social change I will discuss briefly; geographic specificity makes 'Islam in one country' possible.

The problem of geographic specificity

In the Islamic mission there seem to be two approaches to the problem of scope. Sayyid Qutb and some others see Islam as a universal and total ideology, so that the mission itself must be international and have universal principles.[12] The Ganusi–Shariati line, on the other hand, argues for geographic specificity, due to the different cultures and histories each country has experienced since the early days of Islam.[13]

In *Girişim* both arguments are presented but with a clear preference for the latter. Metiner argues in an editorial: 'To be specific to yourself (or to the community or the nation) is not nationalism. Nationalism appears as a feeling of superiority or self-sufficiency. This [the acceptance of specificity] has of course a quality that leads to the universal.'[14] The mission should therefore recognize existing conditions realistically, but this 'specificity' should be eliminated for the universality of Islam if the mission is ever to be accomplished.

What are the elements of this specificity? First of all, from the time of Muhammad to present-day Turkey, this culture has been shaped by a history which includes the Ottomans, the War of Independence, Westernization, and the Turkish Republic. Muslims have fought wars of independence in different parts of the world, including Turkey, and this has made a major impact on their culture. Turks were the leaders of the Islamic world, another dimension of their cultural heritage. The second element to be recognized and analysed is the 'cultural and spiritual' resources, that is, the existing culture. Turkey has long been dominated by supporters of Westernization and nationalism, who have put the people in a position where they are asked to vote periodically in the present system (democracy) without any resistance. In recent years this has been supported by a new dimension, de-politicization. In Turkey, however, the people are Muslims, whereas the élite is not. This brings us to the third element, that is, a search for identity, an identity not specifically national or racial or ethnic, but Islamic.

Girişim recognizes that this geographic specificity argument is not widely accepted in other Turkish Islamic revivalist circles, for four reasons: the other movements are afraid of nationalism; they seek leadership for Turkey among other Islamic countries; they despair of the extent of Western influence in Turkey; and lastly because there is no leadership of the Learned in Turkey. But *Girişim* clearly rejects this indifferent, detached attitude, and claims to propose a 'specific, innovative and multidimensional' solution.

Pluralism

Social science associates pluralism in a modern society with the articulation of interests based on class or social group differentiation. *Girişim*, however, while occasionally mentioning social classes, does not consider their organization or interests. But in its manifesto there is a clear proposal for a kind of ideological pluralism which is called 'multi-colouredness' (*çok renklilik*), a pluralism in the mission of the Islamic movement. Two kinds of limits to this pluralism are set: first, there must be agreement on the basic principles of the Koran, Sunna, and belief (*iman*) – a limit so wide that it will include all believers independent of sect and tarikat. Secondly, there should be no attempt to align the Muslim movement with the Western bloc, as they are incompatible; attempts to bridge Islam and democracy are doomed to failure.

The source of pluralism is the faculty of 'reason' (*akıl*) that Allah has given to man. *Girişim* argues that the main aim of the Koran is to motivate individuals to think about humanity, nature and history. This can be achieved by inquiry, investigation and learning. As ordinary people think, observe their environment, read, learn and use their judgment, they will come to different conclusions, which is possible given the specificity of societies and cultures. The nature of *fıkıh* is comparison and analogy (*kıyas*) with the Koranic text in specific situations. Differences of opinion are inevitable; if there is love for Muslims, and if they are considered a brotherhood, a community, then with good will these differences should be tolerable. Moreover, even ordinary believers should be given the right to choose, and they are entitled to a fair picture, to know all differences of opinion. 'To be "single-coloured" is not only to defend a part or a party, it is to be afraid of different choices and of the presentation of these choices in public, and not to trust the believer's reason.'[15] 'Now we want our men to choose and criticize; what we do not approve of is mere acceptance and approval.'[16]

In such a pluralism *Girişim* finds many advantages for its mission. In the first place it becomes an inclusivist ideology; once basic premises are agreed, no group is left out because of any conflict or difference. The exclusivist method of the tarikats had been criticized by both Mawdudi and Shariati[17] as an obstacle in the path of the movement. This inclusivism can even overcome Shi'a–Sunni differences, which *Girişim* sees as a construction developed by the old traditional interpretations, still being used politically so as to hinder Muslim unification. 'Even if they do not think like us, even if they are not part of our Muslim community and followers of our Imam, we should not forget that all Muslims are part of the Muslim Ummah.'[18]

Secondly, it is argued that this pluralism brings dynamism to the movement when new perspectives, new ideas, new interpretations are brought in. The editors indicate that previous attempts at Islamic resurgence quite often found themselves in deadlock. Movements which overrule dynamism cannot find solutions to contemporary problems. The repeated failure of various movements has led Muslims to an unnecessary urgency, because they are afraid that they will never experience victory. The flexibility proposed in the model will obviate this haste and bring a new synthesis whenever problems appear.

Thirdly, because each individual group was introverted and over-involved with its own problems, the general perspective has been lost. Tolerance of differences will lead to a better understanding of each other, easier co-existence and a global perception of the Islamic movement. In this respect, only Asrı Saadet (the Muhammadan age) can be used as a common language where everyone will find their own differences and similarities.

Leadership and the people

'Partition on the basis of groups, cliques and factions, self-assertions on the basis of "I said and it happened", are so widespread and common among us that we cannot form a global outlook. *Girişim* has pointed out its position on this by saying, all we Muslims who believe in the oneness of Allah make up a family, and we are part of that family.'[19]

Girişim notes that, especially as a result of tarikat influence, the group of people who call themselves the Learned (the Ulema) and the leaders (shaikhs) are separated from those who are in general asked to emulate and obey them. In principle this kind of division is rejected which gives a special position to the leaders *vis-à-vis* the people and believers. In this respect, the authors of *Girişim* are clearly anti-authoritarian. They recognize no right to lead, either innate or acquired through learning. They argue that all Muslims are equal on two grounds, that belief can be measured only by Allah, and that all Muslims are equally responsible for themselves and each other in Jihad, so that there is no inequality even in terms of political responsibility. Moreover, *Girişim* introduces another notion, that of social equality. They propose that Allah shows a clear preference for the poor, and in this respect they introduce an egalitarian leftist interpretation into the Islamic mission. 'What these circles [imperialist and capitalist] do not know, and probably will never accept, is the fact that prior to everything and everyone Allah will be together with the poor and oppressed.'[20] Muslims, who are of equal status and rank before Allah, make up a community (Umma) which has a solidarity and integration which is specific to them and distinguishes them from Western society.

This does not, however, solve the problem of how existing society will be made into an Umma. The old tarikats solved the problem through the leadership of the shaikhs, whom they obey and emulate. *Girişim* rejects this on the basis that it is a model of slavery (*kapıkulluğu*), where the believer is treated as though he has no reason and is not entitled to consider different opinions and to choose among them. They also argue that this can lead to factionalism in the Islamic movement, where leader and followers become involved in power struggles, to the point where individuals are idolized, and followers begin to argue that if their leader is not recognized or obeyed the Islamic movement is doomed to failure. Similarly, the hierarchical model of Shi'a tradition, which leads to the emergence of priests as a class, is rejected.

To make *fıkıh* decisions, however, which is reserved for the Learned, and to initiate and direct the 'calling' and the Jihad, there is still a need for leadership; so there is a distinct and very important position for leadership in the theory of calling. *Girişim* differentiates three kinds of leaders. *Intellectuals*, first, are influenced by Western principles, acquire knowledge for its own sake and are alienated from the existing system, but they are also isolated from the people. *The Learned*, secondly, have a profound knowledge of Islam, the Koran, Sunna, and *fıkıh*; their faith and knowledge of Koranic principles are enough for them to exercise *fıkıh*; and they are an integral part of the *ictihat meclisi* (the Shura assembly), though not necessarily politically involved. Finally, *a political leader*, they argue, is essential for the mission; this leader must be obeyed, but not blindly: 'exactly as being a slave (*kapıkulu*) is forbidden for Muslims, obedience to those who are capable of leadership is required in Islam'.[21] The qualities of a leader are described as follows: 'He must be capable of evaluating both Islamic principles and the political conditions of society, he must be capable of using all available opportunities, whether positive or negative, he must be devoted to the mission of calling, he must strictly apply Islamic principles and the decisions and principles of the Shura in his personal life.'[22] This definition, of course, stresses the purely political rather than the religious side of the leadership.

With this leadership, a method of calling is suggested too. Islam, *Girişim* argues, can be diffused from an enlightened cadre to the people, therefore, unlike tarikats which preach withdrawal from the non-Islamic community, they recommend that leaders should associate with the people. This will bring dynamism to Islam, protecting the religion from over-centralization and rigidity. *Girişim* is also aware, however, that it may lead to populism, whereas Islam is a religion of Koranic principles, a religion of Allah. The solution is for the leader to accept the people's problems as his own, and to preach to them the Islamic truth. Leaders are Mujtahids, messengers for the future.

Means of preaching 'calling'

The most important means of preaching 'calling' is of course mass-communication. But *Girişim* also considers theatre and cinema as means for creating an alternative culture, which can be acquired in the home, where new generations are integrated into the Islamic tradition. Universities, labour unions and all kinds of organizations can also be used. In all of these, opportunities emerge through private enterprise, because the secular state and its organs will be the biggest barrier to the Islamic mission. Private initiatives in Islamic theatre and cinema should be supported. The introduction of courses of religion in schools is not a step forward, because it is teaching the secularist religion of the Turkish republican state.

Summary

Girişim represents the independent Islamic movement that became prominent in the 1980s. The outstanding features of the movement are adaptability to and usage of the conditions of the modern world, as well as appeal to the masses through an intellectual group that has undergone the influence of Westernization. Acceptance of democratic values such as tolerance and pluralism, efforts to accommodate Western political institutions to Islamic principles (parliament and Shura), and recognition of a complex and differentiated social structure, all remind one of a 'modernist' approach.

Girişim is a new periodical, representing a new movement. The periodical to be discussed next represents one of the oldest orders in Islam.

İSLAM

İslam is a monthly periodical published in Ankara by the İskender Paşa Dergâhı, one of the biggest lodges (*dergâh*) of the Nakşibendi order. It has a circulation of about 100,000. Of course this does not show how much it is read, because the followers of the Shaikh are usually asked to buy several copies and to distribute them to friends. Publication began in 1983, and has been uninterrupted since. The contents of any one issue are highly varied; clearly the editors want to cover all aspects of life, and to offer solutions to every problem. Each issue contains between 48 and 64 pages; one third is reserved for 'File of the Month', made up entirely of news from Muslims around the world, including interviews with Muslims well known for various reasons. A second section of between about 8 and 10 pages is called 'research', which addresses issues ranging from problems in organizing time to the techniques of nuclear war. There are usually another 2 and 4 pages on economics. A further major section is reserved for Islamic history and 'Ideal Muslims', where all the articles are stories from Asrı Saadet. Then there are between 2 to 4 pages on 'Women and Home', including a special section called 'Catechism' (*İlmihal*) with detailed descriptions of Islamic practices. Every issue also has at least 8 pages of advertisements, clearly indicating the financial back-up for the journal.

Unlike *Girişim*, *İslam* provides its readers with an opinion about Islam as a religion. It may be only one version, but it certainly gives an idea: there are descriptions and discussions of practices, beliefs, sins. Nor does *İslam* hesitate to use Islamic concepts, though Western terms are not disregarded. One often meets terms such as *şirk* (associationalism), *tağut* (idolatry), *haram* (forbidden), *günah* (sin). Indeed, readers are usually assumed to have a profound knowledge of Islamic belief and doctrine. The editors are probably aiming at a more homogeneous group of readers, followers of the Nakşibendi order and graduates of Imam–Hatip schools and the Faculty of Theology.

İslam is a sophisticated periodical, but instead of preparing its followers for discussions with Western intellectuals as *Girişim* does, it is more of an internal communiqué that aims to raise the level of understanding of its followers and to give them social, economic and political instructions. By reading *İslam*, however, an ordinary Muslim can be converted to the tarikat line, and a non-Muslim can become a believer. It has a strong didactic tone; but as there are separate sections, ordinary believers probably read those that interest them and ignore the others.

Another characteristic of *İslam* is its optimism. In every issue there are at least ten 'good-news' stories from the Muslim world; they may be on major issues, such as how the Western bloc is in crisis and deadlock, or minor affairs, such as an Islamic conference or news from an Islamic Bank. From a reading of the volumes, one might imagine that the Islamic movement will succeed in a few years' time, not only in Muslim countries but probably even in Britain. This optimism is focused on youth, one of the two categories of society that are specifically addressed, who are given a special role in the Jihad, and the recent Islamic revival among the youth is seen as a significant omen for the future. The second special category is women, who are seen in the same perspective: they can be part of the Jihad by making their homes into schools of Islamic belief and by bringing up Muslim children.

İslam, unlike *Girişim*, has a very clear model of society for emulation in the future, that is Asrı Saadet, which is frequently referred to and described in detail, with the lives of Muhammad and his Companions depicted as ideals. As human nature has not changed, there is no reason why the rules which applied then should be changed. This idealization leads to frequent reference to Islamic history and doctrine. In every issue at least one hero is chosen from among the early Muslims, his or her basic deeds are described and praised, and readers are advised to draw lessons from them. Usually these are stories of extreme devotion, obedience to Muhammad, and self-sacrifice.

The essence of Asrı Saadet, *İslam* argues, is valid in the present world. This validity will be more profound if Koranic principles and Sharia are practised and people are allowed to live Islam fully. Of course they realize that the world has changed, and there is more differentiation and complexity today; but society was created by Allah, and, exactly like an organism, every group in society has a function and these functions are programmed to work in harmony. Today's society is one of conflict and chaos, because Koranic principles have been abandoned; to restore harmony and order we must refer back to Asrı Saadet. Asrı Saadet is an ideal model, where one can find solutions to even the most modern problems. Although Muslim society has diverged from the 'correct path' of Sharia, none the less there has been improvement in the doctrine. Doctrine, the accumulation of Islamic literature, is accepted as an integral part of tradition. One very important aspect is that in *İslam* there is little discussion; one usually finds solutions and instructions, which can be about anything from the elimination of time-wasting during work to techniques for fighting the propaganda of Westernization.

Unlike *Girişim*, *İslam* is not specifically political, but it has a political model integrated into its global and holistic system. This model is future-oriented, but takes its principles from Asrı Saadet. An overall evaluation clearly indicates a self-confidence derived from the centuries of tradition of the Nakşibendi order. It is determined, bold and ambitious, aiming to appeal to all Muslims in the world, but it is still presented in the context of a proposal for a social morality rather than a political programme. However, some themes arise repeatedly which hint at a political stance: anti-Westernism, internationalism, totalism, relations of authority between leader and believers, means of communication and proposed routes of Islamic action.

Anti-Westernism

The editors of *İslam* see Western society as a bloc, without differentiating between socialism and capitalism, both of which are regarded as materialist. They are clearly anti-Marxist, and claim that socialism is incompatible with Islam. The capitalist world consists of two complementary components: one is the consumer society, which impoverishes people and countries through inflation, interest and waste; the other is culture and science. They argue that the West is trying to create a sense of inferiority in Islam, particularly through 'modern science', the source of imperialism since it imposes the universalism and superiority of Western civilization. They claim that the cultural aspect of Westernization is more important than the economic, because it is culture that Muslims are trying to incorporate, and it is culture that leaves Muslims with a feeling of inferiority.

İslam accepts that Western culture is dominant in the world now; but this situation is temporary, and there are clear signs that it is changing. One sign is the degeneration of Western culture: problems such as AIDS, the alienation of the individual in the consumer society, the loneliness of the elderly. Another sign is the appeal of Islam in Western society. In every issue there is a story of conversion to Islam. Great pride is taken in the conversion of Yusuf Islam (Cat Stevens) and Roger Garaudy, and it is argued that some distinguished Westerners do understand the deterioration of the West, and become devout Muslims. Islamic societies have previously had periods of relative decline which they used for gathering energy for a resurgence to take what Allah has promised them.

So what is to be done? First of all, Muslims must go back to history and search for their own culture and identity, which must be purified from Western values, otherwise they will be assimilated to the West. Secondly, Muslims should give priority to economic development. Non-developed, non-industrialized societies are vulnerable to imperialist exploitation. The reason why there has been no development until now is that Muslims have been under the influence of Western culture, whose purpose is to leave them underdeveloped. So moral purification will bring the urge for development. Thirdly, Muslim countries should join forces to fight the materialist world, so an Islamic community is proposed to counter the European Community.

Internationalism

İslam lays such stress on the internationalist aspect of the movement that in the first two volumes it gives the impression of not being aimed at a Turkish readership at all; but three countries in particular are marginally or occasionally mentioned: Iran, Saudi Arabia and Turkey. In all four volumes the editors maintain their critical position towards both Iran and Saudi Arabia, but in the third and fourth volumes attention is increasingly turned to Turkey, due, I think, to internal problems in the Nakşibendi order and their political alliances, rather than to a change in their internationalist approach.

İslam argues that in every existing Muslim society, whether among the minorities of the Soviet Union or in Saudi Arabia, there is an identity problem which is due to Western domination. Yet Muslims live in the richest parts of the world, therefore there is no reason why they should not take the lead. There is no attempt to discuss Islamic resurgence in one country; all Muslims are part of a community (the Ummah) and resurgence can be achieved only by a united movement. In this they attribute great importance to Sayyid Qutb and his theory of Jihad.

Turkey's role in this unity is leadership. Turkey has two advantages, the first of which is history: 'Our nation for a long period has carried the flag of Islam and been the representative of Muslims; we have raised great and important personalities, improved Islamic civilization, helped Muslim brothers everywhere around the world, protected them fiercely, ruled in three continents, and received love and respect from all communities because of our good deeds.'[23] Secondly, in Turkey there is a wide community of the Learned who can lead the Muslims.

Political barriers such as nationality and national border problems, and economic barriers such as trade and investment tariffs should therefore be eliminated, and a common cultural and economic medium should be organized and implemented. In this unification, language is an important problem, but Arabic is not insisted upon. İslam proposes an Islamic United Nations for political purposes, an Islamic common market, a single monetary system and a common Islamic politics of development. In all of these, it is implied, Turkey, the most developed, will provide the leadership.

Totalism

İslam has a unitary interpretation of the Islamic religion. It recognizes few problem areas except trivial issues related to conduct; even here, the believer is offered few choices and no initiative in interpretation. Moreover, Islam is presented as a total ideology. 'It is not economic. It is not political, it is not social, it is not academic, but Islam presents a cosmos and a global model. You cannot divide the lives of Muslims into parts.'[24] The division into parts is considered a Christianization and laicization of Islam, because then it becomes possible to argue that the faith is embedded in the individual's heart, and to separate practice and belief from the political. On the contrary, Islam has a different model for agriculture, trade, unionization, politics and so on. Through this, *İslam* can also be critical of other Islamic movements that stress one aspect of society over others. Islamic movements that are not holistic enough, and not patient enough to wait for a holistic revival, cannot succeed.

The self-confidence of *İslam* is striking compared to *Girişim*. It is very evident that its authors not only preach a unified ideology but, relying on 600 years of experience, they seem positive that their group has found the correct Islam. They say they can live with the infidels, as Muhammad did for tactical reasons, and they can tolerate believers' misdeeds, warning them of their sins, but if the sinful believer carries it too far even his belief (*iman*) should not be a reason for tolerance; religion cannot make concessions. *İslam* is critical of all other new movements in Islam, including the Nurcus.

So *İslam* proposes that its readers should:

> list all the Islamic activities in their environment, to comprehend the ideas, know the people and the groups, and even make a well-documented inventory of them. Without cutting your ties with the others, support the side that you think is the most firm and strong, and, instead of serving in one area and thus being rivals, make sure that you are

distributed in different kinds of functions so that there is a division of labour, a plan, a programme and followers oriented to all important areas of service.[25]

Thus we can see that İslam not only conveys a totalistic ideology but can also propose rational plans of organization for spreading its ideology in the present-day world.

The individual, the community and the leader

For İslam, with its tarikat background, the linkage between follower and leader (the shaikh) is very important. There are frequent detailed descriptions of this relationship, emphasizing that to be a true Muslim is impossible without a leader.

As a basic premise, however, each individual is responsible for his own choice in faith. Belief is not separated from action, and all are equal in faith, practice and Jihad, the main components of religion. An ideal believer is the one who has purified himself from Western values, such as ambition, avarice or seeking profit without input of labour; instead, the individual should rely on labour and hard work rather than on luck, show good will towards Muslims, pray for salvation and be charitable. Rather than involving himself with other people's sins, he should try to purify himself, but also warn others. The faithful Muslim is responsible in three dimensions: awareness of his environment, responsibility to others and living in a unified community.

Individual believers therefore cannot practise Islam alone; they need a community where they support each other and are considered brothers, like parts of an organism. This organic unity gives them love of each other and a sense of solidarity. The feeling of community integrates believers as the basis of both social justice and social control. The responsibility imposed on the believer, irrespective of race, nationality or lineage, urges him to intervene in the non-Islamic deeds of other Muslims. Moreover, even if he himself is sinful, he is still required to intervene to stop others from sinning. In this community, he is responsible for others' welfare. The unjust world, for example, where workers are exploited by employers, makes people cruel; cruelty can be prevented only by helping the poor, for which Islamic charity institutions are offered as the best examples.

Being a good Muslim, like any branch of knowledge, has to be learned from a teacher. 'The individual when left alone has a limited capacity. His zeal and intelligence are not enough when he is alone. Then he has to confess this weakness and search for someone to hold his hand.'[26] This is the shaikh (the *rabıta*) whom one must emulate, the leader of religious faith who can take one to heaven or hell. Therefore, it is important whom you follow and emulate because he is responsible for your afterlife; but he is also responsible for improving the community, and thus he is the leader of conduct in this world. İslam clearly states that leadership is required in every Islamic group, but it also implies that the shaikh is a political and military leader, though it does not stress this. The construction of the community is given priority because this seems more relevant in the present world. For this, every follower is asked to make contact with different people; amongst the strategies devised are: to help others, to be nice to people, to understand them and to be patient and to wait for an approach from others.

Communication

According to İslam, the reason for creation is to search for Allah. Any knowledge acquired becomes relevant only if it is oriented towards that search. This may be scientific knowledge, but will not be a value in itself unless it helps the search for Allah. The Western world is trying to stop this search by imposing the view that its values and knowledge are superior, and by giving false information and interpretations of events.

İslam proposes to fight this in two ways: first, by creating a new medium of communication based on Islamic information and the wider circulation of Islamic knowledge. To unite Muslims, this communication network, including all Muslim communities, should be given utmost priority. Muslim news agencies must be established, independent of Western sources that are not impartial. Radio, television and video are not intrinsically bad, but they are used by Westerners for the wrong purposes. Therefore, private Muslim foundations must be organized for such activities; these may include private radio and television stations, clubs and training schools for journalists.

The second tactic is that, in bringing up children, ties with the existing educational system should be cut. Two educational centres are proposed, first homes and mosques, where the principles of Islamic life are taught, and secondly private institutions, community schools where secular teaching is kept to a minimum.

Islamic action

There are two parallel stages of Islamic action: Hijra (*hicret*, 'withdrawal') and Jihad (*cihad*, 'struggle'). Hijra means to purify oneself from foreign values and society, to be a pure Muslim, a true believer. Non-Islamic aspects of life such as nationality, race and all Western values should be eliminated. Hijra has two components, the fight against the self and selfish desires, but, more important, the formation of an ideal community of believers, that is, a model society. There are even hints that this may also be reflected in space, as in a suburb or a village.

But to be a Muslim by yourself is not enough, not even in a community. All believers, not only the leaders, are responsible for the diffusion of Allah's message, which can be carried out through mass communication, by donations, and in warfare – all three are considered appropriate by *İslam*. Jihad should begin at once, but which way to take first is a matter for planning. The secret of success is in planning one's time and in belief. The size of forces is irrelevant, as even the enemy's forces are the property of Allah. However, *İslam* often gives detailed descriptions of armaments, presumably technical information for the believer's armed struggle in Jihad.

İslam gives special prominence to Afghanistan. There is no issue in which the Jihad there is not mentioned and praised. The authors see the importance of the Afghan Jihad in its puncturing of the myth of the superpowers, showing that even a small group of the faithful can make life very difficult for them.

Summary

İslam represents a new interpretation of an old movement; its outstanding features are an awareness of the modern Western world, and a strong resistance to it. Although the technical facilities that come with modernization are to be used as blessings from Allah, the culture that is diffused through them is to be rejected. *İslam* is trying to find an image to be emulated in the Muhammadan period, but whether this can be located in the present world is not elaborated. Lack of discussion, and a didactic style, are prominent throughout the periodical. This is of course an outcome of the patriarchal, authoritarian leadership style of the order, and the total ideology that is being proposed.

CONCLUSION

Two intellectual Islamic journals have been compared. *Girişim* seems to be influenced by recent currents of thought in secular leftist circles: it is anti-étatist, anti-authoritarian and pluralist. It is new, as reflected in the timidity it shows towards its movement and ideology. It is mainly political, but this focus provides no security. It lacks networks and organized backing, with which rival groups are very well equipped. *Girişim* seems likely to remain an intellectual movement for a long period. Trying to be part of the intellectual tradition in Turkey in the 1980s, it seems to be affected by current ideologies mainly as part of Western discourse, such as anti-authoritarianism, realism and geographic specificity.

İslam, on the other hand, argues from a position of confidence, with a 600-year-old ideological tradition and an organizational network extending beyond the boundaries of Turkey. It is very rational in its approach, and claims to be at a stage where it can propose solutions, programmes and models. Interestingly, although at first sight *İslam* is not purely political, it is more oriented towards political action, even showing that it has the potential to mobilize people for that cause.

It is also interesting that *Girişim*, being oriented towards Turkey, under the influence of the new political culture of the 1980s is preaching discussion and theory, while the internationalist movement of *İslam* is calling for action, if not in Turkey, certainly in Afghanistan. *Girişim*'s conflict model of society leads it towards pluralism, while the organic model of society in *İslam* is used as support for Jihad.

Although *Girişim* has a firm stance as a strict supporter of scripture rather than tradition and Sufism, its sensitivity to the dialogue between Islamic and secular ideologies, its positive attitude towards modern technology, the meticulous attention with which it adopts modern Western political institutions such as parliament and values such as freedom, equality and pluralism, suggest that this periodical's ideology can be considered fundamentalist but modernist. Its modernism becomes more obvious when it considers the impact of Western ideologies, even if it shows reluctance to adopt them.

İslam, on the other hand, has a neo-traditionalist approach. Although it does not refute modernism as a whole (it accepts modern technology), its opposition to the culture and political system that accompany modernization indicates a strong reaction and retreat to traditional religion with its totalism, Sufism and authoritative figures.

These two periodicals are very different, both in their approach to Islam and in the methods they propose to revive it, as well as in their strength. *İslam* has great popular appeal because it is backed by the Nakşibendi order and its networks. But periodicals such as *Girişim* have also expanded their influence among urban educated groups. The rivalry and lack of compromise between them is accentuated as each one consolidates its own stronghold. The dimensions of variation are action or inaction, totalism or pluralism, authoritarianism or participation, whereas anti-Westernism is the main common denominator. Whether these differences can be resolved is highly dependent on both the internal dynamic of the movement itself and its interaction with both popular religion and secular ideologies.

NOTES

1. Bernard Lewis, 'Islamic revival in Turkey', *International Affairs* 28, 1952, pp. 38–9. Howard Reed, 'Revival of Islam in secular Turkey', *Middle East Journal*, 7, 1954, pp. 267–82. L. V. Thomas, 'Recent developments in Turkish Islam', *Middle East Journal*, 6, 1952, pp. 22–40.
2. Binnaz Toprak, *Islam and Political Development in Turkey*, Leiden, Brill, 1981. Jacob Landau, 'The National Salvation Party in Turkey', *Asian and African Studies* 11 (1), 1976. Ali Yaşar Sarıbay, *Türkiye'de Modernleşme, Din ve Parti Politikası: MSP Örnek Olayı*,

Istanbul, Alan Yayıncılık, 1985. Ahmed N. Yücekök, *Türkiye'de Örgütlenmiş Dinin Sosyo-Ekonomik Tabanı*, Ankara University, Siyasal Bilgiler Fakültesi Yayınları, 1971.

3. H. Costa, 'Jeune Islam turc. Neo-conservatisme au subversion', *L'Afrique et l'Asie Modernes*, 150, 1986, pp. 105–15. Emelie Olson, 'Muslim identity and secularism in contemporary Turkey: the "headscarf dispute"', *Anthropological Quarterly*, 58 (4), 1985, pp. 161–71. Deniz Kandiyoti, 'Emancipated but unliberated? Reflections on the Turkish case', *Feminist Studies*, 13 (2), 1987, pp. 317–38. Şerif Mardin, 'Culture and religion towards the year 2000', in *Turkey in the Year 2000*, Turkish Political Science Association, Ankara, Sevinç Matbaası, 1989, pp. 163–186.

4. H. M. Federspiel, 'Islam and development in the nations of Asean', *Asian Survey*, 25 (8), 1985, pp. 804–7. J.-C. Vatin, 'Popular puritanism versus state reformism: Islam in Algeria', in James P. Piscatori, ed., *Islam in the Political Process*, London, Cambridge University Press, 1983.

5. J. Casanova, 'The politics of the religious revival', *Telos*, 59, 1984, pp. 3–33. J. Voll, 'Revivalism and social transformations in Islamic history', *The Muslim World*, 76 (3–4), 1986, pp. 168–80. Henry Munson, Jr., 'Islamic revivalism in Morocco and Tunisia', ibid., pp. 202–18. Yvonne Haddad, 'Muslim revivalist thought in the Arab world: an overview', ibid., pp. 143–67. M. Yadegari, 'Liberation theology and Islamic revivalism', *Journal of Religious Thought*, 43 (2), 1987, pp. 38–50.

6. James Piscatori, 'Introduction', in Piscatori, ed., *Islam in the Political Process*.

7. The following points of analysis have been compiled from the usage of the concepts in Bassam Tibi, 'The renewed role of Islam in the political and social development of the Middle East', *Middle East Journal*, 37 (1), 1983, pp. 3–13. W. E. Shephard, '"Fundamentalism" Christian and Islamic', *Religion*, 17, 1987, pp. 355–78; idem, 'Islam and ideology: towards a typology', *International Journal of Middle East Studies*, 19, 1987, pp. 307–36. James Piscatori, 'Ideological politics in Saudi Arabia', in Piscatori, ed., *Islam in the Political Process*.

8. A. Sachedina, 'Ali Shariati: ideologue of Iranian revolution', in John Esposito, ed., *Voices of Resurgent Islam*, Oxford, Oxford University Press, 1983.

9. C. Adams, 'Mawdudi and the Islamic state', in ibid., p. 117.

10. M. Metiner, *Girişim*, no. 19, p. 2.

11. Sachedina, 'Ali Shariati'.

12. Yvonne Haddad, 'Sayyid Qutb: ideologue of Islamic revival', in Esposito, ed., *Voices*.

13. Sachedina, 'Ali Shariati'.

14. M. Metiner, *Girişim*, no. 99, p. 2.

15. Idem, *Girişim*, no. 3, p. 46.

16. 'Editorial', *Girişim*, no. 1, p. 1.

17. Adams, 'Mawdudi'; Sachedina, 'Ali Shariati'.
18. M. Metiner, *Girişim*, no. 16, p. 58.
19. *Girişim*, no. 13, p. 14.
20. A. Seçkin, *Girişim*, no. 3, p. 38.
21. M. Metiner, *Girişim*, no. 16, p. 51.
22. Taham Mustafa, *Girişim*, no. 24, p. 30.
23. H. Necatioğlu, *İslam*, no.12, p. 48.
24. K. Kahraman, *İslam*, no. 22, p. 10.
25. H. Necatioğlu, *İslam*, no. 22, p. 4.
26. H. Algar, *İslam*, no. 3, p. 33.

12

WOMEN IN THE IDEOLOGY OF ISLAMIC REVIVALISM IN TURKEY:
Three Islamic Women's Journals

Feride Acar

THE FRAMEWORK

Until recently, the religious sphere has found conspicuously little representation in the ranks and products of the civilian–military élite of the 'centre' in Republican Turkey. In fact, it has been claimed that throughout Ottoman–Turkish history élite groups of diverse and often contrasting nature have exhibited the common feature of privileging state over religion or being outrightly secular, although such non-religiousness may have been reflected, at different times, in various attitudes and ideologies of anti-clericalism, statist-reformism, 'secular Jacobinism' or positivist-Kemalism.[1] It was thus expected by many that the secular civilian–military coalition at the 'centre' of Turkish politics, despite some concessions and compromises, would continue effectively to keep out the religious contingent of the 'periphery'. It is in this sense that the rapid advent of Islamic groups on the Turkish political scene in the last decade has caused concern, consternation and even alarm among secular natives as well as Western observers.

The Islamic Revolution in Iran, and the general upsurge of Islamic revivalism in the Middle East, have been popularly indicated as external factors contributing to the ascent of Islam in Turkey. Also among the internal causes of this phenomenon some analysts have cited the pragmatic policies of the post-1980 military regime, seen as tolerant and concessional towards the Islamic groups.[2]

A more structural explanation is suggested by an analysis of the complex dynamics of social forces in Ottoman–Turkish history. Accordingly, the rise of Islamic groups may be seen as a gradual process, which has benefited from facilities provided by the secular reforms of the state and structural transformations of society, as well as the cultural void created in the process.[3] Consequently the Islamic groups' acquisition of legitimacy and incorporation into the ranks of the élite by the late 1970s and 1980s are related to their ability to re-introduce Islam as an alternative ideology.

In the analysis of the nature of this ideology and the strategies of contemporary Islamic revivalist movements in Turkey, their attitudes and messages regarding women acquire a central importance for several reasons. First of all, orthodox Islamic ideology in its effort to conquer ground on the issue of women has had to face a strong counter-ideology in republican Turkey, a society that has been exposed to an élite-directed radical transformation of traditional values regarding women. The secular élite's adoption of and commitment to the ideology of women's emancipation has also helped elevate this issue to the symbolic level, despite the fact that not all groups and sectors in Turkish society have internalized the secular reformist ideology of the Republic. Thus, the issue of women has emerged as a major battle-ground in the struggle between secularists and Islamists in the past, and it promises to persist as such in the future. It is not coincidental or insignificant, for instance, that today the most emphasized issue on the Islamic movements' agenda, and the most overt focus of Islamic activism on the national political scene, is the 'head-scarf dispute'. Undoubtedly, this selection of the 'woman issue' also draws from the fact that the Islamic position on women's roles and dress is often difficult to separate from the merely traditional stand on these matters. As such, Islamists' claims here are expected to receive wider support in society.

Secondly, Islam reflects a genuine sensitivity to the question of women's rights, position and roles in society. As a comprehensive social regulator, Islam is particularly careful and elaborate on the issues of family and relations between the sexes as forces that are crucial in the maintenance of order and assume central roles in the process of societal regeneration. In this context, women in their capacity as wives, mothers and home-makers are viewed as social agents responsible for creating and maintaining harmony in family life and socializing the young in line with Islamic principles. This attributes paramount importance to women in the ideology of Islam.

Thirdly, the importance of women in the analysis of the revivalist movements is also due to their active participation in these movements in Turkey. Here, those trained in the Kemalist discourse often raise a critical question: what motivates women to participate actively in the propagation of an ideology that by definition relegates them to a secondary position in its fight against an establishment officially identified with women's emancipation? I believe that in Turkey, as an outcome of the secular Kemalist reforms, women particularly have been exposed to contradictory, dissonant messages and practices and filled with false expectations and aspirations, and have thus been rendered vulnerable and receptive to an ideology that simplifies reality and promises escape from role conflict and ambiguity.

The Kemalist élite emphasized women's emancipation as a sign of the country's level of secularism and modernity, and equated the two latter concepts with social justice and individual happiness. Significantly, a denial of this equation is used in the ideological discourse of Islamic revivalism in Turkey for mobilizing women: secularism and modernity, perceived as the twin evils of contemporary life, are particularly blamed for the misery and unhappiness of womankind. In other words, the banner of women's 'rights' and 'emancipation' is now raised by Islamic groups to attack secularism and modernity, which are perceived as reasons for women's 'exploitation' and 'degradation' in a manner reminiscent of the position of original Islam *vis-à-vis* the Jahiliye system. Hence the Islamic groups' call on women to the front lines of Islamic Jihad.

These considerations lead one to expect the analysis of women's roles in the ideology of Islamic revivalism in Turkey to be a window promising a penetrating view of the world of Islamic movements.

WOMEN AS PORTRAYED IN ISLAMIC JOURNALS[4]

This chapter reports on the findings of a content-analysis of a selection of Islamic monthly publications for women. In this analysis, the guiding concern has been to identify similarities as well as variations among these monthlies as regards issues selected for emphasis and de-emphasis, messages conveyed, and styles of presentation.

For the purpose of this research, the contents of three Islamic women's magazines were systematically analysed: *Kadın ve Aile* (Woman and Family), *Bizim Aile* (Our Family) and *Mektup* (Letter). To provide a general framework, four other publications were studied which are not women's magazines but have women's pages or sections or regularly publish material for and about women: *Köprü* (Bridge), *İslam*, *İcmal* (Epitome) and *Öğüt* (Advice). All these journals are known to represent major orders and groups in the Islamic world.

A breakdown of the affiliations of these periodicals shows that *Kadın ve Aile*, published since April 1985, is the largest Islamic women's magazine (reputed to sell 60,000) and is closely associated with that branch of the Nakşibendi order whose major mouthpiece is *İslam* (circulation 100,000).[5]

Bizim Aile, a more recent addition (published since February 1988) to the repertoire of Islamic women's magazines, is a spin-off of *Köprü*, a monthly published since 1977 representing the views of a section of the Nurcu order. *Bizim Aile* carries the Nurcus' message regarding women.

Mektup, published in Konya since February 1985, does not seem to be so clearly associated with any order, and appears to disseminate a more activist and radical message. It is categorized by some observers as being 'close to Nakşibendi views', while others decribe it as 'independent'.[6]

Öğüt and *İcmal*,[7] finally, are known as publications of the Kadiri order.

This chapter presents a description and analysis of the prominent themes, approaches and messages of *Kadın ve Aile*, *Bizim Aile* and *Mektup*, and contains insights gained through the analysis of the other journals, even though their contents are not discussed explicitly.

KADIN VE AILE

Kadın ve Aile appears to have organized its message against the background theme of opposition to the image of the Westernized, modern woman in Turkey. The main thrust of its ideological stance is criticism and active rejection of anything and everything associated with modernity, Westernization and secularism, by painting the picture of a doomed West.

A typical editorial runs:

> A number of Western thinkers and philosophers clearly state that Western civilization is mentally and spiritually sick and is leading humanity to disaster. They are looking for ways of saving themselves. . . . In Western civilization people use principles in a one-sided manner for their own interests, they do not respect the rights of others, they exterminate innocent and defenceless nations cruelly. They have risen to a climax of pride and exhibitionism, and have taken the road poxed with syphilis and AIDS to pleasure and hedonism. Concepts of honour and family are trampled on constantly in the process. Ties of love and respect among individuals have disintegrated, generations have been sacrificed to alcohol, narcotics and lust, have become hippies and punks. . . . It is time that we realized the superiority and perfection of our belief and culture. We should stick diligently [to our inheritance] and stop imitating the West in order to raise our children as ethical, loving-respectful, enlightened, responsible, industrious and productive, pure Muslims. We should be very careful that the West's spiritual diseases are not spread to our descendants, our family hearths are not dissolved, and our nation does not decline materially and spiritually.[8]

A review of 660 articles, interviews and other items published in this monthly between April 1985 and May 1988 shows that a large number (100) are on topics such as women's roles in resisting Westernization and changes of traditional values. In this context, there is particular stress (66 of the 100) on opposition to watching television, taking summer vacations, using make-up and keeping up with fashion.

To complement its stand on anti-Westernization, *Kadın ve Aile* devotes nearly half its space (295 items) to material on women's roles in the household, in other words to presenting the image of the ideal woman:

For the Muslim woman, shame and honour are of primary importance. She is completely devoted to her husband and her home, she does not show herself to strange men, does not look at them. Her house has separate quarters for men and women. She does not go out without her husband's permission, and does not receive any male or female guests at home without his approval. [For her] premarital courtship and extramarital sex are forbidden.... [The Muslim woman] covers the beauties of her body in a veil, does not adorn herself outside of her home, does not show her treasures to strangers. She covers her head and wears a loose dress.... [For her] the main obligation is to establish a family and raise children. She is a loyal wife to her husband and an affectionate mother to her children. She looks after the house, does the chores, cooks, and strives for the proper upbringing, education and socialization of her children.[9]

Describing the ideal Muslim women in these terms, *Kadın ve Aile* interestingly enough devotes considerable space to items appealing to women as home-makers (176 of the 295) rather than mothers (85) or wives (54). Items on women's role as home-maker include entries on such topics as cooking, home decoration, plant care, craftwork, sewing, embroidery, home economics and family health care. The nature and abundance of the material in this category indicate two underlying themes. Obviously, they project *Kadın ve Aile*'s ideological stress on women's place as the 'home', and its restriction of women's duties to home-making, cooking and child care. However, they also give the magazine a distinctly 'this-worldly' appearance.

The magazine's treatment of women's motherhood role involves extensive discussions of child-rearing practices and children's health care. Although the message about raising children as proper Muslims is easily identifiable in some articles, this category seems dominated by interminable discussions of children's health care and practical issues such as 'bed-wetting' and 'thumb-sucking'. Such an approach also contributes to the magazine's appearance as a comprehensive, all-round women's monthly, almost balancing its emphasis on women's roles as pious practitioners of Islam. In fact, precisely such a balance is indicated by a count of items dealing with women's three major role-categories in the household (i.e. wife, mother and homemaker: 295 out of 660 items) as opposed to those dealing with women's roles as believers and practitioners of Islam (i.e. piety, observance of Muslim rules of dress and behaviour: 236 items).

Furthermore, while some articles on women's role as wives provide information on the Islamic conception of the institution and process of marriage and divorce, most dwell on the issue of women's place in Islamic society. In this context, women's equality, freedom and happiness are discussed and defined either within the boundaries of their wifely role or in the context of their status as 'believers'; never as aspects of their position or relationships as individuals in society. To these ends, one encounters frequent statements emphasizing women's equality with men in the other world as devout Muslims, and the relevance of 'justice' as opposed to equality in organizing gender relationships in this world:

> Man and woman are total equals in obeying Allah, in following the Prophet, in being human beings deserving humane treatment, in the sacredness of their honour and integrity. If they fulfil their obligations [in this world] they will both go to Heaven and have equal rewards; and if they forget their duties and are submerged in sin they will be equals in punishment. . . . Islam has separated the areas of work for man and woman through a division of labour. In this manner, it has prevented a war of inequality between them.[10]

> By distinguishing the duties of man and woman Islam has not obliterated woman's rights. On the contrary, it has protected them. Islam does not burden the woman with both the responsibility of earning money and that of her home and children. . . . Woman's special nature is protected by her special social position.[11]

In fact, the magazine's name indicates its perspective concisely.

The main mission of *Kadın ve Aile* appears to be to mould the image of a proper Muslim woman in Turkish society, building on the critique and rejection of the image of Westernized, secularized woman. Thus, while on the one hand it concentrates on elaborating the sources of women's 'exploitation' (for example pornography, women in advertisements) and 'misery' in Western society, diagnosing Westernized women as 'degenerate', 'immoral', 'discontented' and 'unhappy', on the other it provides the recipe for a life of happiness and contentment to be found in Islam and at home.

Parallel with this mission, *Kadın ve Aile* radiates a very prescriptive didactical message. For instance, there are numerous items (79) on the Islamic behaviour code and etiquette, telling readers what to do and what not to do in rather simplistic black-and-white terms, without much discussion of the justification or consequences of such behaviour. Combined with its emphasis on 'this-worldly' issues such as health care and home-making, such a prescriptive attitude almost defines a 'women's Islam'.

Kadın ve Aile's version of 'women's Islam' at first glance does not contradict the norms of a certain type of traditional social life regulating the lives of many women in Turkish towns and cities. In other words, while it clearly opposes and challenges the secular, 'modern' establishment and its norms in Turkish cities, it gives the reader the impression of falling in line with the values and life-styles of the more 'traditional' sectors of the Turkish urban population, that is, the small-town and Anatolian city 'bazaar' groups and their metropolitan counterparts.[12] In this sense the magazine's message strikes one as espousing an instrumental ideology for the perpetuation of traditional urban social order and relationships rather than the mobilizing ideology of a change-oriented movement.

However, to the extent that what is 'traditional' in the Turkish context is neither homogeneous nor dominant and widespread in any one form, but on the contrary highly heterogeneous, complex and changing, the model to which the ideological message of *Kadın ve Aile* conforms is far from being descriptive of a pervasive 'traditional' reality. Furthermore, I believe, today *Kadın ve Aile*'s Islamic message, despite its appearance, not merely propagates the consolidation of the 'traditional' way of life for women but in fact suggests a new and different Islamic existence. Born out of the confrontation of Islam with the secular world, this proposed order is a contemporary creation.

For instance, the conservative message of Islam is presented in

Kadın ve Aile through a more or less Western medium. One can almost discern a resemblance between this magazine and relatively conservative Western women's magazines, in terms of the issues they dwell on and their general appearance. This indicates that, while Islamic revivalist movements are appealing to women in secularized society by blaming and militantly rejecting the institutions and ways of this society as evil and dangerous, they recognize and make use of resources and norms characteristic of it.

It is noticeable that *Kadın ve Aile* devotes some space to the discussion of such 'public' aspects of women's existence as occupation (16 items) and education (13) – though admittedly much less than to women's domestic roles. Often the arguments on these issues reflect the conventional Islamic viewpoint, yet sometimes there are significant modifications, or noticeable variations in the treatment of different issues. For instance, in *Kadın ve Aile*, women's work outside the house is tolerated only as a last resort in cases of absolute financial need, and even then is clearly restricted to work in the proper environment, that is, sex-segregated localities. In fact, rather than go out and work to earn more, women are told to stay at home, be better home-makers and save their husband's earnings, or at best to practise homecrafts for supplementary income.

However, so far as education is concerned, although segregation is obviously preferred, women's attendance at secularized and co-educational institutions is not altogether rejected. In *Kadın ve Aile*, in the debate over women's education and segregation, the latter is effectively replaced by the concept of veiling. Although Islam's insistence on spatial segregation of males and females is not overtly rejected, *Kadın ve Aile* authors present their arguments as education with or without Islamic dress.

I think one can safely assume that among the secularizing reforms of the Turkish Republic co-education has been more effectively applied and commonly accepted by large segments of the population than has women's work outside the home. In this society, selling the idea of 'separate education for girls' is undoubtedly more difficult than the idea that 'women stay at home'. This is for reasons of both economic feasibility and cultural acceptability. Thus, even though Islam's sensitivity on the segregation of the sexes and the seclusion of women would apply equally to places of education and work, it is treated with very different emphasis by a publication like *Kadın ve Aile.*

Further evidence of this is the fact that the magazine has taken a clear political stand and opened a campaign for segregated transportation on municipal buses in metropolitan areas, despite its ambiguous attitude over segregation in education. Segregated transport is an issue likely to generate greater public support than school segregation, because it responds to the immediate demands of many people who are dissatisfied with this service. *Kadın ve Aile*'s noticeable avoidance of the issue of polygyny – a topic one would assume central for the women of a Muslim society – should I think also be explained in this light.

I believe such selective use of issues and arguments on the basis of the concrete sociological realities and experience of Turkey and Turkish women indicates that the agenda and strategy of Islamic revivalist movements are largely influenced by the 'successes' and 'failures' of the secular establishment. In other words, contemporary Islamic revivalist movements often, through their apparent divergencies from orthodox Islam and their variations from one another, reflect the constraints, requirements and peculiarities of the socio-cultural system of which they are a part.

It is in this sense that we may identify some elements in the ideology of such movements in contemporary Turkey that help define them as significantly different products of the Turkish experience, rather than as reflections of fundamentalist Islam. However, the salience of such apparent differences of a 'Turkish Islam' from fundamentalist or 'traditional' Islam depends largely on knowing whether such variation is confined to mere strategy or whether it reflects deeper-running ideological issues. It is not easy to assess this at this point.

Finally, to judge from the huge number of articles on medicine and health, and sections on literature and history, which assume a certain educational background, and items on topics such as dress patterns, food recipes or consumer tips, which assume an affinity with the 'bourgeois' life-style, *Kadın ve Aile*'s target group of readers can be described as middle-class women of the cities and towns. Since, as relatively well-educated women, they have been subjected to contradictory messages of gender equality and freedom on the one hand and the centrality of marriage and motherhood on the other, they are likely to experience role conflict, problems of identity definition and unfulfilled expectations. Through simultaneously portraying Westernization as the cause of moral downfall and psychological misery, and idealizing the image of Muslim woman, painted as devoted wife and mother, perfect home-maker, pious and obedient believer, and epitome of personal fulfilment and social responsibility, *Kadın ve Aile*'s message can be perceived as a harbinger of happiness by women who have an ambiguous definition of their place in this rapidly changing and not very consistent cultural environment.

BIZIM AILE

Bizim Aile is a new periodical with only four issues published as of May 1988, so it is more difficult to pin-point the distinctive features of its message and to identify possible differences from *Kadın ve Aile*. However, since it is a spin-off from *Köprü* and disseminates an obviously consistent message, interpreting its ideology does not depend solely on a content analysis of these four issues.

The difference in appearance is immediately obvious. *Kadın ve Aile*'s cover usually has photographs of flowers or children, or occasionally women, but only from a distance, from behind and almost always engaged in some religious or semi-religious activity such as prayer or meditation. By contrast, all four issues of *Bizim Aile* feature on their covers frontal and close-up photographs of women – in Islamic dress. These women are depicted in different activities and localities such as at home during Koran recitation, in the family context with a Western-looking husband (wearing a neck-tie), or in an office using a computer.

An initial look at the contents of this monthly reveals that a concern with veiling takes precedence over other topics. Eleven items of the total of 34 deal with women's modesty and veiling. They approach the issue, however, from a different perspective from *Kadın ve Aile*. While the latter emphasizes the merits of veiling for preventing Muslim women from being sexually attractive to strange men and thus threatening to the social order, *Bizim Aile* stresses veiling as an outcome and reflection of 'belief' (*iman*) in Muslim women:

Therefore, the first condition of being subject to [the call for] veiling is belief. The development of a true belief is essential for the implementation of the rule for veiling. . . . First belief, then veiling.[13]

In fact, this magazine's emphasis on 'belief' and believing seems to define its central outlook. The message is that 'belief' holds the key to the solution of women's problems, including that of modesty. One could even think that the publications *Bizim Aile* and *Köprü* express greater tolerance regarding veiling than any of the others, even though they do not explicitly diverge from the fundamental Koranic message:

> Moreover, it is pointed out that women should not be pressured to abide by the veiling rule, because Allah who has decreed the veiling command is forgiving of sins and infinitely merciful. Therefore, veiling cannot possibly be an issue of coercion. In fact, the principle of 'there is no coercion in Islam' should be remembered here. According to the formula of 'first belief, then veiling', if there is any hesitation, reluctance, or a condition of 'being unable to practise despite willingness' [on the part of the woman], what is first needed is serious reinforcement of belief.[14]

As opposed to the prescriptive attitude of *Kadın ve Aile*, stating details of what is to be done and what is not to be done by Muslim women, *Bizim Aile* has a distinctly more intellectual approach in appealing to its readers. The length of the articles, their style and the fact that, rather than reciting 'dos' and 'don'ts', they attempt to discuss the justification and higher meaning of issues such as veiling and women's roles as wives and mothers, give *Bizim Aile* a distinctive character. While this magazine also attempts to appeal to women via an alternative to the present social order, there are hints of a more abstract, more belief-oriented appeal here. The alternative, in other words, is defined at the level of 'belief' rather than that of behaviour:

> What we shall point out here is that regardless of what the woman is doing [in life], a materialist orientation will not

only fail to answer the fundamental questions but will also lead [her] away from the light of truth, towards the darkness of meaninglessness and emptiness. But should she work under the light of Islam, whatever the subject is, she will find the path to learning the truth about this world, herself and her duties.[15]

Also attempted in *Bizim Aile* (and *Köprü*) is a conceptualization of Muslim woman's rights as an issue in the politics of modern society. In contrast to *Kadın ve Aile*'s unquestioning, normative approach to women's issues, *Bizim Aile* attempts to deal with such matters by using the ideological tools of pluralist democratic thought – a product of secular society. In fact, the ideology expressed in *Bizim Aile* appears quite integrated into the present system, as symbolized by its cover photographs.

For example, when *Bizim Aile* publishes articles entitled 'Veiling is Freedom', 'A Scene Unbecoming to Secular Turkey', 'Law's Answer to an Informant Newspaper', to express its defence of Muslim women's rights to dress as they see fit, it openly uses the values, logic and vocabulary of pluralist democratic thought, the arguments of civil society and the tradition of the secular state. Thus the Muslim woman's head-scarf is presented as a symbol of the rights of the oppressed, and defended in the name of democracy and freedom. In the final analysis, somehow the demand for freedom to live an Islamic life becomes synonymous with the demand for women's emancipation. Both are ideals approved by the normative order of the existing political system but unfilfilled in reality by its mechanisms; hence, they open the door to alternative Islamic suggestions.

Ultimately, in its appeal to educated, urban women, *Bizim Aile* represents in style and appearance a more 'liberal' and conciliatory attitude that can be interpreted as an indication of the movement's potential for integration into the system. Further support for this interpretation may be found in the fact that *Bizim Aile* authors participate in forums and discussions organized by their secular counterparts, and engage in dialogue with secular writers and thinkers on issues of popular – even feminist – interest in the secular world, for example wife-beating. Their stand on these issues also appears to be shaped and expressed in the logic and language of secular politics. For example:

'If being beaten is women's problem, beating is men's. Women should not be beaten, but also men should not beat.' The way to achieve this is to develop individuals' personalities, to work for the acceptance and implanting of basic human rights in a democratic system through education and persuasion.[16]

On the other hand, in the specific contents of its message on women's issues, *Bizim Aile* (taken together with *Köprü*) often comes across as no more liberal than *Kadın ve Aile*. Moreover, its message is often contradictory. For example, its stand on women's work out of the home conforms to the mainstream Islamic position (a woman's place is in the home) despite the impression it creates by its covers depicting women in the office setting:

The argument that women can only be happy if they work [outside the home] is a fallacy; because for women to work outside without any need or obligation to do so means neglect of their home, family and children. This influences the psychological well-being of future generations.[17]

Moreover, *Bizim Aile*'s stand on some critical issues is very ambiguous. This may well be deliberate and tactical for political and legal reasons, or it may reflect a genuine difficulty at the level of movement ideology. An editorial expresses the nature of this ambiguity. The anonymous author is responding directly to one of the main anxieties of secular groups in Turkey – what would be the position of non-practising or non-believing women in an Islamic society?

In a society where in the name of the minority the rights of the majority have been tyrannically oppressed for a long time and continue to be so, this is not a question that should be thought about at this time. . . . In reality, our belief is that rights are rights regardless of whether they are the majority's or the minority's.[18]

It appears that, while the author clearly states the movement's ideological stance at the abstract or 'philosophical' level, he/she makes a point of refraining from applying this stance directly to the real-life situation.

MEKTUP

Mektup, despite its subtitle 'From Women's Pen to Everyone – Men and Women', is distinctly a women's monthly. In fact, even compared to the others, the message of this particular journal strikes the reader as what one might call 'womanist', as distinct from feminist. This message is both much more extremist and radical in content and presentation than the others; it is also more woman-based and activist.

First of all, because it publishes no photographs and uses only hand-drawn pictures of human figures with blank faces, *Mektup*'s appearance is very different. Its covers depict such scenes as symbolic hands of Satan with long manicured fingernails grabbing at a woman in Islamic garb who, instead of a face, has a picture of the Ka'ba surrounded by flowers; or a pair of hands, symbolizing the USA and the USSR (as indicated by signs on their shirt-sleeves), peeling the face of planet Earth with a knife symbolizing Israel, to turn the world into a bomb with the fuse already lit. There is a lot of blood on the cover-pictures, and frequent reference to the martyrs of Islam, such as on the cover of one issue where a hand holding the Koran rises out of a pool of blood on which there appears the sentence 'martyrs, those who died but did not die'. This highly dramatic and simplistic style of presentation reflects the contents and target of *Mektup*'s ideological message.

Mektup addresses women of the poorer strata, making specific calls to working-class women, women of the *gecekondu*, small-town women, and even peasant women. Frequently using Koranic terms, glorifying pain and capitalizing on the concept of 'accountability in the other world', *Mektup* seems to appeal to women who by joint consequence of their gender and their socio-economic position find themselves in extreme oppression and exploitation in contemporary Turkish society. It is obvious, however, that as a medium of written communication with a relative emphasis on women's 'public' roles, its target readership may be defined within this category as women who are relatively educated, albeit perhaps through Koran courses or religious schools of some kind.

Mektup's choice of subjects gives clues as to the nature of its readers. It contains endless expressions (fictional or non-fictional) of pain suffered by Muslim women at the hands of infidels. These accounts imply that Muslim women who are not allowed to live as their biological (*fitri*) characteristics require (i.e. veiled) go through terrible suffering under idolatrous (*tağuti*) systems but are that much more exalted in the eyes of Allah. Among such devilish rulers who subject Muslim women to oppression and pain are infidel husbands and 'pharaohs' – secular political authorities. This earthly suffering is viewed as normal but glorified as a trial or an examination leading believers to salvation in the other world, thus making heroines of the 'persecuted' Muslim women.

Furthermore, of all the Islamic publications reviewed here, *Mektup* most stresses such negative aspects of life in the other world as hellfire and 'grave-torment' (*kabır azabı*) for disobeying the rules of Islam. Complementing this emphasis are the very strict norms which the publishers advocate as regulators of life in this world. For instance, like the other magazines, *Mektup* devotes considerable space (35 out of 128 items) to veiling and segregation. However, interpreting the Koranic verse on veiling to mean covering the face and hands as well as all other parts of the body, *Mektup* publishes articles that advocate, as proper Islamic dress for women, the *çarşaf*, the face-veil and gloves, as opposed to merely the head-scarf and a long loose coat. Their stand on the issue of veiling is clearly more extremist and intolerant of deviation, as the following excerpts illustrate:

> Which scholar or which reasonable person can claim, in this day and age, that it is appropriate for women to display their face and hands? Whether the face and hands of women are to be veiled or not may be discussed only in the 'House of Islam' (*Dar ul-Islam*) where one is safe from temptation (*fitna*), since only then are one's life, religion, property and lineage protected. Otherwise, since these securities do not exist in the 'House of War' (*Dar ul-Harb*), the 'House of Pagans' (*Dar uş-Şirk*) or the 'House of Apostasy' (*Dar ur-Riddet*), temptation abounds [and women need to be thoroughly covered].[19]

To go around unveiled and to be free of sins are clearly impossible, because in Islam veiling is compulsory *(farz)*. Compulsory means that if one does not believe in [this type of rule], one is a non-believer. If the belief [in a *farz*] is there, one would be committing a cardinal sin when one does not fulfil the command. . . . Thus any Muslim woman will have to admit her position as a sinner, if she accepts the rule [of veiling] yet fails to practise it.[20]

In *Mektup*'s conceptualization, if a woman cannot cope with the demands of Allah, or is ignorant of Islam, there is always also the initial this-worldly outlet of recognizing one's misdeeds and feeling guilty. In fact, *Mektup* features a regular page entitled 'Guilty Conscience' (*Vicdan Azabı*), where detailed stories are told of women suffering from the sins they have committed in their lives. Remarkably, most of these are rather unusual 'horror-stories' of women from lower socio-economic strata and marginal walks of life, such as prostitutes, drug-addicts, convicts. While such a selection may indicate the publishers' assumption that *Mektup* readers will somehow identify and empathize with these fallen women and their experiences, it also illustrates how central such notions as pain and guilt and their graphic articulation are in the discourse of this magazine.

Mektup writers also argue to extremes proper Islamic attitudes and behaviour on consumption – such as rejection, in the name of frugality, of home furniture and what they consider luxury foods, such as cakes and cookies. Obviously this attitude indicates strong asceticism, but it also implies a definition of the social class position of the magazine's clientele as poor. In this respect, too, *Mektup*'s message contrasts with those of *Kadın ve Aile* and *Bizim Aile*, which assume a middle-class, less spartan existence among their readers. The contrast between *Mektup*'s perception of women and that of the other two journals becomes even clearer when one examines the distribution of items concerning various role categories for women. Items on women's roles as prac-titioners of Islam add up to 78 (out of 128), while only 19 deal with women as wives, two with women as mothers, while no item on women as home-makers could be identified. Thus the ideal Muslim woman painted by *Mektup* is a human being who is materially deprived and spiritually wronged in the unjust and ungodly world in which she lives. Her only support and hope come from her piety and strict observance of the rules of Islam, promising her heaven in the other world.

As radical and intolerant as it is in matters of women's seclusion and observance of Islamic practices, *Mektup* attributes an especially active role to women in the Jihad for the propagation of Islam. Items on Jihad, and on women as active participants in this effort (as *mücahide*), constitute the second largest category (22 out of 128) in the magazine during our review period. Some examples are:

> Consequently, women believers have to fight against idolatrous governments which are rebellious against Allah or Allah's kingdom. Women believers cannot be bound by marriage to men who believe in idols and fight in their name. As women believers we want to be able to use our rights and powers within the boundaries drawn by Allah and his Messenger . . . to raise our children as good believers. . . . Regardless of who they are, those who want to deprive us of these rights are rebellious against Allah. All forces rebellious against Allah are idolatrous and all Muslims are ordered to disobey such idols. Thus the struggle of Muslim woman is not a struggle between the sexes but her struggle to keep her promise to Allah.[21]

This message can be expected to give women, through the exalted role of *mücahide*, an alternative identity of respectability. By making the emphasis on women's role in the propagation of Islam its fundamental mission, *Mektup* may be presenting a message that is very attractive to women suffering from precisely such a lack of respectability in their social positions.

In *Mektup*'s ideology, the *mücahide* who is a practising believer and active propagator of Islam is entrusted with the responsibility of protecting her husband and family in a society filled with the dangerous and evil forces of Westernization and secularism. While this implies an emphasis on the nuclear family, what is probably more significant is the emphasis on the concept of protecting the husband. The husband is the sole provider and guarantor of the woman's security; as such, he is to be protected from the potentially threatening influences of contemporary secular institutions and relationships, and the appeals of Westernized women in society. In other words, in *Mektup*'s message to its readers we can identify manifestations of a gender ideology that offers Islam and its restrictive social norms as safe-haven against the dangers which the outside world holds for the woman's husband and her marriage, that is, her own security. The following statement is a clear reflection of this viewpoint:

> Ladies! . . . To increase our attractiveness for our husbands at home, and to decrease it outside, is our fundamental principle. That is, we shall be attractive at home and repulsive outside.[22]

Hence the magazine's radical and uncompromising attitude on veiling and sex segregation can be seen as an attempt to enhance woman's security by minimizing competition from other women.

Mektup writers also express approval of a non-traditional division of labour between spouses at home. They legitimize and encourage the husband's participation in household chores and child care through arguments built on the Prophet's life. They also propose a greater and more active participation of women in family decision-making and in work outside. For example:

> In Islam, men's superiority is out of the question. Men and women are each other's helpers and spouses. Neither is superior to the other. Whoever is better is superior; whoever speaks the truth is right. Men who 'live' Islam are their wives' helpers. They help their wives in all household chores and taking care of the children.[23]

> Neither women nor men can stay home. It is stated in the Koran that human beings are put on earth to work. Women who do not stay idle, that is women who work according to Islam, are engaged in Jihad, in worship. . . . In short, [the rule is] women should work in all fields permitted by Islam.[24]

The implications of such a more activist attitude appear to be different from the passive, traditional wife–mother image developed in *Kadın ve Aile*.

CONCLUSION

Despite differences in style and content, all three Islamic journals reviewed here aim basically at creating and/or increasing the Islamic consciousness of Turkish women through the development of an alternative culture of Islam in Turkey. To this end, opposition to the norms of secular culture constitute the main banner of all three magazines.

Such opposition is undoubtedly rooted in conformity to such basic Islamic perceptions as the priority of women's roles in the private sphere, the centrality of justice rather than equality in regulating relations between the sexes, and the necessity of veiling and segregation for guiding the social and personal lives of Muslim women everywhere. In fact, in all three publications, rejection of the norms of secular culture and a Western style of life is justified by reference to Koranic verses and the conduct of the Prophet.

Yet the conception of women and their place in society promoted by the ideology of Islamic revivalism in Turkey also reflects the realities and experiences of direct interaction with secular norms in this society. The interaction of Islam with the Turkish secular experience manifests itself in a series of values and attitudes articulated by different wings of the Islamic movement. They range from uncompromising, militant fundamentalism to world views that suggest no more than a conservative social existence and pious individual behaviour.

Islamic revivalist discourse on the topic of women reflects this range of convictions too, as I have tried to demonstrate in this chapter. In this context, while *Kadın ve Aile* and *Bizim Aile* appear as the Islamic counterparts of secular conservative women's magazines, *Mektup* sends out an openly radical message to women in the name of Islam.

The treatment of women as merely extensions of the family institution underlies the discourse of the two former journals, as is perhaps symbolically expressed by their names. An Islamic conceptualization that assigns women passive roles, stressing predominantly their confinement to the private sphere as wives, mothers and home-makers, may appear readily reconcilable with the norms of a significant part of the traditional order. It is further noticeable that alongside their conservative stand regarding many aspects of modern life, *Kadın ve Aile* and *Bizim Aile* both appear to 'take into account items in the daily life of Turkey which are strongly anchored',[25] even when the reconciliation of these with Islamic principles is debatable. A case in point is the fact that both monthlies refrain from openly opposing co-educational institutions. Of the two, dialogue with the secular world is more obvious in the pages of *Bizim Aile*, as discussed above.

Both these magazines, in the format and content of their message, reveal an acknowledgement of the secular world and reflect, with different degrees of ambiguity, a reluctant acceptance of co-existence with its institutions.

To what extent this situation indicates an eventual synthesis of the Islamic with the secular at the level of movement ideology is difficult to say at this point. Although concepts of pluralist democracy and human rights are often invoked by both magazines, this rhetoric may be merely a tactical utilization of the resources and tools of the secular culture by the Islamic movement, to disseminate a message which, in essence, is irreconcilable with the fundamentals of secular democracy. Both magazines' careful avoidance of the expression of a clear stand on several key issues, such as polygyny, a husband's physical punishment of his wife and the treatment of non-practising Muslims in an Islamic society, does nothing to alleviate doubts about the extent to which Islamic ideology is able and willing to compromise with the secular sphere. Thus, so long as Islamic discourse refrains from stating its position on such key issues, explanation for the overlap of the two worlds must be sought at the level of movement strategy and tactics rather than ideology.

Among the periodicals reviewed here, *Mektup* reflects a discourse that least incorporates elements from secular culture. Its anti-hedonistic emphasis, the hostile and vengeful undertones of its appeal, as well as the nature of its language, are indications of its isolation from the secular world. *Mektup* perceives the conflict between the secular and Islamic worlds as absolute and irreconcilable; in this 'war of the worlds' women have a special role to fulfil, that of *mücahide*.

Women's activism in the propagation of Islam, underlined in the definition of the *mücahide* role, and the asceticism of *Mektup*'s ideology, attribute a different identity to women from the conventional wife–mother–homemaker. This identity is defined more by the woman's personal commitment to Islam and less by conformity to Islamic norms governing her social role, although such conformity is by no means rejected by the publishers of *Mektup*. Thus, paradoxically, *Mektup*, the most radical of the periodicals reviewed here, comes across as more tolerant and supportive of progressive – if not feminist – notions such as the non-sexual division of labour at home or women's activism in the public sphere. As such, it may even appear to share certain themes with such secular movements as feminism. Similar overlaps have been observed elsewhere in the case of other Islamic publications.[26] The significance of such overlaps is doubtful, however, when evaluated within the framework of a radical orientation such as that propagated by *Mektup*. Perhaps this is why phrases such as 'feminist Islam' or 'Islamic feminism', used by the popular media in Turkey to describe the likes of *Mektup*'s discourse, misconstrue what may well be coincidental intersections as convergences of fundamentally opposed ideologies.

Consequently, I believe, a thorough analysis of the ideology of the contemporary Islamic movement and its perception by its adherents is needed before the secular world decides on the compatibility of the movement's discourse with such fundamental values as equality, democracy and human rights.

NOTES

1. Şerif Mardin, 'Religion and politics in modern Turkey', in James P. Piscatori, ed., *Islam in the Political Process*, London, Cambridge University Press, 1983, pp. 138–59. Binnaz Toprak, 'The state, politics and religion in Turkey', in Metin Heper and Ahmet Evin, eds, *State, Democracy and the Military: Turkey in the 1980's*, Berlin and New York, de Gruyter, 1988, pp. 119–36 (specifically pp. 121–2). İlkay Sunar and Binnaz Toprak, 'Islam in politics: the case of Turkey', *Government and Opposition*, 18, 1983, pp. 421–41 (specifically pp. 421–8).
2. Gencay Şaylan, *İslamiyet ve Siyaset: Türkiye Örneği*, Ankara, V. Yayınları, 1987, p. 106.

3. Mardin, 'Religion and politics'; Binnaz Sayarı, 'Türkiye'de dinin denetim işlevi', *A.Ü. Siyasal Bilgiler Fakültesi Dergisi*, 33 (1–2), 1979, pp. 173–85 (specifically pp. 177–81).

4. I would like to acknowledge the contribution of Mr Bülent Arıcı, who helped with the content-analysis of the journals discussed here.

5. See Chapter 11 (Güneş-Ayata).

6. Şaylan, *İslamiyet*, p. 96; anon., 'Türkiye'deki İslamcı dergilere bir bakış', *Yeni Forum*, 8 (191), 1987, p. 14.

7. See Chapter 10 (Ayata).

8. M. Esad Coşan, 'İslam ile Batı'nın arasındaki derin farklar', *Kadın ve Aile*, November 1985, p. 4.

9. M. Esad Coşan, 'Asil kadın yetiştirelim', *Kadın ve Aile*, August 1987, pp. 10–11.

10. 'Kadın erkek eşittir', *Kadın ve Aile*, April 1986, p. 7.

11. Aişe Aslı Sancar, 'Müslüman kadın hakkında yanlış kavramlar', *Kadın ve Aile*, November 1985, p. 7.

12. For a discussion of the concept of 'bazaar' groups and their role *vis-à-vis* Islamic revivalism, see Şerif Mardin, 'Culture and religion towards the year 2000', in *Turkey in the Year 2000*, Turkish Political Science Association, Ankara, Sevinç Matbaası, 1989, pp. 163–86; and for an elaboration of the characteristics of small-town women see Mübeccel Kıray, 'Small town women', in Nermin Abadan-Unat, ed., *Women in Turkish Society*, Leiden, Brill, 1981, pp. 259–74.

13. Meral Kaçar, Sevim Tezcan and Yasemin Yavuztürk, 'Örtünmek hürriyettir', *Bizim Aile*, February 1988, p. 16.

14. Ibid., p. 21.

15. Şükran Vahide, 'İlim nasıl saadete götürür?', *Bizim Aile*, March 1988, p. 10.

16. Zehra Zeybek, 'Elele'de bir açık oturum', *Bizim Aile*, March 1988, p. 12.

17. Meral Kaçar, 'Söhbet: Yavuz Bahadıroğlu', *Bizim Aile*, February 1988, p. 33.

18. 'Feminist gözüyle başörtüsü', *Bizim Aile*, March 1988, p. 16.

19. Z. Mümine Yüksel, 'Tesettür meselesi', *Mektup*, July 1987, p. 23.

20. Mevlude Uçar, 'Hem açık gezmek hem de günahkar olmamak mümkün mü?', *Mektup*, January 1988, p. 11.

21. Melahat Aktaş, 'Mümin kadınlar Allah'a iman etmeyen bir erkekle evlenmemez', *Mektup*, January 1987, pp. 21, 22, 23.

22. Hatice Tuman, 'Çiçekler rahmetle büyür', *Mektup*, August 1987, p. 27.

23. Ayşegül Aktürk, 'Cihad eden kadın feminist Müslüman mı?', *Mektup*, January 1988, p. 4.

24. Emine Şenliklioğlu Özkan, 'Muhammed Abbasi ile röportaj', *Mektup*, November 1987, p. 7.

25. Mardin, 'Culture and religion', p. 180.

26. Nükhet Sirman-Eralp, 'Turkish feminism: a short history', paper

presented to the symposium on *The Plural Meanings of Feminism*, 12th Congress of IUAES, Zagreb, July 1988.

NOTES ON CONTRIBUTORS

Richard Tapper has degrees in social anthropology from the Universities of Cambridge (BA) and London (PhD). Since 1967 he has taught at the School of Oriental and African Studies, London, where he is now Reader in Anthropology with reference to the Middle East, and Chair of the Centre of Near and Middle Eastern Studies. He has carried out field research in Iran, Afghanistan and Turkey, and published books and articles on pastoral nomadism, tribe–state relations, ethnicity and history, symbolism and ritual in Islamic cultures, and political and religious ideologies.

İlter Turan studied at Oberlin College (BA), Columbia University (MA), and Istanbul University (DrSc Econ). He has been member of faculty at Istanbul University since 1966 and is now Professor of Political Science in the Faculty of Political Science. He has held visiting appointments at the universities of Iowa, Kentucky, Arizona, Wisconsin and California (Berkeley). His research and writing have been on political culture, political behaviour with emphasis on legislative behaviour, and Turkish foreign policy.

Nancy Tapper took her AB in anthropology from Washington University, St Louis, and MPhil and PhD degrees at the University of London. At present she is Lecturer in the Anthropology of the Arab World at the School of Oriental and African Studies, and involved in research on Syria, but previously she carried out fieldwork in Iran, Afghanistan and Turkey. Her publications include books and articles on marriage, politics, gender, ritual and symbolism in Middle Eastern cultures.

Lâle Yalçın-Heckmann studied sociology at Boğaziçi University (BA) and anthropology at the London School of Economics (PhD). She carried out fieldwork in Hakkari, and wrote her doctoral thesis on the kinship and tribal organization of Kurds in Hakkari. She is now a research fellow at Bamberg University, conducting a project on the religious socialization of Turkish youth in Nürnberg.

Akile Gürsoy-Tezcan has a BA in anthropology from the University of Durham, and PhD in anthropology from Hacettepe University, Ankara, where she worked as a research assistant for five years. Between 1980 and 1982 she worked for UNICEF in a primary health care project whose pilot area was eastern Turkey. She is Associate Professor at Marmara University, Istanbul, and in 1990–91 is visiting Associate Professor at the Center for Middle Eastern Studies, University of Texas at Austin. Her research and publications are in the fields of women's labour force participation, cultural causes of infant mortality, family studies, gender relations, and factors contributing to the quality of life.

Şerif Mardin has a PhD from Stanford University. He taught at the Political Science Faculty in Ankara, then at Boğaziçi University in Istanbul, and now holds the Chair of Islamic Studies at the American University, Washington DC; he has also been Visiting Professor at Columbia and Princeton Universities and at the University of California at Los Angeles, Research Fellow at Harvard and Visiting Fellow at St Antony's College, Oxford. His main research interests have been in the sociology and history of knowledge, and in religion and nationalism in late Ottoman and republican Turkey, on which he has published numerous books and papers.

Bahattin Akşit took a BS in sociology at the Middle East Technical University, Ankara and holds MA and PhD degrees in sociology from the University of Chicago. He is now Associate Professor in the Department of Sociology at Middle East

Technical University, where he has taught and researched for 18 years. His major publications include books in Turkish on the penetration of capitalism into Turkish villages, and social change in Turkish villages, towns and cities; and articles in Turkish and international journals on rural and urban transformations, secularism and the revival of Islam, the sociology of health and the sociology of sociology in non-Western societies.

Ayşe Saktanber is Research Assistant in the Department of Sociology, Middle East Technical University; she is completing her PhD dissertation in the same Department on the theme of urban Islam in Turkey. Her main research interests are ideology, religion, media and gender, and she has published articles in German and Turkish on women in the Turkish media.

Michael Meeker took a PhD in anthropology from the University of Chicago. He is currently Professor of Anthropology at the University of California, San Diego. He did fieldwork in Turkey during the late 1960s, when he resided in small towns in the Turkish provinces and studied the relationship of nationalism and religion. From 1986 to 1988 he returned to Turkey to conduct a study of the new publishing and writing strategies of Turkish believers in Istanbul. In addition to his work on Turkey, Meeker has also published books and articles on patterns of religion, society and identity among pastoral peoples of the Middle East and East Africa.

Sencer Ayata has a BS in sociology from the Middle East Technical University in Ankara, and a PhD in sociology and social anthropology from the University of Kent at Canterbury. He is currently Associate Professor in the Sociology Department at Middle East Technical University. He has carried out research on various social processes in rural and urban areas, and has written books and articles on social and cultural problems of urbanization, the role of religion in Turkish culture and politics, and on the informal sector.

Ayşe Güneş-Ayata received the BS in sociology from the Middle East Technical University in Ankara, and her PhD in sociology and social anthropology from the University of Kent in

Canterbury. She is Associate Professor of Sociology in the Department of Public Administration, Middle East Technical University. She has done research on Turkish political structure and culture, including ethnic and religious movements, and has published articles on urban ethnicity, religious revivalism, the internal structures of political parties and voting behaviour.

Feride Acar received her BS in sociology from the Middle East Technical University in Ankara, and her MA and PhD in political sociology from Bryn Mawr College, USA. Currently she is Associate Professor of Political Sociology in the Department of Public Administration, Middle East Technical University. She has also taught in Yarmouk University, Jordan and Bilkent University, Ankara. Her areas of academic interest are social and political change, social movements and women's studies. She has done research on Turkish political life and conditions of women in Turkey. She has published several articles on women and Islamic movements in Turkey, comparative characteristics and conditions of Turkish and Jordanian women academics, and Turkish political parties.

INDEX

Abdülhamid II (Sultan) 5, 11, 132, 224
Abdulhuda, Shaikh 132
Abu-Manneh, Butrus 124
Acar, Feride 20, 280–303
accommodations
  compartmentalization and balance 62–6
  hidden accommodations 67–71
al-Afghani, Jamal al-Din 131
Afghanistan 275
  migration to 234, 236
ahistoricity 77
Ahmed of Süleymaniye, Shaikh 131
Ahrar, Ubaidullah 125
Akbar (Mughal Emperor) 124
Akşit, Bahattin 16–17, 145–70
Algar, Hamid 122, 124
Âli Pasha 132
alienation 213
ANAP see Motherland Party (ANAP)
AP see Justice Party (AP)
Arvasi, Shaikh Abdulhakim 133
asceticism 231–4, 235
Asrı Saadet
  Girişim (journal) views 259
  Islam (journal) views 268–9
At Which End is the Egg to be Broken (Özdenören) 207
Atatürk see Kemal, Mustafa (Atatürk)
Atatürk and Religious Education 162
Atatürk Supreme Council for Culture, Language and History 51

authoritarianism 47–8
  authority of father 177, 178, 183, 232
  leadership and the people 264–6
Ayata, Sencer 19, 165, 223–53

Babai group 128
Bachelard, Gaston 138
Badie, Bertrand 47–8
Balaam 230, 233–4
Barr, James 76
Barzani movement 109–10
Bayar, Celal 62
Bayezid I (Sultan) 128, 129
Bekkine, Abdulaziz 133
Bektaş, Haci 67
Bektaşi order 58, 67, 129
Berkes, Niyazi 78, 150
Bey, Sati 155, 156–7
bilgi 73
bilim 73
Bizim Aile (journal) 20, 283, 290–4
Bloch, Maurice 69, 77
books
  children's see children's picture books
  Exhibition of Islamic Books 148
  Islamic education in 161–5
  see also individual books and publications
Bukhari, Shaikh Muhammad Murad 129

Bulaç, Ali 18, 197–205
Büyük Doğu 133

Caldwell, JC 92
calendar 6
Caliphate, abolition of 6
calling theory 257–66
capitalism 8, 199–200, 243
Castoriadis, Cornelius 138
Cevdet, Abdullah 157
Cevdet Pasha 131, 154, 158
Chen, LC 88
children's picture books 17, 171–88
CHP *see* Republican People's Party
    (CHP)
Christianity 241
    missionaries 38, 245
civic religion, nationalism as 7
civic rituals 67, 69
civil code 34
class conflict 199
clothing *see* 'head-scarf' dispute; veiling
    Westernization of 6
communication, *Islam* (journal) and
    media 274–5
community
    Islam journal and 273
    political *see* political community
    religious *see* Ulema
Concepts and Orders of Our Time
    (Bulaç) 197, 198–201
consensus 49–51
'constructed society' 194, 195–6
Coşan, Esat 134
craft guilds 4
cultural differences 206–10
    Western cultural invasion 244
    see also political culture
Cumhuriyet 98
davet see calling theory
de Certeau, Michel 138
Deeb, ME 92
delegation 47–8
Democrat Party (DP) 2, 8, 9, 45, 60,
    146, 254
depoliticization 262
deserving poor (*gizli fakir*) 68
Dihlavi, Mujeddidi Shaikh Abdullah
    129
din-ü devlet 41
Directorate of Religious Affairs 10,
    42, 58, 133, 146, 162, 230
dissent, religion as avenue for 44

divinely ordained leaders 40, 47–8
DP *see* Democrat Party (DP)
DYP *see* True Path Party (DYP)

Edremit 57–8
education 16–17, 59, 71–5, 145–70
    in books and journals *see individual
        books and journals*
    children's picture books *see*
        children's picture books
    çolonial rule and 245–6
    Islam (journal) and 275
    self-perception and 38
    women, of 288–9
    see also Imam-Hatip schools,
        medreses
Education and Instruction in Islam
    162–3
*Education in Islam, with a comparison
    with the Western System of
    Education* 164
Eğirdir 56–83
eğitim 73
Eickelman, Dale F 71–2
emancipation 281, 282, 292
Emir Kulal, Seyyid 129
Emir Sultan 129
Emrullah Efendi 159
equality before God 48, 286
Erbakan, Necmettin 15, 134
European Community
    proposed Islamic Community to
        counteract 271
    Turkey and 23, 24, 46
Evans-Pritchard, EE 104
extremists 60–1, 65–6
    see also fundamentalism: religious
        fanatics
Eygi, Mehmet Şevket 134

Fallers, Lloyd 57–8, 71
families, infant mortality and structure
    of 90, 91–2, 93
father, authority of 177, 178, 183,
    232
fatwas, secular 68
'fear of God' 208–9
feudalism 241
fıkıh 259, 265
Fleischer, Cornell 137
Freudian thought 242
Frey, Frederick W 38
Friedmann, Yohanan 125

friends, choice of 183–4
fundamentalism 76, 256
 see also extremists: religious fanatics
 and individual orders eg Nurcu
 order
funding, sources 10, 22

gecekondu 13, 14, 84–101
 source of readership for *Mektup*
 294–5
Geertz, C 118, 225
Gellner, Ernest 67–8
Gemeinschaft, society as 194, 196,
 216–17
gender roles
 children's picture books 176–9
 Imam-Hatip schools and 151
 see also women
Gesellschaft, society as 194, 196, 217
al-Ghazali 258
al-Gilani 239, 246
Girişim (journal) 19, 256–67, 276–7
GNP, infant mortality and 85–6
Gökalp, Ziya 17, 155–6, 157
Grant, James 85
Great Struggle, the 232, 237
 see also Jihad
Gross, Jo-Ann 125
Gümüşhanevi, Ziyaeddin 131–2
Günaltay, M Şemsettin 159
Gündüz, Irfan 122, 124
Güneş-Ayata, Ayşe 19–20, 164–5,
 254–79
Gürsoy-Tezcan, Akile 13, 84–101

Hakkari 14–15, 103, 109–18
Halid Baghdadi, Mevlâna 129–30,
 136
Halidi order 130, 131, 135, 136
Halveti order 129
Hayri Effendi, Mustafa 159
'head-scarf' dispute 281, 292
health centre, replacement by mosque
 94–7, 98
Heper, Metin 9, 10, 21, 41, 44
hicret see Hijra (withdrawal)
Hijra (withdrawal) 20, 231–4, 235,
 275
Hizbullah (party of God) 235–6, 237
Hizbüşşeytan (party of Satan) 236,
 237
hoca 73
humanism 191, 192–3, 209

Hürriyet 98

Ibn Khaldun 152
Ibn Rüşd 152
Icmal (journal) 19, 225, 239–49, 283
identity
 Kurdish
  ethnic identity 114, 115
  non-islamic sources 117–18
 search for 21–2, 23, 262
 Western domination and 271
ijma 49
İlahî, Molle 129
Ilim ve Sanet (Science and Art) 134,
 164
'ilm 71–3
Imam-Hatip schools 145–70
Incident of 31 March 1909 121
industrialization 46
inerrant texts *see* Kemal, Mustafa
 (Atatürk), sayings of
infant mortality 13, 84–101
inferiority complex 208
Intellectual Issues in the Islamic World
 (Bulaç) 201–3, 214
intellectuals 17–18, 56–80, 189–219
Intellectuals' Hearth (Aydınlar Ocağı)
 11
interest 46
Introduction to Education and the
 values Islam Contributes to
 Education 163–4
İran 259
İskender Paşa Dergâhi 267
Iskenderpaşa mosque 133
Islam
 Hakkari Kurds and 109–18
 in Ottoman Empire 4
 political culture and *see* political
  community, culture, ideology,
  legitimacy, values and styles
 see also Islamic revival: Islamic
  rituals: religion
'Islam of the Ancestors' 227–9, 230
Islam (journal) 19–20, 164–5,
 267–77, 283
Islamic education *see* education
Islam intellectuals *see* intellectuals *and*
 invidividual persons
Islamic morality, in children's picture
 books 175–6, 182–4
Islamic revival 3, 9, 10, 255
 divisions among groups 255–6

fundamentalism 256
funding from abroad 10, 22
militant Islam and 31–2
modernism 256
search for identity, as 21–2, 23
traditionalism and neo-
traditionalism 256
see also Girişim (journal): *İslam*
(journal)
Islamic rituals 67, 69

JIhad 20, 275
women and 268, 297, 300–1
see also Great Struggle, the *and*
Lesser Struggle, the
journals 19–20, 254
Sufi orders and *see İcmal* (journal)
and Ribat (journal)
women in 280–303
see also individual periodicals
Justice Party (AP) 8, 60, 146, 147,
148

Kadın ve Aile (journal) 20, 283–90
Kadiri order 2, 10, 11, 19, 130
see also İcmal (journal)
Kalender brotherhood 128, 135
Kandiyoti, Deniz 93
Kazım Efendi 160
Keloğlan 174, 177
Kemal, Mustafa (Atatürk) 50
cult of 75–7
sayings and speeches of 50–1, 67,
76–7
secularism under 2–3, 5–8
see also Turkish Republic
Kemal, Namık 158
Khalid, Mevlâna *see* Halid Baghdadi,
Mevlâna
Khalil (Sultan of Transoxiana) 125
Khomeyni, Ayatollah 238
Kinberg, L 241
Kısakürek, Necip Fazıl 133
Konya *see Ribat* (journal)
Koopman, D 70
Köprü (journal) 283, 290, 291
Kotku, Mehmed Zahid 15, 133–4,
139
Kurdish Workers Party (PKK) 116,
117
Kurds 6, 60, 68, 102–20

laicism 2, 3, 56, 67

see also secularism
language, use of Turkish 62, 71–4
leadership
calling theory and 264–6
divinely ordained leaders 40, 47–8
İslam (journal) and 273
sayyids and shaikhs 112
'Lesser Struggle' 235
Limon 98
literature *see* books: children's picture
books: intellectuals *and individual
books and publications*

Mahmud II (Sultan) 131
Maliki, Imam 258
ma'lûmat 73
Mango, Andrew 73–4
Mardin, Şerif 4, 6, 15–16, 22, 34, 38,
39, 41, 47, 67, 71, 121–42, 172,
224
ma'rifa 71–3
martyrdom 238
Marxism 242, 260
Ma'sum, Muhammad 129
materialism 228, 229–30, 242–3,
270–1
Mawdudi, S. Abul A'la 258, 259, 263
media
İslam (journal) and communication
media 274–5
see also books *and individual books
and periodicals*
medreses 6, 34, 150, 152–61
see also education
Meeker, Michael E 17–18, 189–219
Mehmed II (Sultan) 129
Mehmed Pasha, Kıbrıslı 132
Mektup (journal) 20, 283, 294–9
mela 111–12
Mélikoff, Irène 129
Menemen incident (1920) 122
Metiner, M 262
Mevlevi order 58, 129
mevlûd 64, 69, 70, 77, 115
migration
rural-urban 8, 195
to Afghanistan 234, 236
millets 36, 37
Milli Gazette 46
Milli Görüş 46
Milliyet 98
mims, theory of two 126–7
missionaries 38, 245

MNP *see* National Order Party (MNP)
modernism 256
modernist ideology
  didacticism and discursive practice
    214–16
  Muslim intellectuals and 203–4,
    211–13
Mosley, WH 88
mosques 2, 133
  replacing public buildings with
    94–7, 98
Motherland Party (ANAP) 11, 226,
  254, 261
MSP *see* National Salvation Party
  (MSP)
mücahide 297, 300–1
Mujeddidi 124–7
multi-party politics 8, 44–5
Muslim Brotherhood 224
Muslim intellectuals *see* intellectuals
My Religion 177, 178

Nakşibendi order 2, 6, 10, 11, 15–16,
  19, 58, 121–42, 254, 267
  see also Ribat (journal) *and* Şeyh Sait
    uprising
Naqshband, Bahaeddin 125, 129
Nation Party 45
National Action Party 147
National Order Party (MNP) 8, 11,
  45, 46
National Salvation Party (MSP) 8, 11,
  45, 46, 146–7, 149, 254
National War of Independence 34, 41
  political community and 37
nationalism 36, 61
  as civic religion 7
NATO 24
neo-traditionalism 256
Norton, John 67
Nurcu movement 2, 10, 15, 20, 61,
  75–6, 78, 272
Nursi, Bediuzzaman Said 15, 133

öğretmen 73
Öğüt (journal) 283
Olson, Emelie 67
Ottoman Empire
  Bulaç and 203
  defeat and breakup of 34
  education in 153–4
  historical background 32–4
  Islam in 4

modernization of 33–4
Nakşibendi order in 127–9
secularization 4–5, 33–4
Sultan's *kanun* legislation 4
Tanzimat reforms 4, 5, 37, 131
Young Ottomans 5, 131
outsiders 59–60, 61, 116
Özal, Korkut 15, 134
Özal, Turgut 11
Özdeņören, Rasim 18, 205–10
Özel, İsmet 18, 206, 210–16

Pahlavi, Muhammad Riza Shah 71
Parsons, T 245
patronage 4
Perfect Man 246–7, 248–9
periodicals *see* journals *and individual
  periodicals*
Pharaohs 230, 234, 295
PKK (Kurdish Workers Party) 116,
  117
pluralism, calling theory and 263–4
political community 35–40
political culture 31–55
political ideology 60
  religion and 42–7
political legitimacy 40–2
political values and styles 47–51, 60
politics, multi-party politics 8, 44–5
publishing
  children's books 17
  journals 19–20, 254, 280–303
  revival in Islamic publishing
    activities 10
  *see also individual books and
    journals*

qiyas 49
Qutb, Sayyid 236–7, 261

Rahman, F 226
Reed, Howard A 98–9
religion *passim*
  politics and 35–51
religious consciousness 2–3
religious experience, individualization
  64
religious fanatics 60–1, 65–6, 78,
  103–4
  see also individual orders eg Nurcu
    order *and* fundamentalism
religious personnel 111–12

religious schools *see* education:
   medreses
religious values, rationalization of   65
Republican People's Party (CHP)   8,
   35, 45, 60, 146, 147
Ribat (journal)   19, 164, 225–39
RP *see* Welfare Party (RP)
rural-urban migration   8, 195
Russo-Turkish war (1877–8)   131

Saadettin, Müstakimzâde Süleyman
   129
Sabah   134
Sabahattin, Prens   155
sacrifice   238
   self-sacrifice   269
   suffering   231. 295
Sacrifice, feast of   69
Saktanber, Ayşe   17, 171–88
Sanusi shaikhs   104
Sayarı, Sabri   43–4
sayyids   112
Scheper-Hughes, Nancy   87
sciences in schools   151, 157, 158
script, use of romanized Turkish
   script   74
secularism
   easing under Democratic Party
      government   2
   personal and private nature of
      Islam   6
   separation of Islam from politics   9
   subordination to state   5–6
   Sultan's *kanun* legislation   4
   under Ottoman Empire   4–5, 33–4
   under Republic   2–3, 5–8, 34–5, 41
segregation   288–9, 295, 298
şehit   42
self-perception   38
self-sacrifice   269
Şevketi, M   158–9
Şeyh Sait uprising   14, 103–6, 122
Şeyhülislam   156
Shaikh Sait uprising *see* Şeyh Sait
   uprising
shaikhs   112
Shamil, Shaikh   130
Sharia   11, 33, 137
   abandonment of   6
Shariati, Ali   230, 258, 261, 262, 263
Shepard, WE   238
Shi'a   36, 41
Shi'ites   8

'Short duration'   232
Simko   105–6, 108
al-Sirhindi, Ahmad Faruqi   124–7
slavery   48
Smith, Donald   33, 48
Social Change in the Islamic World
   203
social control   42, 77
socio-economic change, religion and
   44
stereotypes   209–10
suffering
   see sacrifice
Sufi orders   2, 59
   journals affiliated to *see* İcmal
      (journal) *and* Ribat (journal)
   knowledge of   71–2, 73, 74
   see also Nakşibendi order
Sufism   6
suicide   207
Süleyman Efendi   131
Süleymancıs   2, 10, 61, 78, 97
Sultanate, abolition of   6
Sunni Islam   4
Sunnis   8, 41

Tamerlane   128, 129
Tanzimat period of reforms   4, 5, 37,
   131
Tapper, Nancy   13, 56–83
Tapper, Richard   1–27, 56–83
tarikats   2, 4, 9, 10, 121, 224
theodemocracy   259
*Three Problems: Technique,
   Civilization, Alienation* (Özel)
   211, 213–16
Timur *see* Tamerlane
Topçu, Nurettin   197
Toprak, Binnaz   8, 31, 43, 213
totalism, *Islam* (journal) and   272
Trabzon *see* İcmal (journal)
traditionalism   256
True Path Party (DYP)   11, 60
Tuba-tree theory   159–60
Turan, İlter   31–55
'Turk' definition   38
Türkeş, Alparslan   197
'Turkish citizen' definition   38
Turkish language   74
   Turkish Language Foundation   74
Turkish Republic
   multi-party politics   8, 44–5
   national identity   37

nationalism as civic religion 7
secularism under 5–8, 34–5, 41
separation of religious and political
   32
see also political values *etc*
Turkish-Islam Synthesis (TIS) 11
Turkmen tribesmen 127–9

Uftade mosque 133
al-Ukari, Abdulfettah 130
Ulema 4, 49–50, 51, 71, 137, 224,
   259
   authoritarianism and 264, 265
   education and 159
   knowledge of 71, 72, 74
   medrese reform and 153
umma, Ummah 36, 38, 40, 264, 265
Ümmügülsum mosque 133
UNICEF 85

Vahdeti, 'Dervish' 121
Vakf, abandonment of 6
van Bruinessen, Martin 14, 104–6,
   107, 113
veiling 20, 290–1, 295–6, 298
Vergin, N 115
violence, religiously motivated 11
Volkan 121

Wali Allah, Shah 127, 136

Welfare Party (RP) 11, 45, 46, 226
Western sociology, *Girişim* (journal)
   views 258–9
Westernism 34, 50
   calendar 6
   calling theory and 260–1
   capitalism 8
   clothing 6
   Islam (journal) 270–1
   need technology but not culture 46
   women and anti-Westernism 284–5
withdrawal 20, 231–4, 235, 275
women 20, 48, 64, 113, 177–9,
   280–303
Words which Confuse our Thinking
   (Özdenören) 214
work ethic 68–9
World Health Organization 85
writing, use of romanized Turkish
   script 74

Yalçın-Heckmann, Lâle 14, 102–20
Yalman, Nur 7, 58, 72
Yeni Devir 211
Young Ottomans 5, 131
Young Turks 5, 121, 133, 154–5
Yücekök, Ahmed 9–10

Zakariya, Muhammad 98
Zelzele (Earthquake) 181